ESSAYS ON CONSTITUTIONAL LAW

About the Editor

V. Venkataramanaiah, Advocate, High Court of Andhra Pradesh, Hyderabad, was born on 7th September, 1927. He enrolled in Bombay High Court in the year 1951. He worked as junior to Mr. Alladi Kuppuswamy (who subsequently became a Judge and the Chief Justice of the High Court of Andhra Pradesh). He is one of the leading Advocates of the Andhra Pradesh High Court on the civil side. He was the Standing Counsel for the Railways for a period of 2 years. He was the President of the A.P. High Court Advocates' Association (1975-76). He has contributed many papers and participated in many seminars on legal subjects. He is one of the Trustees of the Alladi Memorial Trust under whose auspices this volume is being published.

ESSAYS ON CONSTITUTIONAL LAW
(Alladi Krishnaswami Aiyer Memorial Volume)

Edited by
V. VENKATARAMANAIAH

Foreword by
M. HIDAYATULLAH

CONCEPT PUBLISHING COMPANY PVT. LTD.
NEW DELHI-110059

ISBN: 978-81-7022-061-9

First Edition 1986

Published and Printed by

Concept
Since 1974

Concept Publishing Company Pvt. Ltd.
A/15-16, Commercial Block, Mohan Garden,
New Delhi-110059 (India)
T: 91-11-41101460
E: publishing@conceptpub.com, *W*: www.conceptpub.com

FOREWORD

I AM very happy and feel much privileged to be asked to contribute this Foreword to this commemorative volume in memory of late Sir Alladi Krishnaswami Aiyer. Perhaps I am the only lawyer alive today who can say that he appeared in the Federal Court of India with him and also against him. My association goes back to the very first case in the Federal Court of India when it began functioning. I had a junior brief and Sir Alladi was one of the leading lawyers. Later in the first half of the forties I appeared first on the same side and later against him. Both of us were then Advocates-General of our respective Provinces. There were no more occasions to cross swords as we both would have liked because I became a Judge in 1946. All these events are described by me fully in my Memoirs *My Own Boswell.*

Of all the lawyers of my time with whom I appeard (and they were almost all the top lawyers of the second quarter of this century) Sir Alladi made the greatest impact on my imagination and future life. I learnt to examine with his care and thoroughness a case in which I appeared taking nothing for granted and leaving no stone unturned. Although so much older than me he was ever willing to listen to me and other juniors, with patience and kindness. He always helped and encouraged us. I used to spend considerable time when I was with him in Delhi. I was always made aware of his wide ranging knowledge and intellect. No other lawyer had such a store of knowledge ready at hand, be it Constitutional Law or Civil Law. He could always contribute something new.

The names of great Judges have remained in our memory because their judgments are of perpetual memory. Lawyers cannot evoke memories in the same way as their contribution ends with the case in hand and begins afresh in another case. They leave little or no record of work in Courts except in the memory of persons who watched them function. They can only be commemorated by tributes paid to them and this volume containing some writings of eminent lawyers and men of letters of India and some foreign countries will do this for Sir Alladi. I am proud to be associated with it.

Bombay
February 15, 1986

M. HIDAYATULLAH
B.A. (Nag), M.A. (Cantab),
LL.D ; D. Litt., D.C.L.,
O.B.E, Bar-at-Law,
Bencher, Lincoln's Inn,
Former Chief Justice of
India and Vice President
of India.

PREFACE

THE late Dr. Alladi Krishnaswami was, in the words of Shri V.R. Krishna Iyer, a former Judge of the Supreme Court of India, "during his days a living legend as the ablest lawyer, a professional wonder and an authentic embodiment of jurisprudential versatility". He was the Advocate-General of Madras, India, for over fifteen years. When the Constitution of India was considered by the Constituent Assembly, he was invited by Pandit Jawaharlal Nehru, the then Prime Minister of India, to be one of the members of the Committee which was entrusted with the task of drafting the Constitution and of which Dr. Ambedkar was the chairman. Though there were several members of the Drafting Committee, only five of them took an active part and of these Dr. Alladi was the one who was responsible for almost every phrase and every comma of the Constitution. Dr. Alladi will always be remembered for his priceless part in the Constitution-making process.

Dr. Alladi's son, Shri Alladi Kuppuswami, who was a Judge of the High Court of Andhra Pradesh, India, and who retired as its Chief Justice in 1982, founded the Alladi Memorial Trust in memory of his late father. The Trust was inaugurated by Hon'ble M. Hidayatullah, the then Vice-President of India, on the birth centenary of the late Dr. Alladi on May 14, 1983. He also unveiled the portrait of Dr. Alladi presented to the Trust by Shri S. Ramakrishnan of Bangalore. Hon'ble K.C. Abraham, Governor of Andhra Pradesh, was the chief guest and the Chief Minister of Andhra Pradesh, Hon'ble N.T. Rama Rao, presided. Shri P. Jaganmohan Reddy, former Judge of the Supreme Court of India, who was the Chairman of the Birth Centenary Celebrations Committee, welcomed the gathering. All of them spoke about Dr. Alladi and his valuable contribution as a member of the Constitution Drafting Committee. Shri Alladi Kuppuswami explained the aims and objects of the Trust which are : (1) to promote research in the field of law, jurisprudence and administration of justice ; (2) to undertake or assist the execution of research projects on topics relating to law and administration of justice and the preparation and publication of research papers on such subjects ; (3) to publish or assist in the publication of periodicals, journals and books connected with law and administration of justice ; (4) to establish, start or manage and supervise already established schools, colleges or other institutions connected with law and administration of justice ; (5) to carry on any work connected with law and justice ; (6) to provide financial or other assistance to deserving lawyers, law students, jurists and others associated with law and administration of justice ; and (7) to do all that is necessary for and incidental to achieving all or any of the objects specified above, without any profit motive.

The trust is managed by a Board of Trustees. The Board in pursuance of one of the objects of the Trust decided to bring out a volume consisting of Essays on Constitutional Law by jurists in India and abroad in memory of Dr. Alladi. There was good response from eminent jurists who were gracious enough to contribute to the volume without accepting any remuneration. The Trust expresses its gratitude to the contributors. The Trustees hope that this commemoration volume brought out to perpetuate the sacred memory of the late Dr. Alladi will make a rewarding reading to all.

JUSTICE Y.V. ANJANEYULU
High Court of Andhra Pradesh,
Member, Board of Trustees,
Alladi Memorial Trust.

DR. ALLADI KRISHNASWAMI AIYER

When a proper history of the Madras Bar gets chronicled and the galaxy of its past leaders portrayed, no other figure will engage our attention more than Dr. Alladi Krishnaswami Aiyer with his brilliant forensic powers of debating and his pioneering studies in Constitutional Law. Though endowed poorly by nature in his physique and looks, still by his beaming and glittering eyes and a broad smile, he never escaped notice in any distinguished assembly. For nearly three decades and more, he moved from one to the other of the High Court Halls, and attracted not only a large and varied clientele but an entire world of jurists. His name was on every lip and his unassuming demeanour towards all gained him an enviable popularity. He remained the same likeable gentleman to everybody, despite his day-to-day self-surpassing position in the public eye. Being conscious of his early-life trials and tribulations, penury and his struggle to rise in his profession, he never displaced his wholesome sympathy for others in the same circumstances, in life by any of the intolerances or indifferences usually associated with one so successful in life and enjoying such unusual prosperity.

Born on May 14, 1883, in Nayudupet (Nellore District) of poor parents, he was inculcated from the start in learning. After school, college took him to Madras, where in the Christian College, becoming a favourite of professors like Mr. Kellet, he soon won spurs in history studies. Tutor he remained for some time in the College, but soon entered the portals of the Law College, ultimately to enter the legal profession. Indeed, it needed great courage, confidence, single-mindedness and individuality to choose law for profession with practically no useful social contact nor a sympathizer nor a well-wisher.

He took to law as fish to water, and naturally success came to him in no time. Apprenticed to Shri P.R. Sundaram Aiyar, himself a legal prodigy, Dr. Alladi, with little effort on his part, received the appreciation and encouragement from some of the known leaders in his field. It would be no exaggeration to say he was sought also even by some of the very top seniors to assist them

This article was written by the author for *The Hindu* on the occasion of the birth centenary of the late Dr. Alladi, May 14, 1983. Printed with the kind permission of the author and courtesy of *The Hindu*.

in unravelling knotty problems of law. Hard work during the initial days and his assiduous study of the Reports of both English and Indian decided cases stood him in good stead and added to his natural inclination to seriously discuss legal problems. It was no wonder then that he, in a short time, became known for his incisive intellect and acute skill in debating. In 1907, he was enrolled as a Vakil and in less than two or three years was able to stand on his own legs without undergoing much travail of juniordom. To show how he easily impressed both seniors in the profession and the judges of the High Court, one telling instance may suffice. Once on behalf of his own master, Shri Sundaram Aiyar, he was making a statement on English law before a Bench presided over by no less a judge than Sir John Wallis, when, in appreciation of the aptness of it, the judge queried : "Where from you have got this, is it from any judicial pronouncement or your own ?" At once Shri V. Krishnaswami Aiyar, appearing on the other side, was heard saying, "That young man can himself formulate such a legal proposition." It was a well-deserved tribute from one higher in the profession, and Mr. Alladi long remembered it with pride and gratitude.

From a young junior to be transformed a senior in his turn with an office crowded with juniors and apprentices, it took him not many years to be engaged in any complicated issue of a case, whether it be of Hindu Law or Land revenue or Zamindari Estate. It was said that when Sir Asutosh Mukherjee of Calcutta paid a visit, in 1915, to the Vakils' Association and Sir K. Srinivasa Aiyengar, then a judge, introduced Mr. Alladi as a rising member of the Bar, Justice Sir Abdur Rahim (later to be the President of the Legislative Council at the Centre, in Delhi) who was nearby, corrected him saying, "He has already risen."

The trust was not misplaced. Dr. Alladi was appointed Advocate-General of Madras in 1928, for by then he had established his claim to be chosen the Official Head of the Bar. As Advocate-General he was diligent in acquainting himself with the requirements of the new office. With a sense of resposibility he would even peruse some of the drafted opinions of his predecessors such as Shri P.S. Sivaswami Aiyar and Shri S. Srinivasa Aiyengar in order to be familiar with models of draftsmanship in rendering legal opinions to the Government. He was often overawed by the lucidity of Shri Sivaswami Aiyar's language and the compact terseness of Shri S. Srinivasa Aiyengar's. Himself desirous of wielding a good style, he would write and re-write his statements more to be precise of language and substance. As a matter of fact some of his Farewell Addresses to retiring judges of the High Court were so well prepared with poise and dignity of phrasing that they were collected in a special volume at the time of his *Shahtyabda Poorti* and presented to him.

Dr. Alladi Krishnaswami Aiyer was not known for exhaustive arguments in court. Brief, he was always careful in selecting a few points which alone, according to his judgment, if forcefully pressed, would win the case. No set plan would be employed by him, for his resilient mind often studied the judges and changed his stratagem to suit the occasion. If economy in art makes literature significant, no less was economy in presentation of arguments to him a matter of art. His sound memory and resourcefulness aided him as nothing else.

It was a case for issue of a writ of *scire facias* which came before a Bench presided over by Sir Murray Coutts Trotter. Dr. Alladi began to change his original intention, and canvassed a favourable passage from a book called *Tidd's Practice* of England. Justice Trotter could not restrain his surprise and asked, "How did you get that book ?" The reply astounded the judge even more when Dr. Alladi replied, "We were familiar with that book in Sundaram Aiyar's law chambers when we worked under him." Later he traced the entire course of that writ with various authorities and impressed Justice Trotter of the immense study involved. But soon Dr. Alladi with a wink characteristic of him said to a friend nearby, "Of course the whole *catena* of authorities is well collected in a Calcutta judgment of Justice Asutosh Mukherjee. I purposely made it all look a renewed research for this case."

One other matter demands mention—his quick grasp of details. In the Cauvery Arbitration matter before Justice Page, the judge was taken up with him at the way he piled up points of intimate engineering knowledge. No doubt, the Chief Engineer of the Government of Madras was by his side to brief him on technical points arising. Still, his quick grasp of the subject, or of any unfamiliar subject for that matter, in a moment deserved the compliment offered to Dr. Alladi by the judge.

Even before the Indian Government conceived of the setting up of a Federal Court at Delhi, he had anticipated it and by a regular study of the various Federal Constitutions of the United States, Canada and Australia, sufficiently equipped himself for any contingency that may arise for his services. He loved the subject and was constantly collecting books dealing with the Constitutions of the USA and the USSR and the States of Europe. It was a great pleasure for him to plunge into that familiar field of his later-day studies with enormous zest.

Beyond all his legalistic essayings, there was a core within him which beckoned him to a "Philosophy of Law" which the normal lawyer of any standing never addressed his mind to. If in the Constituent Assembly he was listened to with rapt attention by persons no less than Pandit Jawaharlal Nehru, Dr. Rajendra Prasad and Dr. Ambedkar, it was due to his unfailing alertness to observe a changing world where law became more and more an instrument of social change. Being steeped in law and legalism of every kind he knew also the limits of law beyond which was the life of a people. In an earlier address of his at the Krishna Rajendra Silver Jubilee, 1939, he remarked : "The one important lesson that is learnt by a lawyer in the course of his studies is that the source of all law is to be found in the seething life of the people, that the course of legal development is determined by the progress attained by the nation in the several spheres, and that the legal system in its turn has shaped progress." Dr. Alladi was convinced of the vast population's responsibility for Constitutions proving useful. For answering the real needs of a growing nation he thought of "Adult Franchise" as inev table for its progress. He was found saying, that any day the unlettered man in the street was more educated than the compulsorily educated ones who pose to exercise the gift of franchise.

When all is said of Dr. Alladi's achievement which certainly buoyed up his spirits, he was never proud or exclusive. His child-like simplicity in acknowledging others' excellences, his loyalty to friends who like Shri Subbaraya Aiyar had shared with him his joys and sorrows from the earliest time of their lives, his desire for his own progeny not lagging behind many an ambitious young spirit for achievement in life, his remaining to the last his own self—all these and more draw us to cherishing his memory with admiration and affection.

K. CHANDRASEKHARAN
Advocate, Madras

CONTENTS

THE AUTHORS

Y.V. Anjaneyulu : A Judge of the High Court of Andhra Pradesh and a Trustee of the Alladi Memorial Trust.

K. Chandrasekharan : Advocate, Madras, was one of the Juniors in the Chambers of the late Dr. Alladi.

V. Ye. Chirkin : Professor of Law, Institute for State and Law, U.S.S.R. Academy of Sciences, Moscow.

Rajeev Dhavan : Reader, Department of Law, Brunel University, Uxbridge, Middlessex, U.K.

Bhagwan D. Dua : Chairman and Associate Professor, Department of Political Science, University of Lethbridge, Alberta, Canada ; Visiting Professor, Hokkaiga Kuen University, Japan, in 1984.

V.R. Krishna Iyer : Former Judge, Supreme Court of India. Publications : *Law and the People* ; *Law, Freedom and Change* ; *Environmental Pollution and the Law* ; delivered several lectures including the Alladi Endowment Lecture, on "National Prison Policy" and contributed several articles and papers.

W.H. McConnell : Professor of Law, University of Saskatchewan, Canada. Received his doctorate in Political Science from the University of Toronto, Canada. Has written extensively on aspects of law and legal history. His commentary on the British North America Act is regarded as a standard work on that subject.

Arval A. Morris : Professor of Law and Adjunct Professor of Education, University of Washington, Seattle, U.S.A., Senior Fulbright Lecturer in Law, University of Freiburg, West

Germany, in 1979-80. Author of *The Constitution and American Education* and of a number of articles in various legal and other journals.

N.A. Palkhivala : Senior Advocate, Supreme Court of India. Former Ambassador of India to the U.S.A. Joint author of the well known standard book, *The Indian Income Tax Act '64* (Kanga and Palkhivala). An eminent lawyer and jurist. Some of his important articles and lectures are published in *We, the People.*

P. Jaganmohan Reddy : Former Judge, Supreme Court of India, Judge and Chief Justice, High Court of Andhra Pradesh, India ; former Vice-Chancellor, Osmania University, Hyderabad, India. Publications : *Quest for Justice* ; *Social Justice and the Constitution* (Alladi Endowment Lectures). Delivered the Sir Chimanlal Setalvad Lectures on "Minorities and the Constitution" and Asutosh Mukherjee endowment lectures on "Liberty, Equality and Property in the Constitution".

Peter H. Russell : Professor, Department of Political Science, University of Toronto, Canada. Recently Research Consultant to the committee of the Canadian Bar Association on the appointment of judges in Canada. Author of *The Supreme Court of Canada as a Bilingual and Bicultural Institution.*

Bozo Zepic : Professor, Faculty Law, University of "Dzemal Bijedic", Mostar.

CANADA

ONE

W. H. MCCONNELL

THE CANADIAN DEBATE ON SENATE REFORM

FEW topics in Canadian constitutional law have inspired more heated political rhetoric, or engendered more intricate plans for institutional reform than the vexed question of the reconstitution of the Canadian Upper House.

Since the inception of the Canadian Senate as a 72-member chamber of "sober second thought" at Confederation in 1867, it has increased to 104 members with the gradual addition of Senators representing newly created provinces and the vast northern Territories. The latest change in representation was made on June 19, 1975, when an Act of Parliament[1] provided one Senator each for the Yukon and the Northwest Territories which occupy the far-flung, sparsely inhabited northern landmass of Canada along with the islands of the Arctic Archipelago.

From the very beginning of Confederation, the Senate has been a politically weak body. Canadian Senators were originally appointed for life, but a mandatory retirement age of 75 was set in 1965[2] which applied only to members appointed after that date. There are, of course, no elections for the 104 positions which are filled at the entire discretion of the incumbent Prime Minister. In addition to an office and staff, the position carries with it an annual indemnity of $ 61,000 along with inexpensive meals in Government-subsidized restaurants.

Critics have charged that one of the main purposes of the present Senate is to reward party faithful for their loyalty and political exertions on behalf of the government of the day. In an era of protracted Liberal dominance, the unfettered appointing power can lead at times to disconcerting political imbalances. By 1955, for example, after 20 uninterrupted years of Liberal Party rule, the disproportion had become so glaring that an Opposition of only seven Conservative Senators faced 75 Liberals in the then 102-seat House.[3] Even so, the Prime Minister, Mr. L.S. St. Laurent, refused to relinquish such an important source of patronage, leaving a large number of vacancies to be filled when the Conservatives finally achieved power under John Diefenbaker in 1957. Unlike the case of the Rajya Sabha, no seats are set aside in the Senate for those who have distinguished themselves in various facets of national life and can thereby add to the shared reservoir of experience in the Upper Chamber.

There are three distinguishing characteristics which have emphasized the political supremacy of the House of Commons over the Senate since Confederation. Only the 281-member Lower House is based on direct election, and thus can appeal, in a democratic sense, to actual constituencies of voters ; the House of Commons alone can originate Bills for the raising or spending of money, and by the unwritten convention of responsible government, the Cabinet, which is almost entirely drawn from the Lower House, is responsible only to that House. Accordingly, the Senate can never precipitate the fall of the Government by an adverse vote on a government measure. By contrast, Prime Ministers Meighen (1926), Diefenbaker (1963), Trudeau (1974) and Clark (1979) have been forced to face the electorate once again when they lost votes in the House of Commons. In the subsequent elections, Meighen, Diefenbaker and Clark were defeated while Trudeau was re-elected in 1974 with an increased majority.

Some Constitutional References on the Senate

Although it is rarely in the public limelight, there has been some important litigation on the Senate. The British Privy Council held in 1930 that women were, indeed, "persons" capable of being called to the Senate. Section 24 of the British North America Act stipulated that the Governor-General could summon "qualified persons" to the Upper House, but at the time the statute was enacted by the British Parliament the word "persons" in such a context was restrictively interpreted to exclude females.

Women in England in 1867 could hold no public office, not even that of church warden in the established Church.

Employing his "living tree" metaphor, Lord Sankey ruled that the restrictive 1867 meaning should not govern the interpretation of the applicable section in 1930 : "The British North America Act planted in Canada a living tree capable of growth and expansion within its natural limits."[4] Prime Minister Mackenzie King, accordingly, appointed Mrs. Cairine Wilson an Ontario Senator in 1930. Her reception by male Senators was very cool, however, and King never appointed another woman Senator. After his retirement in 1948, all succeeding administrations have appointed several female Senators to the Upper House.

During the spring of 1978, the Liberal Government of Prime Minister Trudeau brought forward Bill C-60, its comprehensive plan for reform of the Upper House. The new Chamber was to be established along lines radically different from the present Senate.[5] In contrast to the 104-member Upper House appointed by the Governor-General on the recommendation by the Prime Minister, an 118-member House of the Federation was to be elected indirectly, with half of its membership being contingent, respectively, on the share of votes received by the various parties in the last preceding federal and provincial elections. The membership of the new body, consequently, would be constantly changing. While representation of the local units would still be unequal (in contrast to the United States and Australia) some increase was provided for the Atlantic and Western regions, with Ontario and Quebec still retaining their present complement of 24 Senators. The new body, unlike the present Senate, was to have the power to confirm federally appointed judges and senior federal executive appointees. The reconstituted House was also to act as a watchdog of French-linguistic rights with a double majority of English and French-speaking Senators being mandatory for basic changes in language laws.

The Trudeau Government contended that it unquestionably possessed constitutional jurisdiction to reform the Upper Chamber of what was, after all, the national legislature, but in a unanimous reference opinion the Supreme Court of Canada disagreed.[6] One of the main factors impelling the Court to reject the Government's proposal was that the Senate, as originally framed, was designed to represent sectional or provincial interests, whereas no provision had been made for provincial consultation with respect to the reconstituted body. While the Federal Government did not deny that the original concept was for regional representation, it asserted that the Chamber no longer performed such a function. A "federalized" Cabinet, it might be argued, had displaced the Senate in its regional role. It followed from the Court's judgment that a formal constitutional amendment would be required to alter the Upper House in any of its significant features.

An interesting aspect of the Court's judgment was its threefold approach to constitutional powers. While matters exclusively relating to the federal or provincial constitutions could be altered, respectively, by an ordinary statute enacted either by Parliament or the provincial legislatures, some matters affecting both jointly, such as the Senate, could be amended by neither unilaterally but required joint action culminating in a formal amendment to the Constitution.

Other Reform Proposals

Early in 1984, a joint Committee of the Senate and House of Commons recommended that Senators in future be elected, representing major "regions" of the country as well as minority groups.[7] The reform committee suggested that the present Senate be expanded to 144 seats from the present 104 to provide additional representation for some of the smaller and western provinces.[8]

Senators would be elected for a term of nine years, but would not be eligible for re-election, being limited to a single term. One-third of the total number of Senators would be elected at three-year intervals. The reconstituted Chamber would have only a 120-day suspensive veto over most legislation passed by the Lower House. Re-passage of Commons legislation at the termination of the veto period would make it law regardless of Senate opposition. The Senate, however, would acquire an absolute veto over language rights, with a double majority composed of (1) French-speaking, and (2) Senators as a whole, being imperatively required for the passage of such laws.

One of the more contentious features of the above proposal is the limitation of Senators to a single, nine-year, non-renewable term which would sacrifice the fund of experience that members of other Upper Chambers can accumulate over periods of time. The Committee apparently considered that a single relatively longer term would made Senators more independent by relieving them of politi cal pressures and anxieties.

The present Senate has an absolute veto over all matters except constitutional amendments (where it has an 180-day delaying power), but has not exercised its veto power for decades. In 1926, the King Government's proposal to establish non-contributory old-age pensions jointly with the provinces was defeated in the Senate by a vote of 45-21. In the following year, however, the legislation was enacted.[9] Opposition like the foregoing to social welfare measures has reinforced the view of some critics, such as the New Democratic (socialist) Party that the Senate is a citadel of privilege and elitism, and should be abolished. This was the position, in fact, of Manitoba New Democratic MP Rod Murphy on the above Committee.

Others, however, considered that a more substantial regional or provincial presence in the national capital would have mitigated the bitterness of the Canadian debate on the patriation of the Constitution through which the country passed in 1980-82, the lingering aftereffects of which have not yet entirely disappeared.

Some alternative reform proposals share the common feature that appointments to a renovated Senate should be made by the provinces rather than the Federal Government. These proposals envisage the Upper Chamber as a legislative body whose primary function is to review federal legislation having significant regional impact. The Canadian Bar Association, for example, has suggested that a reformed Senate could approve shared-cost programmes with the provinces (e.g. for medical and social services) requiring for passage a two-thirds majority in the Upper House as evidence of a "national consensus". The Chamber would have power to amend or reject any legislation subject to the overriding power of the House of Commons to re-enact it, and would also endorse or refuse the federal use of peacetime emergency powers and other unilateral measures.[10] The *Pépin-Robarts Report* would substitute a 60-member Council of the Federation composed of delegations representing and instructed by the various provincial Governments.[11] Each provincial delegation in the new Chamber would be led either by the Premier or a provincial Cabinet Minister. Federal Cabinet Ministers would be non-voting members, since the function of the renovated Chamber would be to represent *provincial* interests. No province would have more than one-fifth of the total seats allotted. The rapidly growing province of British Columbia has also advocated a Senate in which delegates would represent provincial Governments, with approximate equality between Canada's five regions of which that province would be the westernmost region. Each provincial delegation, moreover, would cast a bloc vote for or against matters expressly designated to be of high provincial interest. In other matters, Senators would be free to vote according to their conscience.

Conclusion : The Historical Background

Our Canadian Upper House was patterned largely on the British House of Lords, and in recent years, like its model, it has attracted sharp criticism. Both Chambers are unelected anachronisms in a democratic age. They each play distinctly secondary roles in the legislative process. Yet to be fair, they also each have reservoirs of experience which enable them to do highly useful committee work. They are forums of sober second thought neither of which, in an age of extensive spending, can initiate money Bills. The British Parliament Act, 1949, provides that any Bill passed by the Lower but rejected by the Upper Chamber can become law after one year, or in the case of a money Bill, after one month. By Section 47 of the Constitution Act, 1982, the Canadian Senate has the power merely to delay constitutional amendments for a 180-day period, at the expiry of which the amendment becomes law if the Lower House again adopts the resolution. Perhaps because patronage appointments are such a central feature of the British and Canadian Upper Houses, they each lack a real political constituency. In any confrontation with the elected Lower House they would have to back down, most probably. It would be only in some great crises, when the House of Commons was manifestly trying to override the will of the people, that the Senate as presently constituted could play an authentic obstructive role. Such a legislative body is essentially a weak body, and there might be forces which would perpetuate its weakness. The House of Commons might not be eager to establish a powerful rival centre of parliamentary authority. Unless there can be real reform, I think the Senate should be abolished ; I would not like to see the present body continued indefinitely. But if we do reform the Senate, how should we go about it ?

The Senate and Parliament generally must acquire greater vitality. The Senate should be an elected body. The substitution of a provincial for a federal appointing power, with leading Senators from each province exercising a bloc vote on matters of high provincial interest, creates too elitist a decision-making process. Citizens must relate more closely to their elected representatives. A senate like the foregoing would merely transpose the federal-provincial conference of first ministers to our central parliamentary institutions. Senators might be elected for six-year terms, with half of the Chamber being elected at three-year intervals to provide an element of continuity. Each province or territory could be regarded as a single constituency with a form of preferential ballot being used.

Equal Representation of Provinces

I would prefer to see a reformed Senate in which the individual provinces were granted equal representation. Representation by population is the rule in the Lower House, and to have an approximation of the same principle in the Upper House (especially an Upper House with significant new powers) would create too much centralization. The weight of numbers will be felt in the Lower House, which alone initiates money Bills, and to which the Government will continue to be solely responsible. Under any new regime, a strong majority of Cabinet members will continue to sit in the Lower House. That great political statesman James Madison discusses the optimum relationship of two Houses in a federation in *Federalist No. 39* :

> The House of Representatives will derive its powers from the people of America ; and the people will be represented in the same proportion and on the same principle as they are in the legislature of a particular state, so far the government is *national*, not *federal*. The Senate, on the other hand, will derive its powers from the states as political and co-equal societies ; and these will be represented on the principle of

> equality in the Senate . . . So far the government is *Federal* not national.[12]

Paraphrasing Madison, we should endeavour to create a genuine federal system by endowing the provinces with equal representation. The danger of imposing a population principle in both Houses would be that we would tend towards an overcentralized national rather than federal polity. As with Australia, I would recommend ten senators from each of our ten provinces, with two Senators from each Territory for a total complement of 104. The three major objections that I foresee to my proposal are : (a) that the disparities in population between the provinces in Canada are too great to allow for equal representation ; (b) that Canada is more properly an entity of five regions rather than ten provinces, and it is the regions that should have approximately equal representation, or (c) that equal provincial representation might ignore Quebec's claim to special constitutional status.

Proceeding first to the argument of population disparity, that is precisely why equal representation in the Upper House is necessary. In an equitable federation, local units of lesser population should not be overwhelmed by weight of numbers. The Lower House expresses the national will on the basis of population, but the Upper House protects the specific federal interests of the local units. In case of disagreement, we compromise. Such dispute-resolving techniques as a joint committee of both Houses, or even a combined session can be used to settle differences.

It should be emphasized that other federations have not found large population disparities among the units an impediment to equal representation in the Upper House. For example, just compare the population of either Wyoming or Alaska with California in the United States. California, in fact, has more than fifty times the population of either Wyoming or Alaska yet each of the three mentioned States has two members in the U.S. Senate. The population disparities in Australia are not as great, but the small State of Tasmania, for example, has only about one-tenth the population of New South Wales. Nevertheless, they each have ten members in the Upper House in Canberra. An excellent philosophical reason for equality of representation is to ensure that provinces or states having certain vital interests will not simply be overwhelmed by a Lower Chamber where seats are allocated exclusively on the basis of density of population. To give a couple of examples from Australia, in 1939 Western Australian Senators helped defeat a gold-tax Bill which would have retarded the expansion of the gold-mining industry in their State—a second Bill at a reduced tax rate was subsequently passed. In 1958, Southern Australian Senators ensured over stiff opposition that their State would get a fair share of water resources from a local hydro-electric project.

The Mythical Nature of Regions

Turning to the argument that it is the regions that should be represented and not provinces, I ask, simply, what is a region? What is this shadowy thing we call a region? How many shared interests, or how much regional homogeneity is there? Alberta and Saskatchewan disagree on the Crow rate; Saskatchewan and Manitoba had major differences on constitutional patriation; Nova Scotia and Newfoundland have deep disagreements vis-a-vis Ottawa on the ownership of off-shore resources. In such cases, who would speak for the region? The differences in industrial development between Prince Edward Island and Nova Scotia, or between Saskatchewan and Alberta make it difficult to logically classify them as members of a common region. Our perspective is typically provincial rather than regional. The northern Ontario hinterland has more affinity with the adjacent prairies than it does with the industrialized south of the province, if Ontario is taken as a region.

But would equality of representation jeopardize the special constitutional interests of Quebec? I don't think so. Where its special constitutional interests were involved, it could be provided that no action derogating from linguistic, cultural or other defined rights would be taken without the assent of Quebec Senators who would be regarded as a unit for that purpose. In this limited case, in other words, the principle of duality would apply.

A reformed Senate could exercise a supervisory role over the plethora of delegated legislation created every year. The Australian Senate ably discharges such a function. Does the conferment of too much rule-making power on officials detract from the rule of law? Or do subordinate regulations conform to the *Charter of Rights and Freedoms*? The Senate might also confirm senior judicial and executive appointments and play a bigger role in the field of foreign policy, if not approving treaties, at least discussing different policy options for Canada.

FOOTNOTES

1. *Statutes of Canada*, 1974-75-76, c. 53.
2. Ibid., 1965, c. 4.
3. W.H. McConnell, *Commentary on the British North America Act*, Toronto, 1977, p. 68.
4. *Edwards* v. *A.-G. Canada* [1930], A.C. 124.
5. See McConnell, "The House of the Federation : A Critical Evaluation", 27 *Can. B. Rev.* 513 (1979).
6. Re : Authority of Parliament in Relation to the Upper House [1980], I.S.C.R. 54 ; 102 D.L.R. (3d) at 1.
7. Parliament, Canada, *Report of the Special Joint Committee on Senate Reform*, January, 1984.
8. The proposed distribution, with the present membership in brackets, would be : Newfoundland, 12 (6) ; Prince Edward Island, 6 (4) ; Nova Scotia, 12 (10) ; New Brunswick, 12 (10) ; Quebec, 24 (24) ; Ontario, 24 (24) ; Manitoba, 12 (6) ; Saskatchewan, 12 (6) ; Alberta, 12 (6) ; British Columbia, 12 (6) ; the Yukon, 2 (1) ; and the Northwest Territories, 4 (1).
9. *Statutes of Canada*, 17 Geo. V., c. 35 (1927).
10. Committee on the Constitution of the Canadian Bar Association, *Towards a New Canada*, Ottawa, 1978, pp. 37-46.
11. The Task Force on Canadian Unity, *A Future Together : Observations and Recommendations*, Ottawa, January, 1979, pp. 96-99.
12. *The Federalist Papers* (Mentor Edition), New York, 1961, p. 244.

TWO

BHAGWAN D. DUA

CANADA :
The Appointment and Removal of Judges

In recent years, particularly after the *Judges Transfer* case,[1] there has been extensive debate regarding the appointment, transfer and confirmation of High Court judges in India. Although a variety of suggestions[2] have been made to limit the power of the central executive in appointment and tenure matters in order to maintain the non-partisan nature of the judiciary, the political and legal community in India has yet to develop a consensus about what should be the rules of the game for this process. While each nation works out its own unique equilibrium among the different branches of government, it is both relevant and instructive to examine another country where the constitutional-institutional arrangements are similar in nature.[3] Both Canada and India are federal-parliamentary systems ; both have Supreme Courts at the apex of the judicial pyramid, which is more or less insulated from the other two branches of the Government, even though the Canadian Supreme Court owes its existence to a simple statute of 1875.

My purpose in this paper is to discuss some of the issues relating to the appointment and removal of federally appointed judges in Canada. More specifically, Part I of the paper will deal with the process of appointment of judges and some of the controversies surrounding that process. Part II will focus on the procedure for removal of judges and summarize a few cases of judicial misconduct. This will be followed by a summary of the paper.

The federal government in Canada is responsible for more than 500 judicial appointments (Supreme Court—9 ; Federal Court—16 ; Provincial Supreme Courts—277 ; District and County Courts—201). Judges are appointed by the Governor-General on the advice of the federal Minister of Justice and/or the Prime Minister[4] and hold office during "good behaviour" until the age of retirement (75 years in the case of judges of the Supreme Court and 70 years in other cases). They can be removed from office by the Governor-General only on Address of the Senate and the House of Commons.[5] Thus, unlike in India where a formal "consultation" mechanism is *constitutionally* in place to recommend senior-level judicial appointments to the executive,[6] the Canadian federal government enjoys exclusive and exhaustive power to staff the federal judicature.

PART I

THE CONTROVERSY REGARDING JUDICIAL APPOINTMENTS

The controversy regarding judicial appointments has invariably focussed on one central question : How to delimit the power of the federal government so as to ensure that (a) all judicial appointments are based on merit ; and (b) the provinces (or regions) have some input in judicial appointments in general, and to the Supreme Court of Canada (which is the final court of appeal in federal-provincial conflicts) in particular.

Patronage v. Merit

A traditional criticism of judicial appointments has been that they have been invariably political and partisan in nature. As R.B. Bennet (Prime Minister, 1930-35) admitted :[7]

> There has been too much political patronage concerned in appointments to the Bench. The result has been that the test whether a man is entitled to a seat on the Bench has seemed to be whether he has run an election and lost it. Very often that has been so. If he has run an election and won it, peradventure he should not look for a seat on the Bench because he can better serve his country in some other capacity.

Although it is not necessarily the case that all appointees ascend to the Bench through the political route, it is nonetheless conceded that partisan service is a desirable asset for judicial appointments. As Dawson and Ward report :[8]

> Party affiliations play a varying part ; but they are not often entirely absent from an appointment, and at times actually prevent the choice falling on those with more desirable qualities. Many potentially able judges have undoubtedly been effectively disqualified for appointment to the Bench because they belonged to the wrong party, and it must be realized that for lawyers who support parties other than the Liberal and Conservative, the disqualification is all but absolute.

Regardless of the substantial evidence to the effect that membership in or association with the political party in power in Ottawa helps, it is important to mention that the government does rate professional and legal expertise highly in making judicial appointments. In fact, the criterion of expertise has become more pronounced in recent years in the case of appointees to the Supreme Court of Canada. As Paul Weiler notes :[9]

> For a long time, political life was the preferred route and a surprising number of Supreme Court judges came directly from the federal Cabinet. In recent years this avenue has receded in importance . . . One would think that an obvious factor in appointments to the Supreme Court would be prior judicial experience in a lower court . . . In the last 35 years or so, this route also has declined in importance and only one-third or so have satisfied this condition . . . A trend in recent years has been the selection of judges with close, continuing association with the law schools . . . culminating in the recent appointment of one of the most distinguished full-time Canadian law professors, Mr. Justice Laskin.

While the above trends augur well for the prestige of the Supreme Court, it has also been suggested that the appointment procedures should be reformed to incorporate some non-partisan mechanism to assess the legal ability of prospective judges. The present accrediting system, initiated in 1967, requires the Government to submit the names of prospective appointees to the judicial committee of the Canadian Bar Association which, in turn, classifies candidates as "well qualified", "qualified", and "not qualified". Although this procedure is sufficiently investigative of judicial talent, it does not bind the government to appoint the most well-qualified persons to the Bench.[10] There is no doubt that the search for talent is now more extensive and that some appointments have crossed party lines, e.g. Thomas Berger, John Osler, Charles Dubin, Davie Fulton, Allan Goodman were appointed to different provincial Supreme Courts even though none of them belonged to the Liberal Party which appointed them. Nevertheless, the lack of a systematic approach to appointments has fostered a continual cry for reforms.

Provincial Representation

Given the peripheralized nature of Canadian federalism (cf. India) and the general perception of the Supreme Court as "pro-federal",[11] the provincial governments have often expressed serious concern about the exclusive power of the federal government to make appointments to the highest court of the land. The principle underlying such a concern was well stated by the authors of the *Tremblay Report* :[12]

> . . . In a federal system, theory and common sense alike demand that a tribunal completely independent of the parties to the suit shall decide, in final resort, quarrels concerning the division of powers. And if this requirement proves either too difficult to meet or contrary to national susceptibilities, at least appointments to the Supreme Court must not be the exclusive appanage of one of the two orders of government.

Although all the provincial governments desire some change in the present system of appointments, the province of Quebec is particularly concerned with the present composition of the Court. The Constitution provides that the federal government must select at least three judges for the Supreme Court from the Quebec Bar or Bench because Quebec has a distinct civil law. However, this arrangement has not been satisfactory to the province. Quebecers have frequently complained that the Court's decisions neither recognize the cultural duality of Canada nor reflect the differences between the civil and common law systems. Hence, a number of suggestions have been made to restructure the Court to improve its legitimacy in Quebec. As one of the speakers before the *Task Force on Canadian Unity* said :[13]

> We need a specialized Supreme Court for dealing with conflicts between the two official languages. And my suggestion is that the only possible fair basis for this specialized Supreme Court is a 50-50 basis, half francophone and half anglophone. And I suggest furthermore that the half francophone should be divided roughly one-half Quebec and one-half drawn from the francophone federations of the rest of Canada.

Another speaker said :[14]

> As a method of calming suspicions, it could be provided that in constitutional matters the Court should have equal representation between the judges appointed from Quebec and from the other regions of Canada.

A third speaker's concern was beyond the question of representation from Quebec ; he suggested that the Court should not only be restructured to provide for greater representation from Quebec but also for regional appointments :[15]

> The composition of the Supreme Court could be altered in cases which are to be decided by the civil law of Quebec. Having greater representation from Quebec in civil-law cases would enhance the legitimacy of the Supreme Court's decisions in Quebec. The Court, for the purposes of federal-provincial issues, should be so structured that provinces and regions would be able to appoint judges directly from their regions. This would allow the provinces some control over the composition of the Court in matters directly affecting their interests and would also lead to greater respect for the decisions of the Supreme Court.

The general thrusts of the suggested reforms have been to adopt the American model of ratification of judicial appointments by an elected Upper Chamber (if an elected Upper Chamber is established in Canada[16]) or the German model of a specialized constitutional court, that is separate from and independent of the present Supreme Court,[17] or a concurrence model where the two levels of government concur in appointments. The abortive 1971 Victoria Charter, for example, provided that (i) appointments to the Supreme Court were to be by agreement between the provincial and federal attorneys-general ; and (ii) failing such an agreement, the issue was to be resolved by a nominating committee consisting of the provincial and federal attorneys-general and a chairman.[18] The 1978 Constitutional Amendment Bill enlarged the idea of concurrence between the two levels of government and proposed that (i) the Court should consist of eleven judges based on regional representation (four from Quebec, and at least one from each of the other four regions, including British Columbia); (ii) nominations for the Bench should be made by an agreement between the federal and the provincial attorneys-general or by a nomination council if no such agreement could be concluded ; and (iii) all appointments should be ratified by a reconstituted Senate (restructured and named as the House of the Federation).[19] In the same year, the Province of Alberta proposed a scheme that approximated the German model : a specialized tribunal to deal only with constitutional issues. The Canadian version of such a tribunal would include seven judges chosen for each case, by rotation, by the federal authorities from a panel of forty to fifty names, established from lists of experienced judges submitted by the provinces.[20]

While the debate among the political leaders over appointments to the Court seems to have settled around the principle of regional input or concurrence, not all the legal scholars are supportive of this model. Paul Weiler, for example, suggested that the Prime Minister should make nominations to the Court but such nominations should be approved by a committee of the Parliament.[21] Bora Laskin, Chief Justice of the present Supreme Court, would like the federal government to seek wider professional advice on appointments rather than to put a prospective judge through a cross-examination by a parliamentary committee. As he stated in an interview :[22]

> I have great reservations about the utility of an examination of a prospective judge's position on various issues in advance of his appointment. I think that to some degree that misstates the judicial function . . . A larger professional input in determination of the qualifications of a prospective appointee is much to be preferred than just indiscriminate exposure of an appointee to a range of questions, some of which may be by people who themselves don't understand that the input from professional associates, from the bar, should be more than adequate.

It will take a long time before any concrete changes in the existing appointment procedures are accomplished. This in part reflects the general nature of the Canadian political system, which is, among other things, too democratic and peripheralized to embrace change easily.

PART II

REMOVAL OF JUDGES

Unlike the civil servants, federally appointed judges are almost in an impregnable position with respect to tenure in office. It is very difficult to remove them so long as they retain full possession of their faculties and are reasonably capable of performing their judicial duties. "Good behaviour or, to use the Latin term, *quam diu se bene gesserint*," writes Shetreet,[23]

> . . . creates an office for life determinable only by the death of the grantee or upon his breach of good behaviour. The grantee holds the office under the conditions that 'he shall behave himself well in it', or in Hawkins' words, that he shall 'execute it diligently and faithfully'. This condition applies by law whether or not it was expressly provided.

In Canada, judges hold office during good behaviour and can be removed by the Governor-General only after an address from both the Houses of Parliament.[24] Although the process appears simple, it is so hedged with cumbersome formalities that it is virtually impossible to implement it. In fact, no judge has ever been removed through this procedure since the beginning of Confederation (1967).[25]

The difficulty of instituting the removel procedure raises the question of how do we get rid of unworthy judges or discipline judges who lack good behaviour ? After all, judges are human and fallible, even though there is a certain element of mystique attached to their functions. Of course, it will be making a mockery of the independence of the judiciary if the judges were to be removed for error in judgment or for misconstruing the law. There must, however, be some workable method to remove judges whose conduct does not befit their high office. The issue of removal involves two things :

(a) what is the workable mechanism for removing judges ; and
(b) what is the definition and conception of "good behaviour" in Canada.

Workable Mechanism

It is healthy if a profession can effectively regulate itself. This argument applies particularly to the judicial profession because of the independence given to it. With the objective of preserving the independence of the judiciary, while at the same time protecting judges from unwarranted criticism of their conduct, Canada has established a Judicial Council,[26] pursuant to the Judges Act of 1970, consisting of high-ranking judges (the Chief Justice of Canada, and chief justices and associate chief justices of all the provincial superior courts) to investigate complaints about their colleagues in the federal judicature. The Council, through an investigating committee, initiates enquiries into cases of alleged judicial improprieties and misbehaviour.

Without going into the details of the various sections of the Judges Act, it is important to note that the Council has wide discretionary powers to oversee the judicial profession. These powers can be assessed from the standpoint of three basic questions that were raised and answered affirmatively in the recent *Berger* case :[27]

1. Does the Canadian Judicial Council have the power to investigate the extra-judicial conduct of a judge without his consent ?

2. Must there first be a *prima facie* case for removal of a judge from office before the Council or an Inquiry Committee appointed by the Council can commence an inquiry as to whether the judge should be removed from office ?
3. Does the Canadian Judicial Council have the power to reprimand or impose some lesser penalty than to recommend removal of a judge ?

Though the Council has no powers to remove a judge from the Bench, its confidential report to the Minister of Justice has sufficient weight, since it is sanctioned by the judicial establishment, to push the Minister one way or the other on the issue. Such a report may either exonerate the judge under inquiry or force him to bow out gracefully.

Since the Council does not have a long history, it is premature to evaluate its preformance (in fact, the Council received no complaints until December 2, 1975).[28] However, its very presence as a guardian of judical discipline and integrity seems to have enhanced, rather than compromised, the independence of judges, who would rather be investigated by their peers than by the executive or the legislative branch of the Government.

Conception of Good Behaviour

The term "good behaviour" is not amenable to precise definition. As early as 1883, the Justice Minister, Mr. Edward Blake, enunciated in Parliament the conditions which could justify removal from the Bench :[29]

> What was the cause, then, which could properly bring this judge's action under our consideration ? It was a charge of partiality, of malfeasance in office—not that the judge erred, for all may err in judgment, but that he degraded his office, betrayed his trust, wilfully and knowingly did a wrong thing, perverted justice and judgment—that is the nature of a charge which could alone make it proper to have been brought here.

While bribery, gross partiality and criminal proclivities clearly violate the requirements of good behaviour in any society, there are other more personal or private activities that lie on the border land of judicial misconduct. It would invariably be the situation, therefore, that the decision to remove a judge for judicial misconduct would depend on the circumstances of the case and on the conceptions of good behaviour of those persons who exercise disciplinary power over judges.

In general, however, it appears that the parameters for the conduct of judges are more restrictive than for other persons in positions of authority. The general code of conduct seems to be all-pervasive, thus penetrating into extra-judicial or non-judicial behaviour. Consequently, the Judges Act provides extensive scope for investigatory powers of the Canadian Judicial Council. Section 40(2) of the Act states :

> The Council may investigate *any complaint or allegation* made in respect of a judge of a superior, district or county court. (Italics mine.)

Section 41(2)(d) of the Act supports the wide degree of latitude given to the Council :

> . . . having been placed, by his conduct or otherwise, in a position incompatible with the due execution of his office.

In the final analysis, this section requires that the judges should not only discharge their judicial duties faithfully but also do nothing that will impair public confidence in the judiciary. In fact, Sir William Anson was of the view that Parliament could extend the principle of "good behaviour" to cover "any form of misconduct which would destroy public confidence in the holder of the office".[30]

Aside from the difficulties surrounding the application of the standard of judicial behaviour, the removal of a judge for misconduct is virtually a non-issue in Canada. It is very rare that one reads anything about the misconduct of judges, much less about their dismissals. This, of course, does not mean that there are no cases of misconduct ; it only means that judges prefer to resign if their conduct is called into question. Therefore, the public may not be aware if a particular judge resigned for reasons of misconduct or for more personal reasons, unless the judge makes his resignation a public issue. Consequently, any attempt to develop a profile on how the concept of "good behaviour" has been interpreted in practice has to be based on those cases of judicial resignations that became public.

1. The Stubbs Case, 1933

Mr. Lewis St. George Stubbs, a Manitoba Surrogate Court judge, was removed from the Bench in 1933 for judicial misconduct.[31]

After the Manitoba Court of Appeal overruled his decision not to grant letters of administration in the estate of Alexander Macdonald (a Winnipeg millionaire) to Macdonald's daughter and son-in-law, Judge Stubbs held a meeting in a public theatre and engineered a resolution to the effect that the Manitoba Legislature should invalidate the Appeal Court decision. Such lobbying in the public arena was too much for the senior judicial establishment to tolerate.

On a complaint from the Superior Court judges, the federal Minister of Justice appointed Mr. Justice Frank Ford as a Royal Commissioner to investigate the conduct of Judge Stubbs. After a 24-day hearing and 600,000 words of evidence (the testimony included the fact that Judge Stubbs had often said: "There is one law for the rich and another for the poor."), the Commission found him guilty of judicial misconduct.

In his own defense, Judge Stubbs said: "I would much rather have done what I did and go off the Bench than not to have done what I did and stay on the Bench." Ironically, three years later, Judge Stubbs was elected to the Manitoba Legislature.

2. The Fulton Case, 1980

Mr. Edmund Davie Fulton was forced to resign from the British Columbia Supreme Court in 1980.

Justice Fulton was appointed to the Bench in 1973 after a long political career (he was a member of Parliament—1945-68, Minister of Justice and Attorney-General in the Diefenbaker Cabinet, and had the makings of a Prime Minister). After six years of service on the Bench, he began to experience great difficulties with alcohol consumption. "The more I drank," he said in a recent interview, "my tolerance for alcohol was becoming less and less and the changes it brought about in my personality and judgment became more and more."[32]

Justice Fulton was found guilty of "drunken driving" twice in 1979. In the first trial, he was fined $ 500, but was allowed to remain on the Bench. In the second trial (which became more spectacular because it coincided with the publication of a book, *The Wendy King Story*, in which a former Vancouver prostitute wrongly identified Justice Fulton as one of her clients—she later publicly apologized for the mistake), Justice Fulton was not only forced to resign from the Bench but also sentenced to 14 days in jail and a $ 700 fine.

Justice Fulton believed that the sentence was harsh. "I still can't help feeling that if I were Mr. Smith down the street it wouldn't have happened. But I guess the Attorney-General felt it was a very public case and he felt that he couldn't appear to be going soft on a judge. But I had resigned and I felt I had paid sufficient penalty."[33]

3. The Berger Case, 1982

Mr. Justice Thomas R. Berger resigned from the British Columbia Supreme Court in 1982 even though the Canadian Judicial Council, which investigated his conduct, did not recommend his removal.

On a complaint from Mr. Justice G.A. Addy of the Federal Court of Canada in 1981, Justice Berger was investigated for making controversial political statements that were viewed as not within the bounds of propriety and the limits of proper judicial restraint. Even the Prime Minister had felt the heat of Justice Berger's comments and urged the judges to "do something about it".

This was the time when many controversial political issues were being debated in relation to the patriation of the Constitution, and therefore, Justice Berger was criticized for intervening in matters of serious political concern. As the Judicial Committee noted :[34]

> Justice Berger's office and experience as a Royal Commissioner . . . obviously made his comments newsworthy. He described the decision of the first ministers to "abandon"

native rights to be "mean-spirited and unbelievable". In his article he criticized the loss of Quebec's veto and argued for one amending formula in preference to another. He again attacked the first ministers for "repudiating" native rights and argued for the restoration of S. 34 "for the recognition and confirmation of aboriginal and treaty rights of Indians, Inuit and Metis."

Justice Berger's response was that while his conduct as a judge was unconventional, it was nevertheless done "with the best interests of my country in mind" and, moreover, the issues "transcended partisan politics". However, the Judicial Council did not accept these arguments :[35]

> We say again if a judge becomes so moved by conscience to speak out on a matter of great importance, on which there are opposing and conflicting political views, then he should not speak with the trappings and from the platform of a judge but rather resign and enter the arena where he, and not the judiciary, becomes not only the exponent of those views but also the target of those who oppose them.

While the Council did not recommend Justice Berger's removal from the Bench, it concluded :[36]

> . . . we view his conduct seriously and are of the view that it would support a recommendation for removal from office. There are, however, in addition to those already noted, special circumstances which make this case unique. As far as we are aware, this is the first time this issue has arisen for determination in Canada. It is certainly the first time the Council has been called on to deal with it. It is possible that Justice Berger, and other judges too, have been under a misapprehension as to the nature of the constraints imposed upon judges. That should not be so in the future. We do not, however, think it would be fair to set standards *ex post facto* to support a recommendation for removal in this case.

Justice Berger's resignation created few headlines in the Press. Moreover, it did not provoke any extensive lament for his innocence, except among a few of his friends and admirers. The Judicial Council did its job with skill and dexterity and laid down some reasonable guidelines (despite the consternation of many outspoken judges) to assess judicial misconduct in the future.

SUMMARY

In this paper, I have provided a general description of the appointment and removal process for federally appointed judges in Canada. Also I have outlined briefly some of the extra-constitutional procedures of consultation and investigation that have been developed in this regard. Although partronage appointments to the Bench are not uncommon, it is generally the case that the professional qualifications of the prospective appointees override purely partisan considerations. Nevertheless,. there is a growing concern to limit the appointment power of the federal government in order to reinforce both the reality and the image of non-partisanship on the Bench. The provincial governments, particularly, are anxious to provide more input in judicial appointments to the Supreme Court of Canada because of its adjudicative role in the federal-provincial relations.

While Canada has not experienced many cases of judges being ousted before their retirement, I have discussed three episodes culminating in the resignation of judges. These cases are inadequate to develop a complete profile of judicial misconduct. Nonetheless, they do provide an aperture to the world of judicial constraints.

NOTES

Since this paper was written, the Canadian Bar Association has drawn the following conclusions in its August 20, 1985, report on *The Appointment of Judges in Canada* :

"The present system of selection and appointments at the federal level is, in several respects, overly dominated by political considerations :

In most provinces politics plays too important a part in selecting candidates for the Bench—in some provinces to the point of abusing the concept of partisanship.

There have been unseemly political confrontations between the federal government and several provincial governments over who should be appointed to judicial office. These confrontations are not only demeaning to those involved ; they also demean the selection and appointment process and, ultimately, all those that hold the office of judge. It is our hope that our suggestions can help governments avoid the situation where certain provinces have refused to co-operate with the federal government and virtually vetoed appointments in an effort to bargain for candidates.

* Some judicial appointments have been made on the eve of a change of government or shortly after a government assumed with such haste as to give the impression that the political authority acted precipitately without the consideration and care that should be given to selecting the best person for the office of judge."

In addition to strengthening judical councils responsible for recommending provincial and territorial judicial appointments, the Canadian Bar Association has recommended that there should be an Advisory Committee (representing five constituencies—the Bench, the Bar, the Federal Government through the Minister of Justice, the Provincial Government through the Attorney-General, and the general public) in each province and territory to advise the Minister of Justice on appointments to Section 96 courts and to the Supreme Court of Canada.

The author is thankful to Professor J. Anthony Long for his helpful comments and revisions suggested during the preparation of this paper.

REFERENCES

1. See *Times of India*, January, 1, 1982 ; *India Today*, January 31, 1982 ; Bhagwan D. Dua, "Study in Executive-Judicial Conflict : The Indian Case", *Asian Survey*, Vol. XXIII, No. 4, April 1983.
2. See N. R. Madhava Menon, "Judicial Appointments and Transfers", *Journal of the Bar Council of India*, VIII (1), 1981 ; *Eightieth Report, Law Commission of India* (New Delhi, 1979).
3. See R. MacGregor Dawson and Ward, *The Government of Canada* (Toronto : University Press, 1973) ; B.D. Dua and McCormick, "The Politics of Federalism : Canada and India",—unpublished paper presented at the Indo-Canadian Workshop, Osmania University, 1981.
4. See Geoffrey Stevens, "Appointment System Improved", in Paul W. Fox (ed.), *Politics : Canada* (Toronto : McGraw-Hill Ryerson Limited, 1982).
5. W.H. McConnell, *Commentary on the British North America Act* (Toronto : Macmillan of Canada, 1977).
6. See Articles 222(1), 217 (1) of the Constitution of India ; also, see B. Shiva Rao, *The Framing of India's Constitution* (New Delhi : Indian Institute of Public Administration, 1968), Chapter 17.

7. *Canadian House of Commons Debates*, May 17, 1932, p. 2999, referred to in R.M. Dawson and Ward, op. cit., p. 404.
8. R.M. Dawson and Ward, op. cit., p. 403.
9. Paul Weiler, *In the Last Resort : A Critical Study of the Supreme Court of Canada* (Toronto : Carswell/Methuen, 1974), p. 20.
10. See Geoffrey Stevens, op. cit.
11. Professor Peter H. Russell writes : "Federal authorities have yet to lose a constitutional decision before an independent Supreme Court of Canada, whereas provincial claims have been defeated on numerous occasions." See Russell, "The Supreme Court's Interpretation of the Constitution", in Paul W. Fox, op. cit. In a recent decision, the Supreme Court ruled that Ottawa owns, and controls the oil-rich ocean floor off Newfoundland's shores. The Premier of Newfoundland called this decision as "manifestly unjust" and added : "The question of rights to the offshore is a political question, not a legal one." See *Globe and Mail*, March 9, 1984.
12. *Report of the Royal Commission of Enquiry on Constitution Problems*, Vol. II (Quebec, 1956), p. 109.
13. *The Task Force on Canadian Unity : A Time to Speak—The Views of the Public* (Quebec, 1979), p. 250.
14. Ibid.
15. Ibid.
16. There has been extensive debate to reform the present appointed Senate to make it truly representative of the provinces/people. See Peter McCormick. Ernest C. Manning, Gordon Gibson, *Regional Representation* (Calgary, 1981) ; *Report of the Special Joint Committee on Senate Reform* (Ottawa, 1984).
17. *Harmony in Diversity : A New Federalism for Canada* (Alberta, 1978), p. 11.
18. *Proposals on the Constitution 1971-78* (Ottawa, 1979) ; also, D.V. Smiley, *Canada in Question : Federalism in the Eighties* (Toronto : McGraw-Hill Ryerson Limited, 1980), pp. 66-90.
19. *The Constitutional Amendment Bill* (Ottawa, 1978), pp. 49-66.
20. *Harmony in Diversity : A New Federalism for Canada* op. cit.
21. Paul Weiler, op. cit., p. 233.
22. *The Financial Post*, September 20, 1980, p. 20.
23. Shimon Shetreet, *Judges on Trial* (New York, North-Holland, 1976), pp. 88-89.
24. The County and District Court judges can be removed, under the Judges Act, by the Governor-General on the recommendation of the Minister of Justice. In case this is done, the order-in-council as well as other documents relating to dismissal must be laid before Parliament within fifteen days if sitting, or within fifteen days of the commencement of the next session.
25. The procedure was initiated in several cases—one recent (1966-67) example being that of Mr. Justice L. Landreville of the Ontario Supreme Court, who resigned when Parliament was about to prepare an address for his removal.

26. See W.H. McConnell, op. cit., pp. 323-324.
27. Canadian Judicial Council, "Report of the Investigation Committee to the Canadian Judicial Council in the matter of s. 40 of the Judges Act ; and in the matter of the Hon. Mr. Justice Berger of the Supreme Court of British Columbia," Mimeo. Ottawa, Canadian Judicial Council, 1982.
28. In addition to its investigative role, the Canadian Judicial Council has also many professional development functions. As Professor McConnell writes : "The Council also has the aims of promoting efficiency in court administration, uniformity in approach to legal problems, improving the quality of judicial service and sponsoring seminars for the education of judges. From time to time, it establishes conference of chief justices." See W.H. McConnell, op. cit.
29. *Canadian House of Commons Debate*, April 9, 1883, referred to by R.M. Dawson and Ward, op. cit., p. 400. Also see, Eugene Forsey, "Removal of Superior Court Judges", *Canadian Commentator*, February 1966 ; W.R. Lederman, "The Independence of the Judiciary", 34 *Canadian Bar Review*, 1956.
30. William Anson, *Law and Custom of the Constitution* (Oxford, Clarendon Press, 3rd edn.), p. 222.
31. Paul W. Fox (ed.), op. cit., (4th edn., 1977), p. 551.
32. *Globe and Mail*, March 9, 1984.
33. Ibid.
34. Mimeo of the Canadian Judicial Council, 1982, p. 18.
35. Ibid., p. 22.
36. Ibid., p. 23.

THREE

PETER RUSSELL

THE SUPREME COURT DECISION
Bold Statescraft Based on Questionable Jurisprudence

ON September 28, 1981, the Supreme Court of Canada released its decision in what is surely the most momentous case in the Court's history. Never before has Canada awaited so expectantly for a decision from its highest court. Indeed, even if we look south of the border to the democracy in whose history Supreme Court decisions have played such a dramatic role, it is difficult to find a smaller occasion when the main stream of national political life flowed so relentlessly up to a Supreme Court decision. Perhaps the *Dred Scott* case is a parallel.

Writing so soon after the decision when a constitutional accord between the federal government and all the provinces except Quebec has been consummated, the political consequences of the decision may appear to be essentially positive. The Supreme Court's decision was the decisive event in paving the way for a federal-provincial accommodation that would enable the Canadian constitution to be patriated in a manner acceptable to the federal government and nine provinces. The split nature of the Court's verdict gave both Ottawa and the provinces a strong incentive to return to the bargainning table they had abandoned a year earlier. While the decision gave Ottawa a legal green light to proceed unilaterally with its constitutional plans, it cast a heavy mantle of political illegitimacy over the constitutional changes that would result from such a procedure. On the other hand, while the decision confirmed the provinces' claim that their participation in fundamental constitutional change was a constitutional requirement, it warned the provinces that if they failed to work out an agreement with Ottawa, Ottawa could go ahead without them and the courts would do nothing to enforce the provinces' right of participation. When the federal and provincial leaders assembled at the Ottawa Conference Centre on November 2, their opening statements testified to the efficiency of the Supreme Court's decision in restoring their interest in reaching an accommodation on the Constitution.

But the risk to Canada inherent in the Court's decision was also apparent as one contemplated the possibility that an accommodation might not have been reached and the federal government might then have exercised its legal option of proceeding unilaterally. If that had occurred, the country would have experienced the worst possible consequences of the Court's decision. Patriation with an amending formula and a charter of rights would have been achieved, but in a manner which our highest court considered to be unconstitutional. One could scarcely think of a worse way for Canada to finally take charge of her own constitutional affairs and inaugurate a new regime of entrenched rights and freedoms.

The risk I have described has not entirely dissipated. It is now clear that the Lévesque government will do all it can to undermine the legitimacy of the November 5 accord and the Canadian Constitution it is likely to produce. As part of this campaign, the question of whether Quebec's consent is a constitutional requirement for changes in the Canadian Constitution affecting Quebec's powers has been referred to the Quebec Court of Appeal.[1] The outcome of this court action is difficult to predict. If the constitutional resolution passed by the Canadian Parliament and now delivered to the Queen[2] obtains a swift passage through the British Parliament, the Quebec Court of Appeal or the Supreme Court of Canada might view the question as moot and refuse to answer it. What is predictable is that René Lévesque's government and the separatist movement will attempt to take maximum political advantage of any judicial outcome. A refusal to answer the question, given the courts' willingness to answer the earlier decisions, will be branded as a gross injustice and an affront to constitutional government. If the courts deny that Quebec has a veto, the judges will be pilloried as *vendus* and agents of the federal government. Finally, there is the possibility that the courts, or at least a majority of their Quebec francophone members, will find that the requirement of substantial provincial consent has a cultural as well as quantitative dimension that makes Quebec's consent a constitutional requirement at least in a conventional sense. Such a decision would do much to undermine the legitimacy of Canada's newly patriated Constitution in the province of Quebec and to increase support for Quebec independence.

Criteria for Assessing the Decision

Given the decision's weighty political consequences it is tempting to assess the decision solely on the basis of its political results rather than on the quality of the judges' reasoning. Certainly the key political actors in the constitutional struggle do not appear to have been greatly influenced by the arguments the Supreme Court judges advanced for their holdings. Federal and provincial politicians were making public statements about the decision within hours of its release. These political leaders looked for what they could use in the decision to enhance their cause—the provincial Premiers (at least the eight who opposed the federal initiative) emphasizing the majority's conclusion that the federal government's unilateral approach was unconstitutional in a conventional sense; federal leaders emphasizing a different majority's finding that there was no legal bar to the federal government's proceeding in this unconstitutional fashion. For the media and the public whose opinion is shaped by the media, the justices' reasoning was of little consequence. The mass media cannot communicate information about as complex a matter as the reasons for a judicial decision. They can only report the "bottom line"—the bare results. Given that the decision had, in effect, two "bottom lines" with no clear winner, the public probably found the decision confusing. Any damage this may have done to the Supreme Court's public reputation was likely offset by the fact that the split nature of the Court's verdict immunized the Court from attack by either group of contending politicians and rekindled interest in seeking a broad Canadian consensus.

Even if short-run political reactions are not influenced by the Court's reasons, it is to be hoped that in the longer run the reasons advanced by the judges as the grounds for their decision will figure more prominently in Canadians' assessments of the merits of the decision. For adjudicative decisions, unlike the decisions of the political branches of government, "the quality of rationality . . . is a prerequisite for their moral force."[3] Judges, especially those who serve on our highest court of appeal, are required to persuade us by their reasons that their findings are based on a wise and accurate reading of our constitutional and legal experience. But, while the nature of the judical process obliges us to examine the soundness of the reasoning on which the judges' conclusions rest, we may well find that the rationality of a decision of this kind might have to be tested on two planes —one, more narrowly jurisprudential and related to the internal logic of the decision, and the other, more politically prudential and related to the exigencies of the national crisis.

Having emphasized the importance of assessing the judges' reasons, I must acknowledge that the central issue in this case is such as to reduce the long-run importance of the majority and dissenting opinions. Normally judicial opinions can have a developmental effect on the law by leaving certain aspects of a question somewhat open and by providing ideas and arguments that might be used by counsel in subsequent cases to persuade judges to revise or further refine legal doctrines. However, aside from the response to Quebec's current court challenge, there will not likely be an occasion for future judicial decision-making on the main point at issue in the case at hand—namely, whether some or all of the Canadian provinces must consent to constitutional amendments affecting their powers. For, if the Canadian Constitution is soon patriated with a comprehensive amending formula, this particular question will henceforth be governed by the written constitutional text.

There is, however, a broader constitutional issue at the very core of this case which will be of enduring importance and is not capable of being definitively resolved by amendments to our written Constitution. That issue is the nature of constitutional convention and its relationship to law. If the Supreme Court's decision in this case is read 50 years from now for more than its "bottom line", I suspect that it will be because of what the judges said on the general question of law and convention. Accordingly, my own comments on the decision will give priority to the Courts treatment of that question.

Should the Court have Answered the Questions ?

Before considering the Supreme Court's decision on the substantial issues, a threshold question must be raised. Were the questions appropriate for a court to answer ? The federal government's position throughout was that the rules and principles concerning Canadian requests to the U.K. Parliament for amendments to the BNA Act were entirely in the realm of convention not law and as such were not appropriate for judicial determination.[4] This is one of the reasons for the federal government's refusal to exercise its option of referring questions concerning the validity of its unilateral approach directly to the Supreme Court of Canada. The Court's holding on the nature of convention may seem to vindicate the federal government. The Court held that conventions, although part of the Constitution, are distinct from the law of the Constitution and that the remedy for breach of convention must be obtained in the political arena not from the courts. If in the Court's view constitutional conventions are entirely political and not at all legal in nature, what, it might be asked, was a court of law doing rendering a decision on a non-legal subject ?

It is no answer to this question to say that the Supreme Court had no choice but to answer the questions put to the provincial courts of appeal and appealed to the Supreme Court. Although provincial and federal legislation establishing the reference case procedure appear to put virtually no limits on the questions which governments can submit to courts, Canadian judges have refused to answer questions considered to be inappropriate for judicial determination. As recently as the *Senate Reference* of 1980, the Supreme Court had refused to answer several questions about Parliament's power to make certain changes in the Senate because these questions were too vague and indeterminate.[5] Also, a majority on the Manitoba Court of Appeal had refused to answer the first question at issue in this case—namely, whether the contents of the constitutional resolution before the Court if enacted would affect federal-provincial relations or provincial powers—because, at the time, the resolution was still being debated in Parliament and there was no telling how it might be amended before it was finally adopted. This objection to the indeterminate nature of the first question had, however, been overcome when the case went on appeal to the Supreme Court by virtue of an all-party agreement in the House of Commons that no further amendments would be made to the resolution submitted to the Supreme Court in April 1981.

Still, the issue remains of whether the Supreme Court should have answered the question about the existence of a convention—a question which, in its own view, was not a legal question. This, it should be noted, is to pose the issue of justiciability in narrower terms than the Trudeau Government's claim that there was no justiciable question concerning the federal government's unilateral procedure. That broad claim was surely untenable. There were a number of important arguments based, *inter alia*, on an interpretation of the Statute of Westminster, to the effect that there was a legal requirement of provincial consent. These arguments clearly raised issues appropriate for judicial determination. Further, the relationship of constitutional convention to law is itself a legal question.

When disputes arise about a person's or a government's rights, obligations or powers, it is the function of courts to provide authoritative rulings on these disputed questions of law. That is the *raison d'être* of the judiciary in our system of government. Thus, the Supreme Court had no difficulty in determining, without dissent, that the questions as to whether provincial consent was a constitutional requirement in a legal sense (one dimension of the third question in the Manitoba and Newfoundland appeals) or whether Parliament was authorized by statute to proceed with certain amendments without provincial consent (one dimension of the second Quebec question) were justiciable.[6]

But the Court could not give the same justification for its decision to treat the question about constitutional convention as justiciable. Here, I think, the Court was "hoist with its own petard". Because it separated convention from law so completely it had difficulty explaining what business it had as a court of law answering a non-legal question. Personally, I am not persuaded by the Court that there is such a complete gulf between law and convention. I will advance my arguments on this point later in this paper. Here I wish only to draw attention to a lack of intellectual coherence in the Court's overall handling of the convention question.

The three dissenting judges on the convention question (Chief

Justice Laskin, Justices Estey and McIntyre) were clearly troubled by the justiciability issue. At the beginning of their opinion they explain that because, in their view (and the view of the majority), convention is not law, questions concerning the existence of convention normally ought not to be answered as "it is not the function of the Court to go beyond legal determinations". Still, they were willing to answer these questions—"notwithstanding their extra-legal nature"—"because of the unusual nature of these References and because the issues raised in the questions now before us were argued at some length before the court and have been the subject of the reasons of the majority."[7] The majority appear less conscience-stricken about justiciability. They adopt the opinion of Chief Justice Freedman of the Manitoba Court of Appeal that even if the existence of a convention is not a question of law it is, nevertheless, a question which is "constitutional in character". Further, they point out that in answering the question, they are not enforcing a constitutional convention but simply recognizing its existence—something which courts have often done in the past when conventions have been used as an aid to constitutional or statutory construction.[8]

Now I can accept the latter argument because, in my view, it is the courts' very use of conventions and the principles upon which they are based in interpreting legal rights and duties that makes it wrong to divorce convention completely from law. But on this point, of course, the Court's view is different from mine. In their view convention is in no sense part of constitutional law. So, I remain unconvinced by their own or Justice Freedman's reasons that, given their views on the nature of convention, they should have answered this part of the reference questions.

To understand why the Supreme Court judges answered the questions concerning convention we have to look beyond the internal logic of their arguments to their sense of the necessities of judicial statecraft. This is hinted at in the dissenting judges' vague reference to "the unusual nature of these References". The circumstances surrounding these References certainly were unusual. The country was caught in a very difficult constitutional impasse. There was a widely shared assumption by the people and the politicians that a Supreme Court decision was the next essential step in resolving the crisis. A refusal to deal with a major dimension of the reference questions might reasonably have been regarded as threatening greater damage to the constitutional fabric of the country than would stretching the notion of justiciability to embrace what the Court regarded as a constitutional question of a non-legal kind.

Partisans of the federal government might contest the view that a judicial decision was needed. Mr. Chrétien, the federal Justice Minister, is reported to have opposed suspending the federal initiative to await a court decision on the grounds that

> such a delay would set a dangerous precedent, whereby any citizen or group could challenge the legality of government action before it was taken and thus suspend the ability of Parliament to pass legislation.[9]

Such an argument is not sound. Among other things, it ignores the fact that the reference procedure can only be initiated by governments and that it has been used many times by both levels of government to obtain advisory opinions on legislative proposals.[10]

No doubt court references are often used by a province or by the federal government partly to obtain some tactical advantage in federal-provincial bargaining. In this case clearly it was the provinces that felt they had most to gain by referring the matter to the courts. At the very least the court cases would slow down the federal initiative. A number of provincially initiated references would entail even more delay than a federal reference directly to the Supreme Court and increase the probability of obtaining a judicial ruling favourable to the provincial position. The federal government's decision not to pre-empt the provinces and initiate its own reference gave the provinces the additional advantage of being able to frame questions in a manner best calculated to elicit answers favourable to their position.

The fact that reference cases may be tactical manoeuvres in federal-provincial controversies does not negate their value in Canada's constitutional system. While they entail the risk of enabling politicians to plunge our higher appeal courts into the thick of the hottest federal-provincial controversies, they have the advantage of making it possible to remove constitutional doubts before implementing major changes in legislation or the constitution. Imagine the situation which would have occurred had Parliament forged ahead in 1979 and replaced the Senate with a House of the Federation only to have the constitutional amendment effecting this change subsequently challenged in the courts. Assuming the Supreme Court would have decided such a case in the same way it decided the 1980 Reference, Canada would have had an unconstitutional House of Parliament.

In the case at hand, where the very foundation of Canada's constitution and a major change in its system of government—a constitutional charter of rights—were at issue, it was in the country's interest to resolve doubts about the constitutionality of these changes before rather than after they were made. Having said this, it must be admitted that the Court's decision was such as to retain the possibility that the changes might still be made in a manner not only alleged by provincial politicians to be unconstitutional but also held by a majority of the Supreme Court to be unconstitutional. This was surely the great risk inherent in the Court's decision : that Canada might find itself in the predicament of having an unconstitutional constitution.

The Nature of Convention

For Canada, and indeed for all democracies whose constitutions combine "unwritten" conventions with "written" constitutional instruments, the Court's holdings on the nature of constitutional conventions have enduring implications. Also, the intellectual coherence of the Court's overall conclusion that provincial consent for amendments affecting provincial powers, while a constitutional requirement, is not a legally enforceable right, depends on the validity of the way in which the Court drew the line between law and convention.

It was clear from the opening moments of the hearing before the Court that this would be a crucial, if not the crucial, issue in the case. Mr. Twaddle, the lead counsel, for Manitoba had just begun to develop the provincial case when Chief Justice Laskin leaned across his desk and asked, "Mr. Twaddle, are you talking about law or convention ?"[11] Clearly in the Chief Justice's view, law and convention belonged to different realms. As it turned out, all of his brethren shared this point of view.

In examining the Court's position on this issue it is useful to begin by setting out what the majority of six (Justices Martland, Ritchie, Dickson, Beetz, Chouinard and Lamer) say about convention that is relatively uncontentious at least in the sense that it is generally consistent with the writings of English and Canadian constitutional scholars. The three judges who dissent on the question of convention agree with much of the majority opinion on the general nature of convention, although they clearly disagree on a few points.

Both the Supreme Court judges and constitutional writers take the discussion of constitutional conventions in A.V. Dicey's *Introduction to the Study of the Law of the Constitution* as their starting point.[12] This is to be expected for it was largely through the influence of Dicey that the concept of constitutional convention came into use. Dicey used the term to refer to precepts or rules of political conduct (to use his own language, "a body of constitutional or political ethics")[13] concerning the proper use of legal powers. He wrote primarily about the conventions relating to Cabinet government, the Crown's prerogatives and the relationships between the three branches of government.

The following passages from the majority opinion captures the essence of Dicey conception :

> The main purpose of constitutional conventions is to ensure that the legal framework of the Constitution will be operated in accordance with the prevailing constitutional values or principles of the period.[14]

It is worth unravelling this conception, for such an exercise will reveal, I believe, four essential features of constitutional conventions that are acknowledged by most constitutional writers, including Dicey's critics.

The first feature is that the constitutional function of conventions is to provide rules concerning the proper exercise of the legal powers of the government. For example, the convention requiring that the Queen or her representative should act on the advice of Ministers responsible to the elected branch of Parliament governs the way in which the Queen should exercise the vast powers vested in her by law. *At least* in this sense, conventions are closely related to laws. As many constitutional writers have pointed out, the existence of some legal powers—for example, Section 9 of the BNA Act which vests "the Executive Government and Authority of and over Canada" in the Queen—would be intolerable if these powers were not exercised in accordance with well-established constitutional conventions.

Secondly, conventions have a strong normative character. Conventions may arise through custom and practice but unlike mere custom or earlier precedents, conventional rules have come to be regarded as obligatory by most of those who are active in the institutions to which the conventions pertain. It may not be easy to discern the extent to which a convention, or a particular formulation of a convention, has come to be accepted as obligatory. Take, for example, the conventions relating to the Crown's prerogative power to dissolve Parliament. In 1926 when Governor-General Byng refused Prime Minister King's request for a dissolution, not all of the political actors involved agreed that constitutional convention permits a Governor-General to deny a dissolution in those circumstances.[15] But the existence of this dispute does not in itself constitute proof that the Governor-General was wrong. Even less does it prove that there is no constitutional convention permitting the Crown in certain circumstances to refuse a Prime Ministerial request for a dissolution.

The three dissenting judges appear not to agree with this point. According to them,

> While a convention, by its very nature, will often lack the precision and clearness of expression of a law, it must be recognized, known and understood with sufficient clarity that conformance is possible and a breach of conformance immediately discernible.[16]

I think this is too exacting a test of convention. It would mean that the normative force of a convention could be destroyed by the mere existence of a dispute about its correct application. This is wrong because the normative force of a convention is derived from acceptance of the principle upon which it is based.

This brings us to the third essential feature of constitutional conventions, namely, that their justification depends on the prevailing political principles of the period. For Dicey the validity of constitutional conventions depended on the fundamental principle of popular sovereignty. He endeavoured to show that the reason for following the conventions of responsible government was to ensure that the exercise of governmental power was, as far as possible, in harmony with the will of the nation.[17] This was a requirement of democratic theory, and democratic theory, by this time, was at the foundation of the British constitution. In this sense, the ultimate justification of constitutional conventions must be in terms of whether a convention serves what has come to be a fundamental principle of the constitutional system.

But note it is the prevailing principles of the period that justify convention. This points to a fourth essential feature of conventions—the dynamic element they bring to a constitution. The observance of convention may avoid the necessity for formal constitutional change or revolution by ensuring that the exercise of legally defined powers is not out of keeping with what the politically active people of the nation find acceptable. In Great Britain the conventions of responsible and Cabinet Government meant that the operation of the British Constitution could be adjusted to the requirements of a political culture that demanded government do much more for the people and be much more responsive to them.

Conventions in a Federal State with a Written Constitution

While all nine judges appear to be, for the most part, in agreement on these basic Diceyan attributes of convention, the three dissenting judges on the convention question took the position that constitutional conventions must have a much more limited application in the context of a federal state with a written constitution :

> In a federal state where the essential feature of the Constitution must be the distribution of powers between the two levels of government, each supreme in its own sphere, constitutionality and legality must be synonymous, and conventional rules will be accorded less significance than they may have in a unitary state such as the United Kingdom.[18]

It is not entirely clear how this statement is meant to apply to the conventions of parliamentary and cabinet government. In the very next sentence the dissenting judges equate "constitutionalism in a unitary state" with the "practices" within "the national and regional units of a federal state." These practices, as is generally acknowledged by Canadian constitutionalists, are based primarily on conventional rules many of which are subsumed under the phrase in the preamble of the BNA Act which states that Canada is to have "a Constitution similar in principle to that of the United Kingdom."[19] If the dissenting judges were suggesting that these conventions are to be accorded less significance in Canada than in the United Kingdom, they were surely wrong. Canadians no less than Englishmen would regard a failure to comply with the rule that the Queen or the Queen's representative act on the advice of Ministers responsible to the elected branch of the legislature as a serious breach of constitutional convention. The conventions of responsible government are as significant in Canada as they are in the United Kingdom.

Nor can I understand a later passage in the dissenting opinion on convention in which "the Dicey convention" is distinguished from the convention at issue in this case on the grounds that the former "does not qualify or limit the authority or sovereignty of Parliament or the Crown" while the latter "would truncate the functioning of the executive and legislative branches at the federal level."[20] The rules which Dicey called conventions do qualify the authority of the Houses of Parliament and the Crown in that they govern in an ethical, if not a legal, sense how the legal powers of these institutions are to be used. The majority attributed no greater force to the convention of provincial consent in the amending process.

It may be that the dissenting opinion's downgrading of the significance of convention in the Canadian context was meant to apply only to those conventions governing federal-provincial relationships. Perhaps the point they were getting at was that because there is a written constitutional text governing most of the important features of those relationships, conventional rules must have less significance in this area. Now if significance here is meant to have only a quantitative meaning, no one could seriously quarrel with the point. In countries which, unlike Britain, have written constitutions a smaller proportion of important constitutional rules will take the form of conventions. But I suspect the dissenters were thinking of significance in a qualitative as well as a quantitative sense. They were, I think, suggesting that where conventions concerning federal-provincial relationships exist, they must necessarily be given less normative weight than is normally given to conventions. This is a much more dubious proposition.

In constitutional systems that have a basic constitutional

text as one of their ingredients, constitutional conventions are often needed to modify or supplement relationships which are fixed in the formal text of the constitution.[21] This point has been made by many constitutional writers. Mr. Colin Munro (one of the Supreme Court's most respected authorities on conventions) points out that Dicey himself came to acknowledge that conventions may play an important role in countries which unlike England have written constitutions. Munro goes even further by suggesting that

> Indeed, it is at least arguable that convention should play a larger role in countries with written constitutions; the greater the degree of constitutional rigidity, the greater the need for the benefits of informal adaptation which conventions bring.[22]

Conventions have certainly played an important role in the development of Canadian federalism. For example, early recognition of the requirement that all regions of the country be represented in the federal Cabinet helped render tolerable the exercise of central government powers over a society marked by sharp regional differences and compensated for the weakness of the mechanism provided for this purpose in the constitutional text, namely, the Senate.[23] Another example is the federal government's refusal in recent years to use its powers of disallowance and reservation over the provinces no matter how much it might be provoked by provincial legislation.[24] This pattern of refusal reflects the growing strength of the federal principle in the operative political ethics of the Canadian constitution.

The last example demonstrates how a formal constitutional text can limit the application of convention. Even those who believe that the non-use of disallowance and reservation should be regarded as a constitutional convention would, I think, agree with the Supreme Court of Canada's holding in 1938 that if such a convention exists it could not legally nullify a power explicitly established by the BNA Act.[25] The incapacity of convention to have the *legal* effect of nullifying established legal powers is not confined to conventions relating to federalism. For instance, although by convention royal assent should be given to Bills passed by the legislature, because royal assent is a strict legal requirement, courts will not give legal effect to a Bill from which royal assent has been withheld even though it has been withheld in defiance of constitutional convention.[26] But, of course, the overriding effect of explicit legal powers does not in itself destroy the normative weight of convention.

Also it is important to note that the legally overriding effect of explicit powers established in the constitutional text is not relevant in a context involving a constitutional power or relationship not explicitly provided for in the written constitution. Precisely such a context is involved in the case at hand. The conditions under which it is proper for the federal Parliament to address requests to the U.K. Parliament for amendments to the BNA Act are not spelled out in that Act. Indeed no power to make such requests or effect amendments concerning legislative powers is explicitly established by the written constitution. So this situation must be distinguished from the disallowance or reservation situation.

The dissenting judges, with their insistence that in a federal state with a written constitution "constitionality and legality must be synonymous", disagreed with the majority that a breach of constitutional convention is properly referred to as "unconstitutional" behaviour. Here they seemed to be maintaining that because in a country like Canada " unconstitutional" can have a distinctly legal meaning—i.e. a violation of the division of powers in the BNA Act—which it could not have in the United Kingdom, the word should be used exclusively for such violations. But this argument ignores the fact that there is much more at stake than mere semantic tidiness in deciding how the concepts of "constitutional" and "unconstitutional" are to be used. To deny that behaviour which is merely a breach of convention can be considered unconstitutional is to take most of the political sting out of the finding that it would be a breach of convention for the federal Parliament to proceed with the proposed constitutional resolution without a substantial measure of provincial support.

The devaluation of the significance of violating conventions is reasonable if one is not prepared to attach importance to the principle upon which conventions are based. Dicey thought it appropriate for an Englishman to refer to conduct violating convention as unconstitutional and mean something different from and often deeper than calling behaviour illegal because in his view these conventions were based on a fundamental principle of the English constitution—popular sovereignty.[27] By the same token, Canadians who regard the principle of federalism upon which the convention at issue in this case is based as fundamental to the Canadian Constitution should agree with the majority that it is appropriate to refer to conduct violating the convention as unconstitutional even though such action might not be illegal.

Identifying the Conventional Requirement

Turning to the substantive issue of whether the majority were correct in finding that convention requires at least a substantial measure of provincial consent, it is essential to consider the methodology used by the Court in answering this question. It may be that the Court's elucidation and application of this methodology is the most significant contribution it makes in this case to Canadians' understanding of their Constitution.

The methodology employed by both the majority and the dissenters follows logically from the Diceyan conception of convention. It is a test which they found neatly summarized in the following passage from Sir W. Ivor Jennings' *The Law and the Constitution* :

> We have to ask ourselves three questions : first, what are the precedents ; secondly, did the actors in the precedents believe that they were bound by a rule ; and thirdly, is there a reason for the rule ?[28]

It is vital to appreciate the multi-faceted nature of this approach. Too often debates about Canadian conventions have been carried on solely in terms of precedent—each side endeavouring to bolster its case with some historical precedents, however quaint, irrelevant or peculiar they might be. Such an approach may be attractive because it seems so thoroughly empirical and therefore objective, avoiding any "value judgments" about which practices are right. But that is precisely the weakness of such an approach. By leaving out of account the reason for following a particular practice—the principle on which the convention is based—it ignores the extent to which questions about conventions are not simply questions about historical facts but are normative or ethical questions. But they are ethical questions of a peculiar kind. A historical component is involved in answering these questions in as much as an acceptable answer depends not on one's personal view as to why a practice ought to be followed but on being able to maintain that the reason for following the practice rests on a principle of government that has come to be an essential feature of the political community in question.[29]

While the majority and the dissenters appear to agree on the threefold test of convention—precedents, attitudes of political actors and principle—they come to very different conclusions in applying each part of the test. The majority opinion follows closely the report of the British Kershaw Committee[30] and the submissions made to the Court by Dean Lysyk as counsel for Saskatchewan. The dissenters follow most of the major arguments put forward by Mr. Chrétien in his paper which attempts to rebut the Kershaw Committee.[31] Kershaw, Dean Lysyk and the majority have much the better of this argument.

Consider first the treatment of precedents. The threshhold question here is—what are the relevant precedents ? For the majority the relevant precedents are those involving amendments which "directly affected federal-provincial relationships in the sense of changing provincial legislative powers."[32] Using this criterion they find only five positive precedents : the 1930 amendment giving the western provinces control of their natural resoures, the Statute of Westminster, and the amendments of 1940, 1951 and 1964 giving the federal parliament jurisdiction in the fields of unemployment insurance, old-age pensions and supplementary benefits respectively. All of these amendments were approved by all of the provinces whose powers were directly affected. Further, in negative terms, they find that "no amendment changing provincial legislative power has been made since Confederation when agreement of a province whose legislative powers would have been changed was withheld."[33]

For the dissenting judges, on the other hand, "the real test of relevance" is the reaction an amendment provoked from one or more of the provinces.[34] Thus amendments concerning central government institutions or federal subsidies to the provinces to which at least one province objected count for the dissenters as evidence that there is not a convention requiring unanimous provincial consent.

Setting aside for the moment the question of unanimity, I think that the dissenters' criterion of relevancy is much too wide. By including aspects of federalism outside the realm of intergovernmental relations it goes beyond the reference in the questions submitted to the courts to amendments "affecting federal-provincial relationships or the powers, rights or privileges" of the provinces. Further such a criterion is not sufficiently sensitive to the question of principle at issue in this case, namely, whether one level of government in the Canadian federation should be able unilaterally to alter the powers of the other level.

Secondly, in considering the attitudes of political actors--the second part of the test of convention—it is essential to consider the historical context in which words were uttered. The dissenting judges do not do this. In their view the existence of conflicting statements in the historical record "adds additional weight to the contention that no convention of provincial consent has achieved constitutional recognition to this day."[35] But, if instead of attaching equal weight to all quotations, these judges had taken historical context into account, they would have found it much more difficult to maintain their agnostic position. For example, at the Dominion-Provincial Conference of 1931, Prime Minister Bennett, in seeking the support of the provinces for the "Canada clause" in the Statute of Westminster exempting the amendment of the BNA Act from that statute, assured the provincial Premiers

> that there would be no amendment to the Constitution of Canada in its federal aspect without consulting the Provinces which, it must be remembered, had the same powers within their domain that the Dominion has within hers.[36]

Now, if Prime Minister Bennett meant to commit the federal government here only to consult with the provinces while maintaining the right to proceed unilaterally with amendments directly affecting provincial powers over the opposition of most provinces, then his statement and general performance at this conference must rank as one of the great confidence tricks in modern history.

The majority's interpretation of two other statements of

crucial historical importance is also much more convincing than the dissenting judges' treatment of the same material. I refer to Prime Minister King's 1940 statement in the House of Commons and the fourth principle as set out in the 1965 White Paper on Constitutional Amendment in Canada. Mr. King's statement was made on a critically important occasion—the first time since the enactment of the Statute of Westminster that the Federal Parliament had considered a resolution addressed to the United Kingdom requesting a constitutional amendment affecting the division of legislative powers. By obtaining the consent of all of the provinces for this amendment, Mr. King explained to the House that his government had

> avoided the raising of a very critical constitutional question, namely whether or not in amending the British North America Act it is absolutely necessary to secure the consent of all the provinces, or whether the consent of a certain number of provinces would of itself be sufficient.[37]

In the majority's opinion the only point about which Mr. King was uncertain was whether unanimity was required. There was no doubt "as to whether substantial provincial support is required". The dissenting judges dismiss King's statement as showing merely that Mr. King thought it was "good politics" to obtain provincial consent.[38] But here they miss the point about convention : conventions are fundamentally about "good politics" in that they embody standards of political conduct that have come to be required by the prevailing sentiment of the political community.

The fourth principle in the 1965 White Paper to which the majority opinion gives great weight is described as follows :

> The Canadian Parliament will not request an amendment directly affecting federal-provincial relationships without prior consultation and agreement with the provinces. This principle did not emerge as early as others but since 1907, and particularly since 1930, has gained increasing recognition and acceptance. The nature and the degree of provincial participation in the amending process however, have not lent themselves to easy definition.[39]

They rightly emphasize that this statement was carefully formulated by the federal government and accepted by all of the provinces. Again, the dissenting judges' denial of this statement's significance is unconvincing. They allude to a sentence in the White Paper referring to all of the principles governing the process of securing the U.K. amendments to the BNA Act as "not constitutionally binding in any strict sense."[40] But, of course, this statement only recognized that these principles belong to the conventional part of the constitution and are not in the written constitution. As the second Kershaw Report points out, if this statement were taken to mean that the principles in the White Paper were not constitutional requirements even in a conventional sense, then Canadians could have no constitutional objections if the U.K. Parliament ignored the White Paper's first principle by amending the BNA Act on its own without any request from Canada.[41] But surely such an action would be regarded by the federal government and by the provinces as unconstitutional.

The minority also maintained that the two sentences following the fourth principle demonstrate an absence of the unanimity and certainty required for constitutional amendments. Taking unanimity first, and setting aside qualms I have about accepting unanimity as a necessary property of conventions (who must be unanimous ? does one successful repudiation or breach of convention destroy the convention ?), the fact that all the provinces and Ottawa accepted the White Paper as a correct statement of the principles governing the amending process shows that by 1965 the most relevant political actors all accepted the convention of provincial consent. As for uncertainty, again it is questionable to regard certainty as a necessary property of conventions. Whose formulations, for instance, of the conventions of parliamentary and cabinet government are to be regarded as certainly the correct ones ? As Dean Lysyk pointed out in his oral submission to the Court, the absence of a precise and universally accepted definition of the conditions under which a legislature's confidence in the government may be said to be lost does not prove that there is no convention requiring the government to maintain that confidence.[42] Besides, the uncertainty in question pertains only to the precise extent of provincial agreement required. That is precisely the issue about which Mackenzie King was uncertain, on which federal and provincial leaders over many years were not able to agree and on which the majority wisely did not attempt to be definitive but left open to resolution in the political arena. Lack of knowledge as to exactly how much provincial consent is required does not preclude a firm belief that for the federal government to proceed against the wishes of eight of the ten provinces would be a violation of constitutional ethics.

It is the statements of the political actors that provide the main basis for the majority's declining to find that convention requires unanimous provincial consent. As all of the relevant precedents, on their face, supported unanimity, without these statements the evidence might seem to favour unanimity. As for principle—the third part of the test for convention—it does not provide a firm basis for unanimity. There have certainly been many Canadian leaders who have regarded Confederation as a compact the terms of which can only be changed with the consent of all the parties. That indeed was the position which seven of the eight provinces opposing Ottawa took in this case. But such a view of the federal principle implicit in Canada's Constitution has not been accepted by federal leaders nor by all provincial leaders.[43] Nor can a requirement of unanimous consent be derived from the general theory and practice of federalism. None of the classical federal systems require that all of the units agree to amendments affecting their powers.[44]

Although the majority do not find that unanimity is required, neither do they reach a firm conclusion that unanimous consent is not required. Their conclusion is that "the agreement of the provinces of Canada, no views being expressed as to its quantification, is constitutionally required . . . ."[45] Thus, it is still open for Quebec to argue that its consent is required on the grounds that unanimity is a conventional requirement. I think a stronger case would be based on the contention that the requirement of substantial provincial consent has not only a quantitative dimension but also a qualitative, dualistic dimension which requires the consent of the province in which most of Canada's French-speaking citizens reside. In considering this claim not only must precedents be considered but, equally, the extent to which federal and provincial leaders indicated that they felt obliged to observe a Quebec veto and the historical acceptance of cultural dualism as a fundamental principle in Canadian political life.

Finally, there is the question of principle—the reason for

accepting a practice as binding. The majority looked upon provincial autonomy in matters constitutionally assigned to the provinces as basic to the federal character of Canada's Constitution. That principle has been recognized as a fundamental principle of the Canadian Constitution in a number of judicial decisions.[46] In the majority's view that principle

> cannot be reconciled with a state of affairs where the modification of provincial legislative powers could be obtained by the unilateral action of the federal authorities.[47]

It is no answer to this to say, as do the dissenters, that "the BNA Act has not created a perfect or ideal federal state", or to point to provisions of the BNA Act that modify the federal aspects of the Canadian Constitution.[48] For the majority position to be sound it is necessary to accept only that as a minimum requirement of the federal dimension of the constitution one level of government not be able unilaterally to alter the powers of the other level. Unquestionably, the BNA Act contains provisions that were based on principles other than those of federalism. Along side the federal division of powers are provisions derived from British imperial history, more suitable to the constitution of a unitary state, with a senior level of government at the centre and inferior local governments.[49] These unitary or imperial elements of the constitution were, no doubt, welcomed by those Fathers of Confederation who, like John MacDonald, did not care for federalism at all. Still, it is reasonable to assume that the Confederation coalition would not have held together had it been understood that the federal element in the new constitution was so weak that the provinces' powers could be altered unilaterally by the central government. It is even clearer that as Confederation evolved, the unitary-imperial provisions so valued by MacDonald's part of the Confederation coalition became increasingly unusable because their operation collided with the deepening and broadening acceptance of federal principles by the bulk of politically active Canadians. In Canada "the prevailing constitutional values or principles of the period" are now such as to require that the federal principle be respected at least to the extent of ensuring that the provinces participate in making decisions on amendments affecting their own powers. Paradoxically, of course, this is evident in the Trudeau Government's commitment to an amending formula that would entrench in a patriated constitution the right of the provinces to participate in the amending process.

The best counter to the majority's position on convention was given not by dissenting judges but by dissenting politicians. This is what one should expect given that conventions are established and developed in the political arena. Prime Minister Trudeau in his initial response to the Supreme Court decision (the televised Press Conference from Seoul, South Korea) acknowledged that a convention requiring provincial consent for amendments affecting provincial powers had existed.[50] However, he went on to argue that unless this convention was set aside, at least for the immediate period, its strict observance would perpetually frustrate the realization of another essential Canadian constitutional value—the full achievement of Canada's self-government. This response has the merit of recognizing that constitutional conventions are a dynamic part of the constitution and further that a constitutional system is based not on a single absolute principle but on a number of political values or normative considerations, the ordering of which may well be shaped by the political exigencies of the country. Mr. Trudeau, as it turned out, did not press this argument to the point of proceeding unilaterally with the patriation package without making one more effort to arrive at a censensus with the provincial premiers. But, I would submit, had the concessions he made in modifying his package not been reciprocated by concessions from a substantial number of Premiers, he would have had a reasonably strong case in terms of constitutional ethics for proceeding unilaterally.

Law and Convention

While the Supreme Court justices did not agree as to whether a convention requiring provincial consent exists nor as to whether violations of conventions in Canada constitute unconstitutional behaviour, they were unanimous that whatever the convention is it cannot be enforced by the courts. This brings us to the most difficult question of jurisprudence in this case—the relationship between law and convention. On this issue the Supreme Court judges may speak as one, but the constitutional scholars clearly do not.[51]

There can be no serious quarrel with the Court's starting point on this issue. The Court was surely correct in drawing a distinction between convention and law. As their quotations from Dicey demonstrate, Dicey introduced the concept of "convention" precisely to distinguish two sets of constitutional rules—one set which he referred to as laws "in the strictest sense" and another, which although forming a "portion of constitutional law" he called conventions. Also it is true that for Dicey, as for the Supreme Court, the key difference between the two sets of rules was that whereas "constitutional laws in the strict sense" are enforced by the courts, constitutional conventions are not.[52] Conventions develop in the political arena and the sanctions for breaching them are administered in that same arena by officials, politicians and ultimately by the electorate.

But pointing out this difference between law and convention does not exhaust what can be said about the relationship between law and convention. As the Supreme Court itself acknowledged, conventions have frequently been recognized in judicial decisions "to provide aid for and background to constitutional or statutory construction."[53] Many cases were cited by counsel for the provinces (most systematically by D.A. Schmeiser, counsel for Manitoba)[54] in which Canadian and English courts have referred to constitutional conventions. However, the Supreme Court insisted that none of these cases constitutes an instance of a Court enforcing convention or of a convention crystallization into law, and that it was "an overdrawn proposition" to say that in the cases cited the court had "given force to convention".[55] The majority on convention went even further and denied that convention was part of constitutional law: "constitutional convention plus constitutional law equal," they said, "the total constitution of the country".[56]

Now I have some difficulty with this portion of the Court's jurisprudence. I see at least two problems in insisting on such an unbridgeable gulf between law and convention. The first is that some of the cases cited do suggest that in certain contexts courts will give legal effect to conventions. The second is the Court's implicit inference that what is not enforceable by courts is not law.

The cases which are difficult to reconcile with the Court's position are those involving conventions which, far from being in conflict with the law, were used to interpret legal rights and obligations. The best known Canadian example is Chief Justice Duff's opinion in the *Labour Conventions* case that the practice of Dominions entering into agreements with foreign states "must be recognized by the Courts as having the force of law."[57] For the Supreme Court this example does not really count as it belongs in the realm of international law which "perforce has had to develop, if it was to exist at all, through commonly recognized political practices of states . . . ."[58] So let us consider a completely domestic example, *Arseneau v. The Queen*.[59] In *Arseneau* the Supreme Court held that a person charged under the section of the Criminal Code establishing the offence of bribing "a member of a legislature" could not escape conviction by claiming that the person who accepted his bribe did so as a Cabinet minister rather than as a member of the legislative assembly. Justice Ritchie, writing for the majority, rejected this distinction because it was not in accord with "the generally accepted practice in this country whereby Ministers are accountable to the elected representatives of the people in Parliament or the Legislature."[60] A similar English example, cited by Mr. Schmeiser, is *Liversidge v. Anderson*[61] where the House of Lords referred to the convention of ministerial responsibility as one of its reasons for not going behind a detention order. In these cases conventions were given legal effect to the extent that they shaped the interpretation of legal powers and responsibilities and the decisions recognizing the conventions became legal precedents.

Outside the context of statutory interpretation there are examples, at least in English law, of the courts giving legal effect to fundamental political principles and making them part of the common law. The most important example is the courts' recognition of the supreme authority of Parliament. In the words of Sir Ivor Jennings, "It is, therefore, *common law* that Parliament can do as it pleases."[62] A much more recent example of the English courts showing a willingness to incorporate convention into the common law is *Attorney-General v. Jonathan Cape* (the Crossman Diaries case).[63] In that case the British government sought an injunction to prevent publication of an ex-Cabinet Minister's diaries on the grounds that publication would violate the convention of cabinet confidentiality. Against this claim the publisher contended that "whatever the limits of the convention of joint Cabinet responsibility may be, there is no obligation enforceable at law to prevent the publication of Cabinet papers and proceedings, except in extreme cases where national security is involved."[64] The government's claim, it should be noted, was not tied to any alleged breach of the Official Secrets Acts or of an oath of office but was based solely on the essential importance of the rule of Cabinet confidentiality in maintaining Cabinet responsibility. After considering a great deal of evidence concerning the existence of the convention in question, Chief Justice Widgery concluded that

> the Attorney-General has made out his claim that the expression of individual opinions by Cabinet Ministers in the course of Cabinet discussion are matters of confidence, the publication of which can be restrained by the court when this is clearly necessary in the public interest.
>
> The maintenance of the doctrine of joint responsibility within the Cabinet is in the public interest, and the application of that doctrine might be prejudiced by premature discloser of the views of individual Ministers.
>
> There must, however, be a limit in time after which the confidential character of the information, and the duty of the court to restrain publication, will lapse.[65]

Because nearly ten years had elapsed since the Cabinet conversations recorded in Mr. Crossman's diaries had taken place, the Chief Justice thought that Cabinet solidarity would not be endangered and therefore refused the injunction.

The Supreme Court tried to explain away *Jonathan Cape* on the grounds that the court was simply "applying its own legal principles as it might to any question of confidence, however it arose."[66] But this does not adequately account for the fact that in this case the English judge stated that he was prepared in certain circumstances to give legal protection to Cabinet information in order to uphold an important convention of the constitution. Chief Justice Widgery's reference to precedents outside of the political context in which the courts had given protection to confidential communications (in commerce and matrimonial relations) does not detract from the fact that he was willing to give legal effect to the convention of cabinet confidentiality in a situation where cabinet solidarity would otherwise be endangered.

The process whereby judicial decisions give some legal effect to constitutional conventions may not be most aptly characterized as "conventions crystallizing into law"[67] or of "the transformation of a conventional rule into a legal rule."[68] These expressions suggest that once the courts have pronounced upon a conventional rule it is no longer a convention, but that is surely not the case. The conventions of parliamentary and cabinet government remain conventions even though they may be recognized from time to time in judicial decisions. Also, these expressions may suggest that once the courts have given legal effect to a convention in one context they would thereby be committed in the future to enforcing the convention in all contexts. But this too would be incorrect. The courts need only treat the cases recognizing convention as legal precedents in situations where similar rights and powers are at issue as were involved in the earlier cases. Also, of course, because conventions are established and changed in the political arena, they can be altered independently of judicial decisions. Thus, for example, if the politicians abandoned the convention of cabinet confidentiality, the courts could not recognize it in subsequent decisions.

The second problem with the Court's categorical distinction between convention and law is its implicit assumption that enforceability by a court is a necessary condition for the existence of law. This proposition which, I take it, is a first premise of legal positivism seems to be taken for granted by the Court. But I find it difficult to accept this positivism as Canada's official philosophy of law without resolving a number of questions it raises. Among such questions are the following: what does enforceability mean ? does it mean giving a remedy ? any remedy, even a declaratory judgment ? who decides what is enforceable ? if it is the judges who decide, how are they to know before they have enforced a rule whether or not it is a law ? or must all law originate in statutes or the written constitution, and if that is so, how do we account for common law ?

Perhaps there are good answers to all of these questions. But until I find acceptable answers I am not persuaded that conventions must be denied any legal status because normally courts do not enforce them. Dicey who as much as any other writer made a distinction between conventional rules and rules that "are in the strictest sense laws" did not go as far as the Supreme Court. While he distinguished constitutional conventions from the "law of the constitution", he referred to both as the "two elements" of the "constitutional law" of his country.[69] By recognizing that convention and the law of the constitution were organically related as twin sources of constitutional law, the Court might have been better able to justify its decision as a court of law to answer the question on convention.

The Incompleteness of Canada's Constitution

Besides the contention that the convention itself was enforceable, there were other legal arguments which the Court (by a seven-to-two majority) had to overcome to be able to conclude that provincial consent was not a legal requirement for an amendment affecting provincial powers. These questions had both a Canadian and a British side.

On the Canadian side the central issue was whether the Canadian Parliament was legally empowered to address resolutions to the United Kingdom requesting changes in the provinces' power. In answering this question the majority rejected the implication in the second Quebec question that the power of the House of Commons and the Senate must be proven by remarking that "it would be equally consistent with constitutional precedent to require disproof."[70] Here they seem to be doing more than asserting a presumption of constitutionality (for which there is certainly precedent). They were also making the more fundamental point that Canada's Constitution is "incomplete" in that not all the powers of government are specified and defined by statutes or the written constitution.[71]

Now even if we concede this assumption about the incompleteness of Canada's Constitution, it does not follow that any branch of government, including the House of Commons and the Senate, can act in relation to those matters on which the Constitution is silent so as to effect fundamental changes with respect to those matters on which the written constitution is quite specific. That is precisely the point emphasized by the two dissenting judges (on the question of law) in insisting that under a system of constitutional government a legislative body cannot do indirectly what the written constitution precludes it from doing directly.[72] As Justices Martland and Ritchie point out, in other areas where the Canadian Constitution might be said to be incomplete such as judicial review, the inter-delegation of legislative powers and, Canadian treaties,[73] the courts have ruled that legislatures are *ultra vires* if they act in a manner that would bypass or defeat the federal division of powers in the BNA Act. This, I think, is a powerful argument which is not adequately answered by the majority.

The majority's position rests on drawing a sharp distinction between passing resolutions and enacting legislation. They accept the federal government's contention that the passing of resolutions is not subject to the division of powers in the BNA Act. Such an activity simply falls under the power of the Houses of Parliament to govern their own internal proceedings, a power which they claim is on the same legal footing as that of the British Parliament and which is therefore beyond judicial review.[74] But nowhere do they consider the appropriateness of transposing this British doctrine to a country like Canada with a written constitution and a federal division of powers. Nor do they consider the implications of the Senate and the House of Commons Act which limits the "internal" powers of these bodies to what is "not repugnant to the BNA Act". It is the view of the dissenting judges that such a restriction precludes a resolution which would have the effect of curtailing provincial legislative powers under Section 92 of the BNA Act.[75] Justices Martland and Ritchie, rightly in my view, go beyond legal formalism. Noting the federal government's repeated assertion that there is a "firm and unbinding convention" that the British Parliament must enact any amendment requested by a joint resolution of the House of Commons and the Senate, they realistically find that the resolution at issue in this case, although only a resolution and not a legislative enactment, will have the effect of altering provincial powers.[76]

The Legal Omnipotence of the British Parliament over Canada's Constitution

There was also a British side to the legal issues. The majority appear to deny this. Near the beginning of the majority judgement on law we find the following statement :

> Secondly, the authority of the British Parliament or its practices and conventions are not matters upon which the Court would presume to pronounce.[77]

Despite this statement, the opinion goes on to discuss at length whether the British Parliament's authority to amend the BNA Act is subject in law to a requirement of provincial consent. The Court could not avoid this question if it was to deal with the provinces' argument that since the recognition in 1926 of the Dominions as "autonomous Communities within the British Empire",[78] the British Parliament had relinquished its supremacy over the sovereign powers (federal and provincial) of the Canadian community. In answering this question concerning the independence of Canadian legislatures from the British Parliament, the Court, regardless of its protestations, was necessarily answering a question about the power of the British Parliament over Canada.

The majority rejected the provincial claims of sovereignty for their legislatures and upheld the federal government's view that the British Parliament has retained its "omnipotent legal authority in relation to the British North America Act."[79] This conclusion is based entirely on interpretation of the Statute of Westminster. The majority, in a rather cursory manner, rejected any suggestion that where the Statute of Westminster recognizes the principle of the modern Commonwealth that laws made by the U.K. Parliament will not extend to a Dominion "otherwise than at the request and with the consent of that Dominion,"[80] the Dominion, in the case of Canada, means not the Dominion Parliament alone, but the federal state of Canada in which sovereign legislative power is distributed between the federal and provincial legislatures. The majority do not explain why those who drafted the Statute of Westminster would have used such an ambiguous word as "Dominion" if their intention was to establish a Dominion Parliament's request as the requisite antecedent condition for Imperial legislation extending to an autonomous Dominion.[81]

The majority go further and, in effect, assert that Canada in law is a British colony so far as authority over her constitution is concerned. This, in their view, is the effect of Section 7(1) of the Statute of Westminster which exempts amendment of the BNA Acts from that statute. This exemption, they hold, leaves the British Parliament's power to amend Canada's Constitution supreme and completely untrammelled. This finding means that not only is Britain free to impose constitutional changes on the Canadian provinces but it is equally free to impose changes on the federal Parliament or to reject changes requested by that Parliament.

The majority's conclusion that Canada, so far as her constitution is concerned, is still, in law, totally subordinate to the U.K. Parliament seems wrong to me because it ignores the right to self-determination which Canada could successfully assert internationally. If Britain were to impose constitutional changes on Canada or refuse to enact changes requested by the federal Parliament and all ten provinces, I am sure that Canada's rejection of this exercise of British power would be upheld by her own courts and by the international community. In other words, it would appear doubtful that the enactment of changes in Canada's constitution by the British Parliament, regardless of the wishes of the autonomous Canadian community, is all that is needed to give such changes legal status in Canada.[82] The Supreme Court majority, like many Canadians who are in a rush to achieve patriation, may find it convenient to forget that the legal procedures agreed to at the Constitutional Conference of February 1971 for achieving patriation called for the passing of identical resolutions by the Parliament of Canada and all the Provincial Legislatures endorsing the amending formula and any substantive constitutional changes. The British Parliament's authorization was then simply regarded as an extra step "to ensure the legal validity of the procedures".[83]

Conclusion

Thus my own assessment of the strength of the arguments advanced by each side of the Court on the questions of law and convention leads me to the conclusion that the provinces should have won the case on the basis of law alone. Although I think the opinions on convention also favour the provinces, still I believe that, given the view put forward by the majority at the beginning of their opinion that convention is *entirely* political and in no sense legal, in strict logic the Court should not have answered the question about the content of convention.

This is a troubling conclusion because, as I have suggested in the introduction to this comment, it may be that the Court's opinion will have had a beneficial effect in bringing about a resolution to Canada's constitutional impasse. If that is so, I would like to be able to congratulate the members of the Supreme Court, especially the four judges, Justices Dickson, Beetz, Chouinard and Lamer who anchored both majorities, for the wisdom of their statecraft. But to do so I am afraid may mean that I am subscribing to a "result-oriented" jurisprudence which assesses judicial decisions in terms of whether they support one's personal political preferences. Such a jurisprudence is scarcely jurisprudence at all, for in denying the relevance of rationality in the judges' reasons it denies that there is any inherent difference between decision-making by courts and decision-making by the political branches of government. And that is a conclusion which neither I nor, I am sure, the Court could accept.

FOOTNOTES

1. The question which the Quebec Government proposed to submit to the Quebec Court of Appeal is as follows :

   "Is Quebec's consent necessary, by convention, for adoption by the House of Commons and the Senate of a resolution whose aim would be to modify the Canadian constitution so as to interfere with : (1) the authority of Quebec's legislature under the Canadian constitution ; (2) the status or role of the legislature or Government of Quebec within the Canadian federation ; and does Quebec's objection render adoption of such a resolution unconstitutional according to convention ?" *Toronto Globe and Mail*, Dec. 3, 1981.
2. The constitutional resolution reflecting the agreement reached by the federal government and nine provinces (with a few modific-ations) was received by the Queen on Dec. 9, 1981.
3. Paul Weiler, "Two Models of Judicial Decision-Making", (1968) 46 *Canadian Bar Review*, p. 419.
4. The argument is set out at pages 29 to 31 of the *Factum of the Attorney General of Canada* submitted to the Supreme Court in this case.
5. (1980) 1 S.C.R. 54.
6. (1982), 125 D.L.R (3d) 1 at 17.

7. Ibid., 107. It should be noted that Justice Hall of the Manitoba Court of Appeal refused to answer the second question put to the Court "because it is not appropriate for judicial determination". *Reference re. Amendment of the Constitution of Canada* (No. 1) 117 D.L.R. (3d) 1 (Man. C.A.).
8. (1982), 125 D.L.R. (3d) at 88.
9. *Toronto Globe and Mail*, Oct. 15, 1980.
10. For a good discussion of the pro's and con's of the reference procedure, see Barry *Strayer, Judicial Review of Legislation in Canada*, University of Toronto Press, 1968.
11. This is based on my own record of these proceedings. There is no official transcript of oral hearings in the Supreme Court of Canada.
12. The first edition of Dicey's book was published in 1885. References to the book which follow are to the tenth edition published by MacMillan in 1959 and edited by Professor E.C.S. Wade.
13. A.V. Dicey, *Introduction to the Law of the Constitution*, p. 417.
14. (1982), 125 D.L.R. (3d) at 84.
15. For a discussion of conflicting views see Peter W. Hogg. *Constitutional Law of Canada*, Carswell, 1977, pp. 158-60.
16. (1982), 125 D.L.R. (3d) at 114.
17. The purpose of conventions, said Dicey, "is to secure that Parliament, or the Cabinet, shall in the long run give effect to the will of that power which in modern England is the true political sovereign of the state—the majority of the electors or (to use popular though not quite accurate language) the nation." Dicey, p. 429.
18. (1982), 125 D.L.R. (3d) at 110.
19. For a discussion of the role and status of such conventions in Canada's constitutional system see R. MacGregor Dawson, *The Government of Canada*, 4th edition, University of Toronto Press, 1963, Ch. 4.
20. (1982), 125 D.L.R. (3d) at 115.
21. See K.C. Wheare, *Modern Constitutions*, Home University Library, 1950.
22. Colin R. Munro, "Laws and Conventions Distinguished," (1975) 91 *Law Quarterly Review*, p. 219.
23. See W.A. Matheson, *The Prime Minister and the Cabinet*, Methuen, 1976. According to Matheson, "The practice of ensuring representation from provinces and groups (in the Cabinet) has now broadened into a rigid convention of the Canadian contribution . . ." p. 27.
24. Some constitutional scholars would still support the use of disallowance at least to protect civil liberties, but others view it as being rendered obsolete by convention. See Peter W. Hogg, *Constitutional Law of Canada*, p. 39, note 37.
25. *Reference re Disallowance and Reservation of Provincial Legislation*, [1938] S.C.R. 71.
26. *Gallant v. The King*, (1949) 2 D.L.R. 425.

27. Dicey, p. 419.
28. (1982), 125 D.L.R. (3d) at 90. Jennings' threefold test was proposed in Saskatchewan's factum. See p. 14.
29. In principle the task of ascertaining the answer to a question about convention is similar to Ronald Dworkin's characterization of the judge's task in deciding "hard cases" about legal rights, a task in which the judge must recognize that "what an individual is entitled to have, in civil society, depends upon both the practice and the justice of its political institutions." Ronald Dworkin, *Taking Rights Seriously*, Harvard University Press, 1968, p. 87.
30. First report of the Foregin Affairs Committee, *British North America Acts : The Role of Parliament*, House of Commons (U.K.), Seesion 1980-81, January 30, 1981.
31. Jean Chretien, *The Role of the United Kingdom in the Amendment of the Canadian Constitution* (Government of Canada, March 1981). The Kershaw Committee produced a rejoinder to this paper. *Supplementary Report on the British North America Acts : The Role of Parliament*, House of Commons (U.K.), Session 1980-81, April 15, 1981.
32. (1982), 125 D.L.R. (3d) at 93.
33. Ibid., 94. The four negative examples were Ontario's and Quebec's refusal to support a proposed amendment on indirect taxation in 1951, the failure to agree on an amending formula in 1960, Quebec's rejection of the Fulton-Favreau amending formula following the 1964 first ministers' conference, and Quebec's rejection of the Victoria Charter in 1971.
34. Ibid., 118.
35. Ibid., 121.
36. Ibid., 105.
37. Ibid., 101.
38. Ibid., 121.
39. Ibid., 99.
40. Ibid.
41. *Supplementary Report on the British North America Acts : The Role of Parliament*, House of Commons (U.K.), Session 1980-81, April 15, 1981, p. xvii.
42. A different point is developed in Saskatchewan's written factum. There it is argued (pp. 37-38) that traditionally in exercising judicial review courts have ruled that in the particular circumstances of the case government activity violates the constitution without providing a comprehensive and precise formulation of a constitutional rule covering all circumstances. For example, in the *Anti-Inflation Act Reference* the Court did not define a precise level of inflation that justifies use of the federal emergency power.
43. See Edwin R. Black, *Divided Loyalties : Canadian Concepts of Federalism*, McGill-Queen's University Press, 1975, Ch. 5.
44. See W.S. Livingston, *Federalism and Constitutional Change*, Oxford, 1956.

45. (1982), 125 D.L.R. (3d) at 107.
46. Numerous decisions were cited in the majority opinion on convention and in the minority opinion on law. See especially ibid., 55-60 and 75-77.
47. Ibid., 104.
48. Ibid., 125.
49. The principal examples of these imperial elements are the federal government's powers of disallowance and reservation, of appointing provincial Lieutenant-Governors, of appointing the senior provincial judges and the federal Parliament's power to declare local works to be under federal jurisdiction and to establish Canada's Supreme Court.
50. *Toronto Globe and Mail*, Sept. 29, 1981, p. D7.
51. Colin Munro's article, *op. cit.*, is a strong statement of the view that law and convention are totally distinct. Sir Ivor Jenning's *The Law and the Constitution* provides a powerful statement of the opposing view.
52. Dicey, p. 24.
53. (1982), 125 D.L.R. (3d) at 88.
54. See *Factum of the Attorney General of Manitoba*, pp. 30-36.
55. (1982), 125 D.L.R. (3d) at 88.
56. Ibid., 87.
57. *Reference re Weekly Rest in Industrial Undertakings Aid*, (1936) S.C.R. 461, at 477.
58. (1982), 125 D.L.R. (3d) at 24.
59. *Arseneau v. The Queen* (1979), 2 S.C.R. 136.
60. Ibid., p. 149.
61. (1942) A.C. 206.
62. Ivor Jennings, *The Law and the Constitution*, p. 109.
63. (1976) 1 Q.B. 752.
64. Ibid., p. 765.
65. Ibid., p. 771.
66. (1982), 125 D.L.R. (3d) at 26.
67. Sir Ivor Jennings attributes the "crystallization" language to the Chief Justice's use of this concept in *Reference re Weekly Rest in Industrial Undertakings Act*. But he states that Duff's use of the concept in this case was "not consistent with the practice of the courts, which is the common law. The constitutional usages which were incorporated into the common law were more of the seventeenth century", op. cit., p. 127.
68. Professor Hogg suggests that "a judicial decision could have the effect of transforming a conventional rule into a legal rule." *Constitutional Law of Canada*, p. 8. The minority opinion on convention appears to repudiate this possibility, (1982), 125 D.L.R. (3d) at 113.
69. Dicey, p. 24.
70. (1982), 125 D.L.R. (3d) at 31.
71. Ibid., 41.

72. The BNA Act does not explicitly prohibit the federal Parliament from amending the BNA Act with respect to provincial powers. However, the fact that in 1949 Parliament obtained a limited amending power (S. 91(1)) which explicitly excludes, among other things, amendments affecting provincial powers provides an overwhelming presumption that Parliament is not empowered to enact amendments affecting provincial powers. Ibid., 61.
73. See cases discussed in ibid., 73-76 and 58-61.
74. Ibid., 30.
75. Ibid., 70-73.
76. Ibid., 69.
77. Ibid., 21.
78. The phrase used in the Balfour Declaration issued from the Imperial Conference of 1926.
79. (1982), 125 D.L.R. (3d) at 34.
80. This phrase is found in the preamble to the Statute. Section 4 of the Statute establishes the same rule.
81. (1982), 125 D.L.R. (3d) at 39-40.
82. For an analysis of "authochthony", the process whereby Commonwealth countries give force of law to their constitutions through action taken in their own territories, see K.C. Wheare, *The Constitutional Structure of the Commonwealth*, Oxford, 1960, Ch. IV.
83. *Final Report of the Special Joint Committee of the Senate and of the House of Commons on The Constitution of Canada*, 1972, p. 8. For a discussion of this issue see Melvin Smith, "Patriation : A Myth or Reality", ? *Policy Options*, December, 1981.

INDIA

FOUR

V.R. KRISHNA IYER

GOVERNOR'S REIGN AND PRESIDENT'S RULE : A Constitutional-Political Critique (of the Legal Conceptions, Pragmatic Aberrations and Futuristic Mutations)

DR. ALLADI Krishnaswami, whose erudite contribution in the field of Constitutional jurisprudence, in the shaping of our nation's Founding Deed and in the drafting of a Fundamental Law for a Free People from the British raw material brings out his creative role as a tall jural statesman, is being remembered in his centenary year and it is an appropriate tribute to him, on this occasion, to brain-scan India's Paramount Parchment from the performance perspective and futuropathic objective, without dubious sanctimony or diehard cynicism. Exposure to sunlight is itself a healing process and constructive debate has a corrective impact. My essay is conceived in this spirit to do reverence to Dr. Alladi Krishnaswami, a legend as a lawyer, a novelty as a nationalist and a walking encyclopedia of legal lore.

A Constitution *is* what a Constitution *does*, not what it professes. Constitutional hardware, not euphemistic software, alone will prevent democratic derailment. Legal mechanisms of ambiguous import break down at critical moments unless the technology is fool-proof. Law and Life are integral and so, sensitive legal controls and imaginative constitutional processes are needed lest the pollutive pragmatics of power shoot down the responsible politics of democracy. The forms and controls of law are too important to be ignored. Alexander Pope echoed common sense but talked poor politics when he said :

For forms of government let fools contest ; Whate'er is best

> administered is best . . .

Realism lies in a viable blend of principle and practice. Law, at once socially symbolic and commanding compliance, must meet current challenges and be potently corrective to gain community credibility and confidence. A continuous assessment of constitutional performance and forces of disruption and an objective debate on needed reforms from time to time is but jural patriotism. From this angle, to be silent when there is a duty to speak is more than default ; it is delinquency, however high you be.

A Constitution is not an omnipotence in the sky or omnipresence among the stars but a politico-legal instrument functionally fundamental, directionally value-loaded and, in practical terms, a regulatory interface between the People and the Power Process. But any Constitution, which is irresponsive to new challenges and old evils and permits itself to be subverted, will prove a tragi-comedy and must suffer eclipse unless periodic mutations update it. Basic constitutional fidelity in its operators and instant popular protest where breach of faith befalls are critical safeguards. Here, the vigilant intellectual goes into social action. This constructive attitude, not negative criticism, persuades me to pick out two interrelated subjects for a close-up from theoretical and practical angles so that instructive conclusions may emerge for a better Indian Constitutional Order. The Governor and his Powers, latterly bitterly controversial, and "President's Rule", which, according to pundits and politicians, has been more abused than used and upsets State Autonomy and Federalism, are the two issues which fall for scrutiny in this article.

These prefatory submissions set our sights on a just critique of the Indian Constitution-in-action, after a whole generation has worked the Founding Deed of the nation and realized where the shoe pinches. Edmund Burke was more than right when he declared :

> I have in general no very exalted opinion of the virtue of paper government.

Once we are rational enough not to be awe-struck by "the

mysterious virtue of wax and parchment" and agree that, in our country, disturbing circumstances have developed, deleterious tendencies have shown up and these pollutions and challenges have distorted the democratic, socialist direction of our polity beyond the foresight of our Founding Fathers, we must reach the determination to redesign the devices and re-condition the processes for the exercise of State Power. For as Burke observed, "the greater the power, the more dangerous the abuse". My endeavour, in this humble contribution to the Centenary Commemoration Volume of a lawyer-statesman, and juridical counsellor in the making of our Fundamental Law, is a futuropathic evaluation of the offices of Governor and his functions as also a brief performance audit of the imposition and administration of President's Rule under Article 356. The two topics are interrelated and are broadly on the agenda of Constitutional amendments before the Sarkaria Commission. Of course, the study of such a highly inflammable subject must at once be alive to current social dialectics and not be drowned in the swirl of passionate polemics. A paradigm shift, if needed, may have to be on the cards. Even in Constitution-making, new perspectives, fresh perceptions and portentous experiences may demand paradigm shifts. A paradigm is a framework of thought (from the Greek *Paradigma,* pattern). A paradigm shift is a call for a different way of dealing with old problems, and, in the constitutional field, it may require rethinking both about old assumptions and assumed sanctions. We are enlivening, in an evolutionary way, a living organic instrument so as to meet unsuspected sabotage situations. The Constitutional parameters must be remembered if the critique is to be a meaningful service to the value constants, even as the specifics of Indian politics must be considered if the exercise is not to lose the warmth of realism. So viewed, what is foremost is the Westminster factor of Cabinet Government, Parliament and the President (the Crown). It is a Raj heritage but absorbed as the political culture of the Sovereign Republic. This Indo-Anglian fundamental, not verbal casuistry, is the political essence and democratic crux of our Constitution vis-a-vis the offices of President and Governor. Since the tyranny of literality has no interpretative veracity while decoding the sense and conscience of a Constitutional provision and since, as the Supreme Court has explicated, the sound-proof, light-proof system of forensic construction, blind and deaf to relevant material based on obsolescent British legal bigotry, cannot hold good when reading the meaning of an organic provision in a value-loaded document, it follows that debates in the Constituent Assembly and other pertinent precedents, later developments and finer factors are valuable aids and guides in arriving at the wisdom and elan of the living words of the Paramount Parchment. My thesis is that Governorship and President's Rule are functional animations, not legal abstractions, and therefore, any sensible evaluation of these institutionalised processes must measure performance with reference to the politics of decentralized democracy which is the cornerstone of our nation. Indeed, in the on-going debate on reform, many maladies have been diagnosed and remedies hawked about with little regard to this credal core. The point is that our Constitutional pathology of negating state autonomy by *Delhi diktat* is our amendatory opportunity to restore people's authority within accepted parameters. The goal is to strengthen the democratic syntropy and to suppress the absolutist entropy of the political system.

The traumatic episodes, with Governors' operational aberrations and President's Rule supersessions, must not stop with deadening our hopes of popular government by frightening portents of reckless misuse but must awaken us into creative exercises to restore the rhythm of State-Union relations. In a system, everyone matters and if it goes awry, everyone has a corrective duty at least to "cry wolf". To suffer in silence is to surrender to fate, to self-alienate from the system to collaborate passively with evil. Democracy is duty too. In this juristic spirit I discuss the delicate issues.

There was a time when Governor and President were glorified and their actions immunized by the aura of office. But the old ideas and assumptions which made institutions legitimate and hallowed are being eroded by dangerous experience. They are slipping away in the face of changing reality, of corroding corruption, and are being replaced by different ideas, doubts and interrogations as yet ill-formed, and not crystallized. Now is the occasion to take stock. We have to be imaginative without being unrealistic, ideologically balanced without being submissively Anglian. The future constitutional history of India desiderates calling the bluff of old dogmas and seeing issues with new eyes, new paradigms, new answers.

The founding fathers who wrote our Constitution were not sages and seers and bequeathed us a document, prolix and complex, wrapped in phraseology which makes meaning only euphemistically. Therefore, with realism untinged by cynicism, we must examine the Constitution to rectify its practical distortions. The current situation, stirred by mass aspirations born of a new awareness, will begin to manifest, on the constitutional screen, a new force, a new consciousness, a new power. In every breakthrough effort, including in the constitutional dimension, political jurists must remember, "We are mid-wives to each other".

The office of Governor is a British Indian transplant with a federalistic flavour. Even so, it is not an altogether otiose office or redundancy. But, thanks to frequent abuses, some political jurists question even the need to keep the Raj Bhavan and its tenant in expensive pomp and panoply and potential for puppetry directed from Delhi. This basic challenge has acquired militancy because Governors are no longer innocent idlers with ceremonial relevance and statesmanly detachment, but ascent torpedoes of State autonomy or artists of superannuated sadistry with gubernatorial ego. Sometimes, they are accused of being shady operators intuitively acting to suit Central appetites. These are grave deviances and serious delinquencies which are contra-constitutional and serious challenges which debunk the State Cabinet's authority, vicariously humiliating State-level democracy, and worse, these dangerous oddities are becoming habitual offences fomenting Union-State frictions and fouling the federal process itself. *No* party in Central Power has been guiltless and the appointments of Governors and their behavioural patterns are an open "trade secret" in extra-constitutionalism. We now need a genetic change in the DNA of the office and its functions so that representative government of State level may not become the political plaything of outsiders.

Again, the problems, relating to President's Rule (Article 356) also desiderate an inside analysis of Raj Bhavan's goings-on with the focus on Central legitimacy in making the "governoring" institution a sort of constitutional satrapy.

Before commencing a detailed study of the anatomy of Governor's office and the technology of Presidential proclamation under Article 356, it may be right to reiterate what I have stated earlier, namely, that no Constitution is too sacred and no amendment too profane ; if progressive changes are mandated by emerging forces and developmental needs, the sensible course is to amend. The only constant in this flux is the radical goal of *democratic* Government actively reflecting the voice of the people. "We, the People of India", is the keynote thought, and nothing is forbidden fruit by way of constitutional mutation if people's power is thus preserved or advanced. I conclude this prologic stage of my paper with the famous quote from Jefferson :

> Some men look at constitutions with sanctimonious reverence and deem them like the ark of the covenant, too sacred to be touched. They ascribe to the men of the preceding age a wisdom more than human, and suppose what they did to be beyond amendment. . . . Laws and institutions must go hand in hand with the progress of the human mind. . . . As new discoveries are made, new truths disclosed, and manners and opinions change with the change of circumstances, institutions must advance also, and keep pace with the times. . . . Each generation . . . has right to choose for itself the form of government it believes the most promotive of its own happiness. . . .
>
> (*Thomas Jefferson* :
> *To S. Kercheval, 1816*)

Now, to the relevant texts of the Articles dealing with Governor's office and the President's powers under Article 356.

Let me make one position clear *in limine* regarding the continuance of these controversial provisions. All things considered, I regard it as desirable that the Governor continues as an institution under the Indian Constitution. How he should be appointed, how his potential for mischief should be robbed, how he can function usefully as a conduit between the State and the Centre, between the Government and the Opposition and in many other ways are matters for discussion, but that the Governor must *remain* seems to be my current view. Likewise, the President's powers in the event of a breakdown of the constitutional machinery may have to be continued, although great care must be taken to forbid the abuses which have anathematized Article 356. I agree with Mr. Seervai's view in his volume III that the abuse of powers conferred by this article does not mean that the powers themselves must be abolished. It is significant that even the 44th amendment to the Constitution passed at a time when an anti-Congress (I) party had the majority in Parliament does not deprive the President of powers under Article 356. My further discussion therefore proceeds on the footing that the Governor will continue as tenant—not as deliquent—of the Raj Bhavan, and the President shall continue to enjoy, under appropriate conditions, the authority to take over the State's administrative and legislative powers. "A power essential for the existence of federal government cannot be said to impair federal principle." This statement of Seervai justifies in some measure the stand I take.

A Categorical Imperative

The Indian polity is federal and, indeed, cannot survive except as a federation. State-level autonomy, not precarious provincialism, is therefore, a categorical imperative and shadow democracy is contra-constitutional. Equally importantly, the political texture of the Indian Republic, both at the Union and the State levels, is secular, socialist and, of course, democratic. Confusion about these fundamentals often leads to obfuscation of thinking. Again, constitutional euphemism, as in the case of the Governor's functions, may endanger the basic democracy of the structure if a certain jural-political maturity in society does not exist.

There shall be a Governor for each State and the Governor is appointed by the President. The executive power of the State shall be vested in the Governor and shall be exercised by him directly or through officers subordinate to him in *accordance with the Constitution*. The Governor's tenure of office depends on the pleasure of the President and he has to affirm (or swear in the name of God) that he will execute the office of Governor and will, to the best of his ability, preserve, protect and defend the Constitution and the Law. The power of the Governor extends to granting pardons, reprieves, remissions, commutations and the like. If the formal phrases of Articles 153 and 162 be read literally one may conclude that the Governor is a mini-monarch of the State with executive supremacy, subject to his being dismissable by the President on the basis of the *pleasure* provision. Such a meaning is a violation of the democratic substance of Cabinet Government, adopted from the Westminster pattern by the Indian Founding Fathers. Article 163, in keeping with the blanket authority the text of the previous 10 articles vests in the Governor, creates a Council of Ministers *to aid and advise the Governor in the exercise of his functions.* A narrow area of discretionary functions is carved out where even the advice of the Cabinet does not run. The Court's jurisdiction is kept out in regard to the scope of his discretionary functions and as to whether any, and if so what, advice was tendered by Ministers to the Government. Again, the temper of servility is kept up in Article 164 which gives the Governor plenary power to appoint the Chief Minister on whose advice the other Ministers shall be appointed. What may intoxicate an arrogant Governor is the extravagant verbalism of Article 164 which says that "the ministers shall hold office *during the pleasure of the Governor*".

Pausing here for a moment, with no aids to interpretation except an old dictionary, a constitutional pundit may hold that the Governor is all in all and his Cabinet of Ministers are but precarious counsellors, with not even the Court to defend the people from such an autocrat when he despises or dismisses the advice of the Council of Ministers which commands a majority in the House elected by the people. All elections become a joke if such be the meaning of the constitutional provisions. Apparently, this is not so because Article 164(2) obligates that "the Council of Ministers shall be collectively responsible to the Legislative Assembly of the State." The minister's oath or affirmation on entering office emphasizes his allegiance to the Constitution, not to the Governor.

Even the legislative powers of the House seem to be in jeopardy if we do not introduce the Westminster connotation into Article 200. This article stipulates that when a Bill is passed by the Assembly (or by both Houses), it shall be presented to the Governor who "shall declare either that he assents to the Bill or that he withholds assent therefrom or that he reserves the Bill for the consideration of the President." If, in the opinion of the Governor, says the second proviso to Article 200, the Bill would derogate from the powers of the High Court, the Governor *shall* reserve such Bill for the consideration of the President. The picture will be complete only if we remember (a) that the

Legislature itself consists of the Governor too and (b) that when the Legislative Assembly of a State is not in session, the Governor, if satisfied in that behalf, may take immediate action by promulgation of such ordinances "as the circumstances appear to *him* to require". When the House is in session, the ordinance making power is in suspended animation. But the session of the State's legislature, its prorogation and dissolution are within the powers of the Governor (Article 174). The verbal width of the provisions I have adverted to make the Ministers and the Legislature itself subordinate creatures of the Governor who "drest in a little brief authority" may "strut and fret the hour", unquestioned by Court or Cabinet or the House. "We, the People of India" could not have produced such a monstrosity. But euphemism may go to the head of some megalomaniac, unless responsible Government, rooted firmly in the people's power and canalized through the Legislature and the Cabinet, becomes an unchallengeable reality. What applies to the Governor, as a grave danger holds good, with greater force, for the President. Indians never struggled for Freedom to create, over again, Chakravarthis and Maharajas. Here comes the supreme importance of the law of the Constitution in its democratic essence and operational conventions. Certain events in recent history stress the need to go to the radical roots of our political culture lest a constitutional coup upset the edifice of the Republic. In the field of fundamental law, verbal *maya* may stultify the reality of democracy. It has happened because a dictionary is on a Rajpal's desk but a constitutional lawyer is uneasy company.

The survival of the Governor as an institution is crucial but, sans functional good behaviour, his trespasses may prove fatal. The folly begins with the choice for the high and delicate office. From this discussion, the following issues may be formulated to clarify the theme :

1. What considerations should govern the choice of Governor and how should he be selected and by whom ?
2. What should be his role *vis-a-vis* the Union Government, the State Opposition, the people and their organizations ?
3. What should be his tenurial security, the Central

control over him and operations through him ?

4. Who should govern the Governor and *when* can he act on his own *vis-a-vis* the Legislature and the Cabinet ?
5. Has he two masters, one in Delhi and the other in the State capital and can he act *independently* under *other* laws if the language warrants ?

These profound questions are of daily but deadly concern and past experience under Congress, Congress-I and Janata eras only deepens the disquiet. The kernel of the problem is the quantum of democracy the Constitution confers on the State. If, on the basics, we do not wobble, the specifics are easy to resolve. The credal core of our Constitution is the Parliamentary System and Cabinet Government.

The Governor is a ceremonial device and *constitutional* head of the State. It is a solemn office, although it involves not much serious business save on one or two critical occasions. He receives the President, visiting heads of other countries, has an honoured rank at summit functions, addresses the House, lends detached dignity to the Administration and imitates Her Majesty the Queen within his micro-cosmos. He deals with the Union, not in secrecy or as a Central spy to play politics, but as the authentic head of his State openly representing his Government (Cabinet) and conveying to the Centre their (not his) views and such other information as the President or the Prime Minister may seek. He must be strictly neutral in State politics and not use his office for politicking from within. He must possess the personality and statesmanship to transcend his individual failings and leanings and resist pressures, temptations, and even if they come from the Union Government, contrary to the integrity and ethics of his high office. Enormous tact is needed in an atmosphere of political polemics to keep up a posture of neutrality and self-effacement. At the same time, not only restraint but activism is expected from the Governor. When his Ministers act rashly, he has the right and duty to counsel reconsideration, seek information from the Chief Minister on controversial actions and inspire confidence in the people that their representations on grievances will be considered by his Government. Inevitably, these attributes demand of the incumbent an elder statesman's capabilities without genuflexion before Central bosses and ambitions for political reincarnations. Nor should he be an unwanted element in politics to be got rid of by gubernatorial assignments. He has to be in lively possession of his faculties, not a faded gerontic and naive, be acerbative, aggressive and partisan or given to pomp and panoply—the stuff that is difficult to get unless there is an intelligent and impartial agency to select. Moreover, he has to act only on the advice of his Ministers and therefore his appointment must broadly command the approval of the State Cabinet.

At this stage, it is appropriate to consider what the powers of the Governor are *vis-a-vis* the State Cabinet. There is no gainsaying the fact that this office is the fulcrum of the Indian federal system. In *U.N.R. Rao* vs. *Indira Gandhi* (1971 SC 1003) Chief Justice Sikri observed :

> If the words of an article are clear, notwithstanding any relevant convention, effecl will no doubt be given to the words. But it must be remembered that we are interpreting a Constitution and not an Act of Parliament, a Constitution which establishes a Parliamentary system of Government with a Cabinet. In trying to understand one may well keep in mind the conventions prevalent at the time the Constitution was framed.

Earlier, in Ram Jawaya Kapur's case, Justice Mukherjea had clarified, "The President has thus been made a formal or constitutional head of the executive and the real executive powers are vested in the Ministers or the Cabinet" (AIR 1955 SC 549). Chief Justice Sikri, in the earlier ruling, had referred to Sanjeeva Naidu's case (AIR 1971 SC 1003) in which Justice Hegde had observed "that under our Constitution the Governor was a constitutional head, and that the administration of the State was run by the Council of Ministers." "The Cabinet is responsible for every action taken in any of the Ministries. That is the essence of Joint responsibility." (Seervai 1818 Vol. III.) Seervai sums up the position by quoting Chief Justice Sikri

> . . . . we receive assurances from the learned authors and the speeches that the view we have taken is the right one, and is in accordance with the conventions followed not only in

the United Kingdom, but in other countries following a similar system of responsible Government.

The Maharaja syndrome, if I may so describe the claim to personal power by Governor or President, has been finally eliminated by Shamsher Singh's case (AIR 1974 S.C. 2192). Chief Justice Ray, delivering the leading judgment, spelt out the constitutional scheme authoritatively :

> 27. Our Constitution embodies generally the Parliamentary or Cabinet system of Government of the British model both for the Union and the States. Under this system the President is the Constitutional or formal head of the Union and he exercises his powers and functions conferred on him by or under the Constitution on the aid and advice of his Council of Ministers. Article 103 is an exception to the aid and advice of the Council of Ministers because it specifically provides that the President acts only according to the opinion of the Election Commission. This is when any question arises as to whether a number of either House of Parliament has become subject to any of the disqualifications mentioned in Clause (1) of Article 102.
>
> 28. Under the Cabinet system of Government as embodied in our Constitution the Governor is the constitutional or formal head of the State and he exercises all his powers and functions conferred on him by or under the Constitution on the aid and advice of his Council of Ministers save in spheres where the Governor is required by or under the Constitution to exercise his functions in his discretion.
>
> . . . . .
>
> 33. This Court has consistently taken the view that the powers of the President and the powers of the Governor are similar to the powers of the Crown under the British Parliamentary system, ... The executive power of the Union is vested in the President. The President is the formal or constitutional head of the executives. The real executive powers are vested in the Ministers of the cabinet. There is a Council of Ministers with the Prime

Minister as the head to aid and advise the President in the exercise of his functions.

. . . . .

48\. . . . . Wherever the Constitution requires the satisfaction of the President or the Governor for the exercise by the President or the Governor of any power or function, the satisfaction required by the Constitution is not the personal satisfaction of the President or the Governor in the Constitutional sense in the Cabinet system of Government, that is, satisfaction of his Council of Ministers on whose aid and advice the President or the Governor generally exercises all his powers and functions. The decision of any Minister or officer under rules of business made under any of these two articles 77(3) and 166(3) is the decision of the President or the Governor respectively. These articles did not provide for any delegation. Therefore, the decision of Minister or officer under the rules of business is the decision of the President or the Governor.

. . . . .

54\. The provisions of the Constitution which expressly require the Governor to exercise his powers in his discretion are contained in Articles to which reference has been made. To illustrate, Article 239(2) states that where a Governor is appointed an Administrator of an adjoining Union Territory he shall exercise his functions as such administrator independently of his Council of Ministers. The other Articles which speak of the discretion of the Governor are paragraphs 9(2) and 18(3) of the Sixth Schedule and Articles 371-A (1)(b), 371-A (1)(d) and 371-A (2)(b) and 371-A (2)(f). The discretion conferred on the Governor means that as the constitutional or formal head of the State the power is vested in him. In this connection, reference may be made to Article 356 which states that the Governor can send a report to the President that situation has arisen in which the Government of the State cannot be carried on in accordance with the provisions of this Constitution. Again Article 200 requires the Governor to reserve for consideration any Bill which in his opinion, if it became law, would so derogate from the powers of the High Court as designed to fill under the Constitution.

55. In making a report under Article 356 the Governor will be justified in exercising his discretion even against the aid and advice of his Council of Ministers. The reason is that the failure of the constitutional machinery may be because of the conduct of the Council of Ministers. This discretionary power is given to the Governor to enable him to report to the President who, however, must act on the advice of his Council of Ministers in all matters. In this context Article 163(2) is explicable that the decision of the Governor in his discretion shall be final and the validity shall not be called in question. The action taken by the President on such a report is a different matter. The President acts on the advice of his Council of Ministers. In all other matters where the Governor acts in his discretion he will act in harmony with his Council of Ministers. The Constitution does not aim at providing a parallel administration within the State by allowing the Governor to go against the advice of the Council of Ministers.

56. Similarly Article 200 indicates another instance where the Governor may act irrespective of any advice from the Council of Ministers. In such matters where the Governor is to exercise his discretion he must discharge his duties to the best of his judgment. The Governor is required to pursue such courses which are not detrimental to the State.

The separate but concurring judgment delivered by me, on behalf of Justice Bhagwati also, exhaustively investigated the position of Governor (and of President) under the Indian Constitution, from the historical, cultural, political and other angles, reinforced by the debates in the Constituent Assembly, later legal literature and rulings of the summit court. Any student entertaining doubt on the issue may read and re-read Samsher Singh's case which crystallizes the proposition that the President (and the Governor) holds an important office enjoying influence but no power. The following excerpts may throw more light on the grey area under scrutiny :

135. The analysis which appeals to us, in the light of this court's rulings, accords with the view expressed by Mr. Keith in his Preface to *The King and the Imperial Crown*:

"It is a conviction of the public in the self-governing Dominions of the Crown that the Governor-General in matters official serves no more distinguished purpose than that of rubber stamp. As for the semantic gap between the verbal and the real, even in England, as William Paley has explained :

"There exists a wide difference between the actual state of the government and the theory. When we contemplate the theory of the British Government, we see the kind vested with . . . a power of rejecting laws. Yet when we turn our attention from the legal extent to the actual exercise of royal authority in England we see these formidable prerogatives dwindled into mere ceremonies ; and in their stead a sure and commanding influence of which the Constitution, it seems, is totally ignorant."

136. In Blackstone's commentaries on the Laws of England, said Dicey, students might read that the Constitution concentrated all executive power in the hands of the King. "The language of this passage", he remarked, "is impressive . . . . It has but one fault : the statements it contains are the direct opposite of the truth."

137. The President in India is not at all a glorified cipher. He represents the majesty of the State, is at the apex, though only symbolically, and has rapport with the people and parties, being above politics. His vigilant presence makes for good government if only he uses, what Gagehot described as, "the right to be consulted, to warn and encourage." Indeed, Article 78, wisely used, keeps the President in close touch with the Prime Minister on matters of national importance and policy significance, and there is no doubt that the imprint of his personality may chasten and correct the political government, although the actual exercise of the functions entrusted to him by law is in effect and in law carried on by his

duly appointed mentors, i.e. the Prime Minister and his colleagues. In short, the President, like the King, has not merely been constitutionally romanticised but actually vested with a pervasive and persuasive role. Political theorists are quite conversant with the dynamic role of the Crown which keeps away from politics and power and yet influences both. While he plays such a role, he is not a rival centre of power in any sense and must abide by and act on the advice tendered by his Ministers except in a narrow territory which is sometimes slippery.

138. Of course, there is some qualitative difference between the position of the President and the Governor. The former, under Article 74, has no discretionary powers ; the latter too has none, save in the tiny strips covered by Articles 163(2), 371-A (1)(b) and (d), 371-A (2)(b) and (f), VI Schedule para 9(2) and VI Schedule para 18(3), until omitted recently with effect from 21.1.1972. These discretionary powers exist only where expressly spelt out and even these are not left to the sweet will of the Governor but are remote-controlled by the Union Ministry which is answerable to Parliament for those actions. Again, a minimal area centering round reports to be despatched under Article 356 may not, in the nature of things, be amenable to ministerial advice. The practice of sending periodical reports to the Union Government is a pre-constitutional one and it is doubtful if a Governor could or should report behind the back of his Ministers. For a centrally appointed constitutional functionary to keep a dossier on his Ministers or to report against them or to take up public stances critical of Government policy settled by the Cabinet or to interfere in the administration directly—these are unconstitutional *faux pas* and run counter to parliamentary system. In all his constitutional 'functions' it is the Ministers who act ; only in the narrow area specifically marked out for discretionary exercise by the Constitution, he is untrammelled by the State Ministers' acts and advice. Of course, a limited free-wheeling is available regarding choice of Chief Minister and dismissal of the Ministry, as in the English practice adapted to Indian

conditions.

140. . . . Indeed, a whole host of such Articles exist in the Constitution, most of them very vital for the daily running of the administration and embracing executive, emergency and legislative powers either of routine or momentous nature. The power to grant pardon or to remit sentence (Article 161), the power to make appointments including (that) of the Chief Minister (Article 164), the Advocate General (Article 165), the District Judges (Article 233), the Members of the Public Service Commission (Article 316) are of this category. Likewise, the power to prorogue either House of Legislature or to dissolve the Legislative Assembly (Article 174), the right to address or send messages to the Houses of the Legislature (Article 175 and Article 16), the power to assent to Bills or withhold such assent (Article 200), the power to make recommendations for demands of grants (Article 203(3), and the duty to cause to be laid every year the annual budget (Article 201), the power to promulgate ordinances during recesses of the Legislature (Article 213) also belong to this species of power. Again, the obligation to make available to the Election Commission the requisite staff for discharging the functions conferred by Article 324(1) on the Commission (Article 324(6), the power to nominate a member of the Anglo-Indian Community to the Assembly in certain situations (Article 333), the power to authorize the use of Hindi in the Proceedings in the High Court (Article 348(2), are illustrative of the functions of the Governor qua Governor.

141. Similarly, the President is entrusted with powers and duties covering a wide range by the articles of the Constitution. Indeed, he is the Supreme Commander of the Armed Forces (Article 53(2), appoints judges of the Supreme Court and the High Courts and determines the latter's age when dispute arises, has power to refer questions for the advisory opinion of the Supreme Court (Article 143) and has power to hold that Government of a State cannot be carried in accordance with the Constitution (Article 356). The Auditor-General, the Attorney-

General, the Governors and the entire army of public servants hold office during the pleasure of the President. Bills cannot become law, even if passed by Parliament, without assent of the President. Recognising and derecognising rulers of former native States of India is power vested in the President. The extraordinary powers of legislation by Ordinances, dispensing with enquiries against public servants before dismissal, declaration of emergency and imposition of President's rule by proclamation upon States, are vast powers of profound significance. Indeed, even the power of summoning and proroguing and dissolving the House of the People and returning Bills passed by the Parliament belongs to him. If only we expand the ratio of Sardarilal (1971) 3 SCR 461=(AIR 1971 SC 1547) and Jayantilal (1964) 5 SCR 294=(AIR 1964 SC 648) to every function which the various Articles of the Constitution confer on the President or the Governor, Parliamentary democracy will become a dope and national elections a numerical exercise in expensive futility. We will be compelled to hold that there are two parallel authorities exercising powers of governance of the country, as in the dyarchy days, except that Whitehall is substituted by Rashtrapati Bhavan and Raj Bhavan. The Cabinet will shrink at Union and State levels in political and administrative authority and, having solemn regard to the gamut of his powers and responsiblities, the Head of State will be reincarnation of Her Majesty's Secretary of State for India, untroubled by even the British Parliament—a little taller in power than the American President. Such a distortion, by interpretation, it appears to us, would virtually amount to a subversion of the structure, substance and vitality of our Republic, particularly when we remember that Governors are but appointed functionaries and the President himself is elected on a limited indirect basis. As we have already indicated, the overwhelming catena of authorities of this Court have established over the decades that the Cabinet form of Government and the Parliamentary system have been adopted in India and the contrary concept must be rejected as incredibly allergic to our political genius, constitutional creed and culture.

. . . . .

145. Before jettisoning wholesale the theory of absolute power of Presidency we must deal with two Articles of the Constitution, one relating to the determination of the age of High Court Judges (Article 217(3)) and the other relating to the Election Commission (Article 361) which have come up for judicial consideration. Counsel for the appellant has relied on passages from these cases which hark back, in a way, to the theory of individual judgment of the Head of State.

148. . . . We are of the view that the President means, for all practical purposes, the Minister or the Council of Ministers as the case may be, and his opinion, satisfaction or decision is constitutionally secured when his Ministers arrive at such opinion, satisfaction or decision. The independence of the Judiciary, which is a cardinal principle of the Constitution and has been relied on justify the deviation, is guarded by the relevant Article making consultation with the Chief Justice of India obligatory.

Literal construction of the articles conferring power on the President and the Governor may lead to political disaster :

"If we read these powers literally as 'personal' to the Head of State, the conclusion is rather disquieting in a country which has already had a long night of imperial subjection and monarchical tradition. Dr. Ambedkar expressed this warning in the Constituent Assembly in words which have contemporary relevance :
This caution is far more necessary in the case of India than in the case of any other country. For, in India, Bhakti, or what may be called the path of devotion or hero-worship, plays a part in its politics unequalled in magnitude by the part it plays in the politics of any other country in the world. Bhakti in religion may be a road to the salvation of the soul. But in politics, Bhakti or hero-worship is a sure road to

degradation and eventual dictatorship.

The omnipotence of the President and of the Governor at State level is euphemistically inscribed in the pages of our Fundamental Law with the obvious intent that even where express conferment of power or functions is written into the Articles, such business has to be disposed of decisively by the Ministry answerable to the Legislature and through it vicariously to the people, thus vindicating our democracy instead of surrendering it to a single summit soul whose deification is incompatible with the basics of our political architecture lest national elections become but Dead Sea fruits, legislative organs become but labels full of sound and fury signifying nothing and the Council of Ministers put in a quandary of responsibility to the House of the People and submission to the personal decision of the Head of State. A parliamentary-style Republic like ours could not have conceptualised its self-liquidation by this process . . . . "

(*AIR 1974 SC 2229*)

In a later case in *Maru Ram v. Union of India* (AIR 1980 SC 2147), the Court repeated that the Constitution breathed life into an Indian Cabinet system of the British pattern :

"61. . . . the President is symbolic, the Central Government is the reality even as the Governor is the formal head and sole repository of the executive power but is incapable of acting except on, and according to, the advice of his Council of Ministers. The upshot is that the State Government, whether the Governor likes it or not, can advise and act under Article 161 the Governor being bound by that advice. The action of commutation and release can thus be pursuant to a governmental decision and the order may issue even without the Governor's approval although, under the Rules of Business and as a matter of Constitutional courtesy, it is obligatory that the signature of the Governor should authorise the pardon, commutation or release. The position is substantially the same regarding the President. It is not open either to the President or the Governor to take independent decision or direct release or refuse release of any-

> one of their own choice. It is fundamental to the Westminster system that the Cabinet rules and the Queen reigns. Being too deeply rooted as foundational to our system no serious encounter was met from the learned Solicitor-General whose sure grasp of fundamentals did not permit him to controvert the proposition, that the President and the Governor, be they ever so high in textual terminology, are but functional euphemisms promptly acting on and only on the advice of the Council of Ministers save in a narrow area of power. The subject is now beyond controversy, this court having authoritatively laid down the law in Shamsher Singh's case (1975) 1 SCR 814 : (AIR 1974 SC 2192). So, we agree even without reference to Article 367(1) and Section 3(8)(b) and 3(60)(b) of the General Clauses Act, 1897, that, in the matter of exercise of the powers under Articles 72 and 161, the two highest dignitaries in our constitutional scheme act and must act not on their own judgment but in accordance with the aid and advice of the ministers. Article 74, after the 42nd Amendment silences speculation and obligates compliance. The Governor vis-a-vis his Cabinet is no higher than the President save in a narrow area which does not include Article 161. The constitutional conclusion is that the Governor is but a shorthand expression for the State Government and the President is an abbreviation for the Central Government."
>
> (*AIR 1980, SC 2169*)

I know that some professional pundits and puritanic brothren, conditioned by regurgitated erudition, have been allergic to my (un)-English because they have decreed that the "robes" must never rise above the dull monotony of pontifical prose. But whoever may bark, the caravan will pass. In my humble submission, the powers of the Governor are a teasing illusion but the role of that office is dynamic and significant. Equally clearly, he is *not* a servant of the Central Government or its subservient agent but an independent office-holder though nominally dependent on the President's pleasure. In *Hargovind Pant v. Dr. Raghukul Tilak* (AIR 1979 SC 709) the Supreme Court spelt out this position :

> "It is no doubt true that the Governor is appointed by the President which means in effect and substance the Government of India, but that is only a mode of appointment and it does not make the Governor an employee or servant of the Government of India. Every person appointed by President is not necessarily an employee of the Government of India. So also it is not material that the Governor holds office during the pleasure of the President. It is constitutional provision for determination of the term of office of the Governor and it does not make the Government of India an employer of the Governor.
>
> "His office is not subordinate or subservient to the Government of India. He is not amenable to the directions of the Government of India, nor is he accountable to them for the manner in which he carried out his functions and duties. He is an independent constitutional office which is not subject to the control of the Government of India. He is constitutionally the head of the State in whom is vested the executive power of the State and without whose assent there can be no legislation in exercise of the legislative power of the State."

(If power to appoint carries with it the legitimacy to interfere in functions, then judicial independence is a giant myth.)

The former Vice-President, Shri G.S. Pathak, way back in 1970, had pertinently observed :

> "In the sphere in which he is bound by the advice of the Council of Ministers, for obvious reasons, he must be independent of the Centre. There may be cases where the advice of the Centre may clash with the advice of the State Council of Ministers" (quoted in Report of the Centre State Relations Inquiry Committee 1971, Government of Tamil Nadu, p. 125). In such cases the Governor must ignore the Centre's 'advice' and act on the advice of his Council of Ministers. That is the clear incontrovertible legal position."

(*White Paper on the Office of the Governor by the Government of Karnataka*)
September 22, 1983

How Should the Governor be Chosen ? and Removed ?

As the Constitution now stands, stripped of healthy political conventions and constitutional insights, it might appear that the President (assuming that he acts on the advice of his Cabinet) may, at his will and pleasure, choose any Indian above the age of 35 and may remove him even if he does not like his face or food (the vegetarianism of a Madras Governor angered a visiting President although one does not know whether it was a factor in the former's summary dismissal later on, without even a minute's notice).

The Governors' Committee rejected the doctrine of the Governments being boneless wonders or blue-eyed babies or hatchet men of the President, and recommended that :

(i) They should be chosen with great care and should be people well-known and respected for their integrity and competence. There is no room now for old and decrepit politicians or Civil Servants, to be made Governors to provide to them comfortable living at the fag-end of their lives, or to make troublesome politicians Governors either to satisfy them or to keep them away from causing mischief in their home States, and

(ii) The present provision, under which the Governors can be removed or transferred at the pleasure of the President, which in effect is really the pleasure of the Prime Minister, should be changed. A Governor once appointed should be removable only in the same way as in the case of a judge of the Supreme Court. It is only then that the States can be assured of the independence of their Governors.

The Constituent Assembly rejected the suggestion of an elected Governor, but there was repeated stress on consultation with the State Cabinet. Said Dr. Alladi :

> "In the normal working of the Constitution I have no doubt that the convention will grow up, of the Government of India consulting the provincial Cabinet, in the election of the Governor. If the choice is left to the President and his Cabinet, the President may, in conceivable circumstances,

with due regard to the conditions of the province, choose a person of undoubted ability and position in public life who at the same time has not been mixed up in provincial party struggle or factions. Such a person is likely to act as a friend and mediator of the Cabinet and help in the smooth working of the Cabinet Government in the early stages. The central fact to be remembered is that the Governor is to be a constitutional head, a sagacious counsellor and adviser to the Ministry, one who can throw oil over troubled waters. If that is the position to be occupied by the Governor, the Governor chosen by the Government of India, presumably with the consent of the provincial Government, is likely to discharge his functions better than one who is elected on a party ticket by the province as a whole based upon universal suffrage or by the Legislature on some principle of election."

. . . . .

". . . A convention of consulting the provincial Cabinet might easily grow up. Such a convention, as the House is aware, has grown up in the appointment of Governors in Canada. In Australia too, though under a different Constitution, a similar convention has grown up and the Governor of a State is appointed on the advice of provincial Cabinet. . . . In our Constitution we must try every method by which harmony could be secured between the Centre and the Provinces. If you have a person who is not elected by province or the State but you have a person appointed by the President of the Union with the consent, I take it, of the provincial Cabinet, you will add a close link between the Centre and the Provinces and a clash between the Provinces and the Centre will be avoided which will otherwise occasionally result."

(*pp. 9-10, White Paper*)

Jawaharlal Nehru made observations relevant to the choice of Governor in the debate on the subject in the Constituent Assembly :

"I think it would be infinitely better if he (the Governor) was not so intimately connected with the local politics of the province, with the factions in the provinces. And, as has been stated by Mr. Munshi, would it not be better to have a more detached figure, obviously a figure that is acceptable to the province, otherwise he could not function there ? He must be acceptable to the province, he must be acceptable to the Government of the province and yet he must not be known to be a part of the party machine of that province. He may be sometimes, possibly, a man from that province itself. We do not rule it out. But on the whole it probably would be desirable to have people from outside eminent people, sometimes people who have not taken too great a part in politics. Poilticians would probably like a more active domain for their activities but there may be an eminent educationist or persons eminent in other walks of life, who would naturally while cooperating fully with the Government and carrying out the policy of the Government at any rate helping in every way so that policy might be carried out, he would nevertheless represent before the public someone slightly above the party and thereby in fact help that Government more than if he was considered as part of the party machine. I do submit that is really a more democratic procedure than the other procedure in the sence that the latter would not make the democratic machine work smoothly."

(*CAD Vol. III, p. 455*)

Nehru positively stated that the "President's nominee must be acceptable to the Government of the Province".

Regarding the removal of the Governor, the Assembly debates were equally clear in negativing the President's arbitrary pleasure. The Rajamannar Committee, dealing with the Governor's office, stated :

"The Governor should be appointed always in consultation with the State Cabinet. The other alternative will be to make the appointment in consultation with a high power body specially constituted for the purpose.

"The Governor should be rendered ineligible for a second term of office as Governor or any other office under Government. He should not be liable to removal except for proved misbehaviour or incapacity after inquiry by the Supreme

Court.

"A specific provision should be inserted in the Constitution enabling the President to issue Instruments of Instructions to the Governors. The Instruments of Instructions should lay down guidelines indicating the matters in respect of which the Governor should consult the Central Government or in relation to which the Central Government could issue directions to him. Those Instructions should also specify the principles with reference to which the Governor should act as the head of the State including the occasions for the exercise of discretionary powers."

Although, there is a term of five years given to a Governor, he does not have even the protection that a peon enjoys in Government service. The humiliating fact is that Governors have taken it lying down, by and large. Many have been hungry politicians of the Party in Central power holidaying in the Raj Bhavan plotting for an opportunity for re-entry.

"The Study Team of the Administrative Reforms Commission, headed by Shri M.C. Setalvad, in its Report submitted in September 1967 likewise observed :

There have been instances of persons appointed as Governors continuing their connection with active politics, and in some cases returning to active politics after ceasing to be Governors. We have no hesitation in recommending that there should be a firm convention that no person who is appointed Governor should take part in politics after his appointment as such.

"The Study Team noted the qualities expected of a Governor and remarked that many of those who have filled posts of Governors during the last 16 years have falled short of this standard. It is our considered view that the real reason for this state of affairs is not the paucity of suitable persons, but the lowly place given to the post of Governor in the minds of those responsible for making the appointments.

"Circumstances devalued the post, and with that there was a logical fall in the standard of selection for Governors. The post came to be treated as a sinecure for medicrities or as a consolation prize for what are some times referred to as

> 'burnt out' politicians. Most of the persons selected were old men of the ruling party at the Centre. All th s should not be construed to mean that no suitable men were appointed but that their number was small.
> "The Administrative Reforms Commission in its Report on Centre-State Relationships submitted in June 1969 made similar observations (vide page 23 of its Report).
> The situation has considerably deteriorated since. At least two members of the ruling party who had to resign from office as Ministers following judicial strictures were subsequently appointed as Governors ; to wit, Shri M. Chenna Reddy and Shri Ramlal."
>
> (*White Paper, pp. 24-25*)

A new danger to democracy when read ominously in the light of frequent use of the Army to suppress civil commotion is the appointment of vintage military veterans as Governors. What happens if they begin to govern by themselves or if a President were also a military boss ?

Even regarding transfers of Governors, the humours, hungers and failures of the party in Central power determined the situation. Dr. Dhawan, in his study *President's Rule in the States*, writes :

> "A Governor should normally be appointed for five years. But this is not always the case. There are various instances where the Centre may have shortened the tenure of a particular Governor for political reasons. Thus in Punjab in 1966, Governor Ujjal Singh was replaced by Dharma Vira, two days before the latter sent his report recommending the imposition of President's Rule in Punjab. Again Governor Dhavan of West Bengal went on 'leave' and later resigned as Governor of West Bengal in 1971 well before his tenure expired. This may have taken place because he invited the Communists to prove that they had a majority in the Legislature with a view to forming a Government, because they were the single largest minority party. . . ."
>
> (*N.M. Tripathi Pvt. Ltd., 1979, p. 118*)

The White Paper prepared by the Karnataka Government quotes

Shri H.M. Seervai, which is pertinent to this point :

> "The events leading upto the resignation of Mr. Antulay and the subsequent events including the sanction given by the Governor to prosecute Mr. Antulay have raised important questions about the position of the Governor. The present position is very unsatisfactory ; however, it will be fully discussed in the chapter on the Union and the State Executive in Vol. II of this book. It is enough to say that the tenure of the Governor's office at the pleasure of the President, which means, in effect, the Union Government, is most unsatisfactory and is liable to grave abuse. The Governor has certain powers under the Constitution. He is not the servant or agent of the President as the Governor's oath of office clearly shows. The exercise of the power to remove or transfer a Governor must cause grave disquiet in the public mind. For example, during the hearing of the petition against Mr. Antulay, culminating in the Judgment of Mr. Justice Lentin, Air Chief Marshal Mehra was the Governor of Maharashtra. Under the Constitution, a report by the Governor on the working of the State Ministry is contemplated ; Art. 356. Sometime after Mr. Antulay resigned, Mr. Mehra was transferred from the office of the Governor of Maharashtra to the office of the Governor of Rajasthan, without any reason being assigned, and he was succeeded by the Air Chief Marshall Latif, who, after the appeal Court judgment, gave sanction to prosecute Mr. Antulay, as stated earlier. Public confidence in the position and authority of the Governor would be gravely impaired by happenings of this kind. It will be suggested in a full discussion on the Governor's position that his tenure of office must be fixed for a period of 5 years. However, as there is no provision in our Constitution for removing a Governor by a process of impeachment, such as there is for the removal of the President, such a provision should be introduced in the Constitution."
>
> (*Constitutional Law of India, Vol. I, 1070*)

These vices have been most prominent during the Congress(I) regime but have not been absent during the Janata rule also.

Appointments and transfers of Governors and their recall and dismissal (sometimes disguised as resignation) have reduced the high office to gross ridicule. The current situation is a shameful stultification of the norms expected by the Founding Fathers and desiderated by the dignified, though ornamental, office. When Governors have genuflected, they have benefited. When they have resisted, they have paid the penalty. Politicization of the powers of the Governor has imperilled the impartiality of the incumbent. Indeed, the functioning of some Governors like Ram Lal in Andhra Pradesh has been a constitutional shock, but he has had close cousins elsewhere.

Having regard to these distortions and remembering the frequency with which the office has been corrupted for dismissing Cabinets and ushering in President's Rule, the time has come for the nation to restructure the process of appointment, functioning and termination of Governor's office. The functional integrity of the State head is integral to the federal process.

I suggest, as a result of the considerations set out above, that Governors must be persons of high calibre, independent judgment, esteemed in society and aware of the constitutional-political tasks and limitations of the office. They should be formally appointed by the President, but the decision about the choice must ultimately belong to the Prime Minister since he and his Cabinet alone have the constitutional right to advise. But fidelity to the constitutional parameters obligates creation of a national mechanism for scrutiny, screening and selection, so that, from a panel so prepared, the Prime Minister may make the crucial choice. What should be that larger representative body which will fit into our federal constitutional framework ? I suggest that it should be an Inter-State Council under Article 263 vitalized in the manner suggested by the Bangalore seminar held on August 5-7, 1983. I have elaborately examined the personnel and processes of such a Council in an article in the *Seminar* on Union-State Relations (Sept. 1984 issue). This Inter-State Council must bear in mind the considerations set out earlier in this paper when preparing the Governors's panel. The Prime Minister must, as a matter of convention, select one from this panel in consultation with the Chief Minister of the State concerned about his acceptability for that State. A Hand Book setting out the guidelines for Governors, must be prepared officially by the legal think-tanks and the Law Commission, approved by Parliament and kept in the Raj Bhavan for frequent reference in the place of an Instrument of Instructions. The constitutional position and functions of Governor, even in delicate situations, must be clearly set out therein. Special attention should be paid to certain mischeifs which have manifested, and Indian adaptation and acclimatization of Crown-Cabinet relations must be evolved as the source and strength of our democracy. Here is a challenge to the constitutional creativity of our jurists and statesmen.

A Few Plain Home-truths

The Governor should not operate secretly in State politics. He should not delay or defy any advice given to him by his Cabinet within the field of State administration. He cannot and should not delay or deny assent to Bills except at the behest of the State Cabinet. Of course, in the narrow category covered by the second proviso to Article 200, he may take the advice of the Advocate-General and the Attorney-General to decide whether he should refer the matter for the assent of the President. Prorogation of the Legislature must be the Cabinet's strategy, not *his*. Even regarding the dissolution of the House, dismissal of the Ministry and the choice of the Chief Minister, he should be guided by established Westminster convention tuned to Indian conditions. It is unfortunate but true that some Governors have run amuck although there is often a method in their madness, in the sense of being "operators" of the party in power at the Centre. Distinguished Governors have brought prestige to the office by their wisdom, impartiality and adherence to healthy conventions. But there has been zig-zag acrobatics by upstart athletes in office in (a) the choice of the Chief Minister, (b) the dissolution of the House on the advice of the Chief Minister, (c) the dismissal of the Cabinet and (d) reporting about imposition of President's Rule. It is regrettable that these confusions have assailed our institutions right from the beginning of the Constitution. And worse, after the resignation of the Desai Ministry, the horrendous happenings in the choice of the Prime Minister and the dissolution of the Lok Sabha have been rather unprincipled. Mr. Seervai is right in his criticism of the induction of Charan Singh as Prime Minister as violative of parliamentary norms. (Even a fine and sensitive person like Justice Khanna was tempted into the two-day folly of being a

Law Minister in that dubious Cabinet.) Constant vigilance is the price of parliamentary freedom. We must hold the flame aloft without selling the Republic's constitutional soul for a mess of political pottage.

It is interesting that there are jurists whose constitutional conscience is conditioned by political allergy. They approved of the dissolution of the Kerala Ministry in 1959 on the specious score that it had lost the confidence of the people forgetting that it had a majority in the House throughout (and polled a substantial percentage in the election that followed) and the mass upheaval which was used as a pretext to read into the situation a wall of separation between the Government and the people was itself a make-believe product of political engineering with the active connivance of the Congress Party (and condemned at once by Rajaji and Justice Patanjali Sastry as a trick). I will deal with the misuse of Article 356 a little later, but content myself with the submission that the conventions in a given situation are easy to discern once the party system and responsibility to the House are underscored as fundamentals. The Constitution makes the Cabinet responsible to the House and parading the legislators in the Raj Bhavan is a vulgar caricature unrelated to the decency and dignity of parliamentary government. The limit was reached where the Sikkim, Jammu and Kashmir and Andhra Pradesh episodes were manoeuvred by the Governors. The majority in the House is to continue the Ministry not the daily arithmatic of head-count tallied on the lawns of the Raj Bhavan adjusted to secret messages from afar ! Save in the rarest of rare cases where the prolongation of the Cabinet for perpetration of stratagems may lead to the demolition of the people's will—inconceivable in any of the aforesaid cases where the Rajpal has dismissed the State Ministries. There may be an honest difference of opinion in particular cases but *mala fides*, when writ large, cannot be sustained on academic quotations.

Living conventions congenial to Indian conditions, rather than pathological imitations of the British system, are the desideratum. Even so, conventions and precedents across the Atlantic may be of immense help since our form of government is patterned that way. Conventions grow or flow, moulded by democratic demands of a given situation. Therefore, it may be useful to see what the British conventions and precedents are, not as binding events but as beacon lights :

> "The historian can tell you probably perfectly clearly what the constitutional practice was at any given period in the past, but it would be very difficult for a living writer to tell you at any given period in his lifetime what the Constitution of the country is in all respects, and for this reason, that at almost any given moment . . . there may be one practice called 'constitutional' which is falling into desuetude and there may be another practice which is creeping into use but is not yet constitutional."
>
> (*p. 13, The British Cabinet, John P. Mackintosh, Stevens & Sons Ltd., London, 1977*)

There may be situations where clear precedents do not exist, but the principle may still help.

> "In the election of December 1923, none of the three parties was returned with a clear majority and the King noted that "there are really no precedents for the present situation. I must use my own judgment as each case arises." Thus a valid precedent and good judgment in a new situation both rest on an understanding of the facts of the case followed by the line of action which is best calculated to further the underlying principles of the current British political system."
>
> (*The British Cabinet, Ibid.*)

The two guiding principles which the King/Queen has followed, and which must threrefore be useful to us too, are that the prevailing political temper of the electorate should be given the fullest means of expression and once the electorate has pronounced its verdict, the Government thus formed should have every opportunity to fulfil its policy with the Crown using its power to keep a strong and stable government and not to toss it in the tumult of frequent elections.

John P. Mackintosh, in *The British Cabinet*, has observed :

> "These two principles also explain the convention governing

the Crown's right to refuse a Prime Minister's request for a dissolution. This request will never be refused if the Prime Minister can claim than an election will reveal a definite change of temper among the electorate or if he can show that the government is likely to be strengthened. The one case where the Crown could refuse is when an election would neither change party representation in the Commons to any appreciable extent nor aid the government. Let it be assumed that there are three parties well represented in the House so that a combination of any two of the parties would have an absolute majority, and that party A has formed a government relying on the support of party B in the division lobbies and opposed by party C. Then, if the government's stock was declining so that a general election would afford no chance of its winning an absolute majority, and yet if neither parties B nor C were eager to go to the country but were prepared to combine in support of an agreed Cabinet, the King would be entitled to refuse a dissolution and to commission a new Prime Minister. This situation almost arose on the defeat of the first Labour Government in 1924. Then George V only granted Mr. Ramsay MacDonald's request with 'the utmost reluctance'. The Labour Party had a reasonable claim to test the electorate's reaction to its first period of rule, and yet George V agreed only after he had ascertained that both the leaders of the Conservative and Liberal parties were unable or unwilling to combine in support of an administration formed out of the existing House. The situation could also have arisen in February 1974 if the Liberal Party had agreed to form a coalition with the Conservatives under Mr. Heath. Had this happened and, a few weeks or months later, this coalition had been defeated and Mr. Heath had asked for a dissolution, the Crown could have refused on the grounds that the Labour Party, with Liberal acquiescence, could have formed a government based on its support in the existing House of Commons."

(*pp. 17-18, Ibid.*)

It is right to note that the role of the "sovereign people" is distinguished from "the sovereignty of Parliament". In the classical sense, the will of the British people was *expressed by the*

House of Commons. Says Mackintosh : "In recent years, with the increasing emphasis on such slogans as 'the will of the People', 'the rights of the majority' and with so much talk of participation, the idea that the public can only express itself in political matters through the House of Commons has declined." Consequently, the finality of the parliamentary majority, as solely reflecting popular sovereignty, is giving place to a more plebiscitary system. Another change which claims our attention is that "it is considered legitimate for a new Prime Minister, even with a clear majority and two or three years to go before a General Election is necessary, to have an election on the grounds that he needs a new mandate ; the direct endorsement of the people." Eden in 1955 and Callaghan in 1976 sought fresh mandates for this reason. One more facet of the relations between Buckingham Palace and No. 10 Downing Street deserves mention. George V, who kept precise proprieties, expressed his views forthrightly, but left the final decision to the politician in power. When he was asked how he was getting on with his first Labour Government, the King replied : "Very well. My grand mother would have hated it ; my father would have tolerated it ; but I move with the times." (p. 417, Ibid.) Very often, objections raised by King George were silenced by the simple statement, "Well, your Majesty, that is the Cabinet decision. . . ." (p. 418, Ibid.) The King felt that he could not reject the advice of a Prime Minister in any other than exceptional circumstances. (*See p. 419, Ibid.*).

Two more observations, and I conclude. King George is said to have been an ideal constitutional monarch "standing aside from the Government of the country, expressing his views on the issues put before him and very occasionally exercising a marginal influence on matters which were not of major political importance. (*See p. 421, Ibid.*).

The abdication of Edward VIII reveals the process of British Government. In connection with his relations with Mrs. Simpson, Baldwin told the King that he must obey his advice or take the resignation of the Government. Indeed, the Ministers refused to permit the King broadcast his case to the people and insisted on a rapid decision. Edward decided to quit.

What I have stated above brings out loudly how important the Prime Minister and the Chief Minister are and how splendidly impotent the President and the Governor are.

This conclusion is topically relevant because Governors, while willing to eat the humble pie when invisibly ordered by the Central Government, have defied the Chief Minister or embarrassed him by assuming autocratic roles. The fact that the President is elected in a qualified way or that the Governor is nominated by the Centre hardly matters. They cannot exceed the Crown. Likewise, the recasting of Article 74(1) is a redundancy because the meaning of the original Article 74(1) and Article 163(1) is not precatory but mandatory vis-a-vis the President and the Governor as authoritatively laid down in *Shamsher Singh* (Ibid.) before and after.

Now, let me express a few thoughts on the bitterly contentious subject of Presidential intervention in the State Government through Articles 355 and 356 read with Article 365.

The Imperial Flavour

The failure of the constitutional machinery at the State level is a special situation where the President, by a proclamation, may assume to himself the functions of the State Government and declare that the powers of the State Legislature shall be exercisable by or under the authority of Parliament. This is popularly known as President's Rule and, so long as it lasts, it stifles State-level democracy, with the poor consolation that not monarchy, but Union-level oligarchic democracy of sorts still flourishes. At least, after the traumatic experience of the Emergency and the mass dismissal by the Janata regime of nine State Governments run in accordance with the constitutional process (imitated more ruthlessly by the successor at the Centre), one should have thought that this provision, seemingly calculated to advance constitutional Government, throws it out of gear and, through misuse, amputates provincial self-government. It has an imperial flavour and the ghost of Whitehall (the hated Section 93 of the Government of India Act 1935) constantly haunts the States and emasculates self-government through the nightmarish 356. The British provisions were severely criticized by the Congress, but the Founding Fathers, without prophetic vision, adopted this authoritarian provision. However, learned men like Seervai have taken the view that these powers uphold the federal principle—*if properly exercised.* A big "if", indeed. In fact, erudite comparisons with the U.S. and Australian Constitutions have been myopically invoked in justification. The minimal reason which may vindicate the power arises only in cases of external aggression. Internal commotion can be arrested by Central assistance to the State, when sought. And Articles 256 and 365, imaginatively interpreted, will justify corrective directives and supersession in chronic defiance. It is a sobering thought that in a situation where the Government at the Union level cannot be carried on in accordance with the provisions of the Constitution, there is no counterpart to Article 356. Why, then, should a second-class status to State democracy, under the guardianship of the Central executive, be imposed is beyond one's understanding, Seervai notwithstanding. After all, outstanding Central politicians often become State Chief Ministers and *vice versa*. For argument's sake, one may treat the submissions of the learned author in Volume III, pages 1617 to 1621 as dubiously good, but the same author has realized the grave abuse of this provision. Be that as it may, the Supreme Court's decision in *Rajasthan v. Union* (AIR 1977 SC 1361) has only made matters worse by legitimizing bastardy, by judicial baptism. The Court has abdicated its jurisdiction and has lent Court concurrence to the contrived collapse of provincial self-governments in nine States at one stroke by the strange plea that when people vote in Parliament elections one way and against the party in power at the State level, they must be deemed to have voted out of their seats the Assembly surrogates. At this rate, if in a State, the panchayat elections result in the victory of a political party in the Opposition, there is a good case for the President to act under Article 356 ! Elections for different tiers are voted on what falls within that dimension and not fanatically for palm or plough or other crude symbol ? Do the Courts sub-consciously follow the polls—a cynical statement substantiated by history. Re-read the *Fundamental Rights case* and the *Rajasthan case et al.*

The White Paper on the office of the Governor published by the Government of Karnataka brings out the President's Rule abuse (although, with partiality, the Janata jettisoning is omitted there) :

> "The record proves beyond a shadow of doubt that, in most cases, the Governors have used their office to serve the interests of the ruling party at the Centre."

The Kerala case of 1959 was a neatly worked out secret plot where the Central Government virtually abetted politically a violent upsurge and benefited by its own wrong through the President disingenuously invoking "the wall of separation" doctrine. The Madras instance of dismissing the DMK Government and the AIADMK Government to suit Central political interest is also a shameful misuse of powers. Of course, the horrendous Andhra imbroglio did not result in President's Rule because puppetry was expected to be a successful adroitry but misfired through mass action. The question is not who was then in office or who came in later. Bhaskara Rao or NTR is not the real issue but Ramlal artistry is the despair of the constitutional calculus. The tragedy is that the power under Article 356 has been used through obliging Governors to achieve the ulterior objective of the Central party in power getting into the saddle at the State level and all Chief Ministers, in mortal fear of the morrow, "stooping to conquer" or to survival. There is no need to repeat the exhaustive treatment in the White Paper (already referred to) except to regret that neither Pandit Nehru nor Morarji Desai resisted the temptation. (In 1959, referring to Kerala, Morarji Desai criticized the "dangerous" appointment of a single additional I.G. of Police as a communist "divide and rule" device. And G.B. Pant nearly warned of Central intervention if the State Government commuted Vasu Pillai death sentence earlier rejected by the President using Article 365 !) There is a marginal hope left in the ratio in *Rajasthan v. Union of India* (AIR 1977 SC 1361) in that a narrow judicial jurisdiction is still left open for striking down *mala fide* Presidential action. Chief Justice Beg has feebly observed :

> "75. .... This Court has not gone so far as that. If it is actually stated on behalf of the Union Government that an action was taken on a particular ground which really falls completely outside the purview of Article 356(1), the proclamation will be vitiated, not because the satisfaction was challenged or called in question on

> any ground but because it was admitted to be on matters outside Article 356(1)."
>
> (*AIR 1977 SC 1389*)

Likewise, Justice (now Chief) Bhagwati has entered a caveat in traditional, half-hearted rhetoric (thanks for small mercies) :

> "But one thing is certain that if the satisfaction is mala fide or is based on wholly extraneous and irrelevant grounds, the Court would have jurisdiction to examine it, because in that case there would be (sic-no ?) satisfaction of the President in regard to the matter in which he is required to be satisfied. The satisfaction of the President is a condition precedent to the exercise of power under Art. 356, Cl. (1) and if it can be shown that there is no satisfaction of the President at all, the exercise of the power would be constitutionally invalid. Of course by reason of Cl. (5) of Art. 356, the satisfaction of the President is final and conclusive and cannot be assailed on any ground, but this immunity from attack cannot apply where the challenge is not that the satisfaction is improper or unjustified, but that there is no satisfaction at all. On such a case it is not the satisfaction arrived at by the President which is challenged, but the existence of the satisfaction itself. Take, for example, a case where the President gives the reason for taking action under Art. 356, Cl. (1) and says that he is doing so, because the Chief Minister of the State is below five feet in height and, therefore, in his opinion a situation has arisen where the Government of the State cannot be carried on in accordance with the provisions of the Constitution. Can the so-called satisfaction of the President in such a case not be challenged on the ground that it is absurd or perverse or mala fide or based on a wholly extraneous and irrelevant ground and is, therefore, no satisfaction at all. It must of course be conceded that in most cases it would be difficult, if not impossible, to challenge the exercise of power under Art. 356, Cl. (1) even on this limited ground, because the facts and circumstances on which the satisfaction is based would not be known, but where it is possible, the existence of the satisfaction can always be

challenged on the ground that it is mala fide or based on wholly extraneous and irrelevant grounds. This proposition derives support from the decision of the Judicial Committee of the Privy Council in King Emperor v. Benoari Lal Sarma, 72 Ind App 57 : (AIR 1945 PC 48) where Viscount Simon, L.C. agreed that the Governor-General in declaring that emergency exists must act bona fide and in accordance with his statutory powers. This is the narrow minimal area in which the exercise of power under Art. 356, Cl. (1) is subject to judicial review and apart from it, it cannot rest with the Court to challenge the satisfaction of the President that the situation contemplated in that clause exists."

Para 144

(AIR 1977 SC 1414/1415/in part)

While the Court has gone all out to support an interpretation which *indirectly* sanctions the potential for abuse—I think this is a ruling which requires reconsideration at the earliest opportunity having regard to the enormity and frequency of abuse by all parties in power—there is a case for limitation on the Presidential power to be legitimately read by a restricted construction of the expression "a situation has arisen in which the Government of the State cannot be carried on in accordance with the provisions of this Constitution." In this connection, Article 365 which has ominous portents must also be remembered. Supposing the direction given by the Central Government is *ultra vires* can it invoke Article 356 to dismiss the State Cabinet ? Only if the Central direction defied by the State Executive results in a grave situation and the Supreme Court holds the direction to be valid, should President's Rule be imposed. It is politically a life-and-death matter for the State, and in case immediate action be needed, the Supreme Court may be moved for special and quick hearing. The Sri Lanka Constitution provides for a few days for challenge of a Bill as *ultra vires* and for the Court to pronounce judgment ? You may have a special Bench, summary hearing, but a speaking not a sphinx-like order. Of course, a *locus paenitentia* to obey may be given to the State by the Centre. This takes away the political sting and convinces the people of the proposed drastic action. Public action for public good is not a secret weapon to produce shock and surprise.

Coming to Article 356 itself the anatomy of the provision needs closer study. "A situation has arisen" means a *critical* situation not a common dilemma or minor imbroglio which, with tact, may well be sorted out. To hold—even for the subjective satisfaction of the President—that the Government *cannot be carried on* in accordance with the *provisions of the Constitution* a secret report of a boneless Governor is not rational material. State democracy is not a plaything of Raj Bhavan conspiracy or federal majority's wish to push out of office an Opposition in State power by means fair or foul. It is a constitutional power, canalized by strict and strong diction, involving serious consequences and fouling Centre—State relations. Everything about it must be above board and, being amenable to parliamentary post-mortem, must be available to preview, within limits, by the summit judicial sentinel. The Court's inspection door must be opened wider than the *Rajasthan case* (AIR 1977 SC 1361) unwillingly agrees to janitor. To hold that the Administration *cannot* be constitutionally carried on is a stringent condition. If the House has confidence, the Constitution issues clearance certificate. If there is a deadlock within the Cabinet or within a Coalition which claims the House majority, the matter can be put to the test by insisting on a confidence vote. If the House throws the Ministry out a new Government will be ushered in according to conventions. Article 356 must go into action in the rarest of rare instances. If the security and unity of the country is grossly undermined by the State Government or the Judiciary is stultified by deliberate defiance, an appropriate constitutional direction under Article 256 read with Articles 365 and 356 may come into play. But merely for opportunistic political advantage or to jettison a Chief Minister who is a thorn in the flesh, you cannot subvert the on-going constitutional machinery, by fobbing off "a failure of constitutional machinery" or fabricating a wall of separation between the "people" and the "Government". And yet, the Rajasthan case has conceded blanket power with political naivete or constitutional pachydermy.

Article 356—Executioner of State-level Democracy

I would conclude my submissions on Article 356 with regurgitating what I had earlier said while inaugurating a seminar on Centre-State Relations in Hyderabad, although the observations overlap, in part, what I have stated earlier.

"It has been said that democracy has a tendency to commit suicide. But under the Indian sun, there is a fatal proclivity for homicide of State autonomy by continued abuse of Article 356. Article 356 read with Article 365 and in the background of Articles 256 and 257, is the executioner of State-level democracy based on *procured* Governor's reports or otherwise. The most misused power under the Constitution is Article 356. Hardly any State has been spared and hardly any occasion free from extraneous political consideration. The Janata Government, for reasons which I consider quite irrelevant (despite the Supreme Court having upheld the action), dissolved nine Assemblies virtually because of allergy to the politics of the governance. The successor at the Centre shot down State Governments likewise. The Article is very widely worded and now judicially protected, although by the grace of the Supreme Court, *mala fide* exercise has been spared for judicial scrutiny. Shri M.C. Setalvad in his Alladi Krishnaswamy Aiyer Lectures observes :

> "It is interesting in this connection to turn to what Dr. Ambedkar said in the Constituent Assembly in regard to the exercise of powers contained in Article 356 :
>
> "I may say that I do not altogether deny that there is a possibility of this Article being abused or applied for political purposes. But that objection applies to every part of the Constitution which gives power to the Centre to override the Provinces. In fact, I share the sentiments expressed yesterday that the proper thing we ought to expect is that such Articles will never be called into operation and that they would remain a dead letter. If at all they are brought into operation, I hope the President who is endowed with this power will take proper precaution before actually suspending the administration of the provinces."
>
> We shall presently see how the hopes entertained by Dr. Ambedkar have been grievously belied."

Indeed, in another part of his lecture, the same great jurist states :

> "A publicist referring to the situation that arose in Pepsu in

1952, in Kerala in 1959, and in some other places has expressed himself thus :

"This history of the working of our Constitution shows that the reports from Governors and advices tendered to the Central Council of Ministers are being turned into instruments in the hand of the ruling Congress party which is determined to see that its own Government is imposed on the people even though they have unceremoniously rejected it.' "

It is well accepted that the existence of powerful Opposition parties capable of taking over the task of forming a Government when necessary is the essence of the Constitutional Democratic Government. It is imperative, therefore, that in order to promote Parliamentary Government there should be built up different political parties commanding respect and confidence. This cannot be achieved by the abuse of its political power by the party which has happened to come into power by the hazard of the polls. Thus unjustified acts of the ruling party which tend to prevent other parties from developing into maturity are a matter of grave concern. Such an attitude forbids disaster to the growth of a real democracy in our country.

Indeed, almost all political parties which have tasted Central power have made blood-thirsty use of Article 356. Now, no Chief Minister in the country can peacefully sleep because he is not sure whether the next morning, Article 356 will pass death sentence on his Ministry. I have not the slightest doubt that if the Central Government's constitutional machinery fails and still India survives as a democracy, as was exemplified a few years ago, there is no reason to apprehend that collapse of Statehood will occur even assuming there is confusion or breakdown, through defection or otherwise, of situations which challenge just administration. In any case, even supporters of Article 356 like Shri Setalvad have grave fears which have since been justified by its gross misuse. He concludes his lecture on this emergency power with sentiments which every democrat will endorse :

"What is needed, however, is the realisation of the true purpose of such provisions and a deep and anxious sense of

> responsibility in the exercise of the power. If the Centre repeatedly supersedes and takes over the administration of States from Ministries formed by parties different from the ruling party at the Centre in the name of the breakdown of the constitutional machinery in the State but really to promote the interests of the ruling party, the country would be heading towards a totalitarian democracy controlled by one party."

The demand for every clear conventions and bold judicial statesmanship is nowhere more necessary than in this grey area.

I am all for freedom from federal friction and a strong Centre, elimination of contra-constitutional forces and weakening by obstructive State operators. But harmonious Centre-State relations cannot be achieved by *in terrorem* tactics from the summit. A vibrant people's voice is a surer guarantee of a democratic constitutional order than the long clauses of a prolix constitution. The States obstreperously protesting against Central intervention do not practise grass-roots democracy. Has there been an election to the Calcutta Corporation or for that matter Hyderabad-Secunderabad, Madras and now Bombay ? Why no Panchayat elections in Kerala, come Congress, come Marxist ? The people matter (in their democratic dictionary) where their votes are in your favour—a strange annotation of government by the people ! My final plea, therefore, is for full-blooded, people-activated democratic forces as the guardian of national unity, integrity and democracy.

From this affirmative perspective, I would plead for a re-examination of the provisions of the Constitution relating to Governor's *Reign* and President's *Rule*. Constitutional Law is pure politics blended with Fundamental Law, as Justice (now Chief) Bhagwati has stated in the *Rajasthan case*. So, we must envision Union-State relations from a higher level and from a holistic perspective. We are in danger of disintegration and must rally the enlightened masses behind the institutions of Government vertically and horizontally.

FIVE

ARVAL A. MORRIS

THE ESSENCE OF THE "ESSENTIAL FEATURES" OF INDIA'S CONSTITUTION
Fundamental Rights and Permanent Revolution

DR. Alladi Krishnaswami Aiyar, an esteemed Advocate-General for the State of Madras and possessed of an unrivalled knowledge of legal principles and case law, played a leading architect's role in creating the whole of the Constitution of India, its Directive Principles, and especially its Fundamental Rights part which was of great importance to him. Truly a father of the Indian Constitution, Dr. Aiyar later delivered a set of brilliant lectures on the Constitution focusing on Part III, The Fundamental Rights. In the course of his lectures, he appropriately claimed that the "institution of adult suffrage (was) by far the biggest step that was taken".[1] That step manifested itself in a representational government. In a bold stroke India transformed herself into a republican form of democracy.[2]

The institution of adult suffrage supplied the remarkable authority that empowered India's constitution makers to write in the name of "WE, THE PEOPLE OF INDIA, . . .".[3] Plainly, Indian sovereignty ultimately rests with the Indian people, themselves, and not with their representatives in the Lok Sabha (the lower legislative "House of the People" directly elected by citizens) or the Rajya Sabha (an upper "Council of States" most of whose members are elected by State Legislatures), nor with the President (who actually exercises the executive power but only with the "aid and advice" of the Council of Ministers), nor the Prime Minister (who is the dominant member of the Council of Ministers which is collectively responsible to the Lok Sabha), nor with India's Supreme Court or the High Courts found in the States. They all are merely public trustees for the people and derive their legitimate power from India's sovereign people.

By demarcating and separating the exercise of power among (and in some cases within) the Legislature, the Executive and the Judiciary, and by creating a system of checks and balances, India's constitution makers sought to safeguard the sovereignty of the people by ensuring that any claim by any partial segment of government to act in the name of "WE, THE PEOPLE OF INDIA" would be carefully scrutinized by the other divisions and could not succeed without their cooperation.

But, securing the recognition that the Indian people ultimately are sovereign was not enough. India's constitution makers had to govern the future as well. Their further task was to create an enduring constitutional structure that would foster a progressive, humane and enlightened development of Indian society, i.e., the "right kind" of future political action was necessary. But, shaping the "right kind" of future is most difficult, at best. How might this be accomplished ?

The beginning of Indian wisdom lay in the clear recognitions by Dr. Aiyar and his colleagues that India's future would not be a glorious re-enactment of its revolutionary struggle for independence and that an unusual, and special, kind of politics unique to India's circumstances was needed. But, this, too, is a dangerous mission because it meant sailing on uncharted seas.

Political action can be of two kinds—abnormal and normal.[4] One—"abnormal" politics—operates at the usurping, revolutionary and highest constitutional levels. It consists of irregularly constituted "elite" groups taking action in the name of "WE, THE PEOPLE OF INDIA", declaring themselves to be the true representatives of the people as they challenge existing authority and act outside of it. If successful, then all previous irregularities and errors are wiped out by later approval by the people in whose name the irregular action was taken. Revolutionary "abnormal" politics are characterized by high-level expressions of altruism and idealism. Revolutionary, "abnormal" politics, it is generally believed, are the highest kind of politics and should be allowed to dominate a people most rarely and then only during periods of intensely heightened political consciousness. Revolutionary politics are potent and can result in attempts at "permanent revolution" as an idealistic and continuing way of life. China's "great leap forward" during its Cultural Revolution is an example.

Dr. Aiyar and other constitution makers saw that India's future needed the idealism and altruism found in the politics of "permanent revolution". But, they also saw that while Indian society could benefit from continual, enlightened development, which requires the politics of public virtue, India could not, and should not, try to sustain the irregular and abnormal politics of "permanent revolution" as a permanent way of life. That path with its singular commitment to a domineering conception of public virtue is quite dangerous. It can easily ignore existing social structures, operate outside them, and degenerate into "benevolent" totalitarianism, led by elites who "know" better than the people themselves what is best for the people. The next step is for the "permanent revolutionary elite" to cast its views into law. Anyone standing in the way of the abnormal politics of permanent revolution becomes a counter-revolutionary and a law-breaker. He is either eliminated or "re-educated". Yet, there clearly is something of value here. The vigour, the idealism and the altruism of this kind of political action, i.e., its public virtue, is a crucial counterweight to the narrow selfishness of "normal" politics, and a necessary factor for India's future economic and social development.

A second and much more frequently observed kind of political action can be called "normal". It consists primarily of groups that are variously well organized, manipulating government and other social structures in pursuit of their own narrow, often selfish, interests. "Normal" politics are characterized by idealistic and altruistic amnesia. True public virtue is lacking. Participating groups pursue their own selfish interests, frequently trying to identify them with virtue. Normal politics must exist in every republican democracy in the name of individual freedom and personal privacy, and when properly confined, normal politics can be valuable to any society.

"Normal" politics are democratically inferior in idealism and altruism to "permanent revolutionary" politics with its emphasis on public virtue. "Normal" politics, like "abnormal" politics, are insufficient by themselves, for sustaining republican democracies like India. Indeed, Montesquieu claimed that republican government would perish unless it could regularly rely on its citizens' public virtue.[5] Without a regular flow of public virtue to guide leaders then, like the ancient Greek democracies, India's new republican government would be beset by "normal" politics. India's government could degenerate into turmoil and despotism as each group sought to use power for its own personal and selfish ends, suppressing other groups seeking to do the same. The public-regarding forms of political activity in which people pursue the common good even if it means sacrificing their private interests are essential. But, as even Montesquieu must have known, a spontaneous and constant flow of citizen public virtue is not something that can be continually expected of the Indian, the American or any people. And "normal politics move in the wrong direction. How, then, may the merits of idealism found in the "abnormal", elite politics of public virtue be built into India's Constitution without their disabling detractions and their tilt toward totalitarianism ?

A Bold Document

India's constitution makers provided an important and unique answer which builds, in part, on an idea found in the Irish Constitution. In language that is general and flexible, Articles 38 to 51 of India's Constitution contain the "Directive Principles of State Policy". Their purpose is to move Indian policy in the "right" direction substantively by focusing the attention of the National and State Legislatures on the goals to be achieved with their enactments. The Directive Principles supply a public purpose. Although not directly enforceable by courts, the principles can be used as a basis for judicial reasoning so long as their interpretation is harmonious with, and does not supersede or limit other judicially enforceable constitutional provisions.[6] The Directive Principles impose binding constitutional obligations upon the state as a whole, and this includes all of the national and local legislators and executives. They are constitutionally obligated to take certain positive actions, to the extent circumstances permit, to promote the welfare of the people and achieve a thoroughgoing economic democracy. Seen in this light, the Constitution of India is a bold document institutionalizing the "abnormal" politics of permanent revolution, drawing on its pubilc virtue and commingling "abnormal" politics with "normal" politics. Articles 38 and 39, as amended by the 42nd and 44th Amendments in 1976 and 1978, are good examples of this vision of permanent revolution :

38. State to secure a social order for the promotion of welfare of the people :

(1) The State shall strive to promote the welfare of the people by securing and protecting as effectively as it may a social order in which justice, social, economic and political, shall inform all the institutions of the national life.

(2) The State shall, in particular, strive to minimise the inequalities in income, and endeavour to eliminate inequalities in status, facilities and opportunities, not only amongst individuals but also amongst groups of people residing in different areas or engaged in different vocations.

39. Certain principles of policy to be followed by the State. The State shall, in particular, direct its policy towards securing—

(a) that the citizens, men and women equally, have the right to an adequate means to livelihood ;

(b) that the ownership and control of the material resources of the community are so distributed as best to subserve the common good ;

(c) that the operation of the economic system does not result in the concentration of wealth and means of production to the common detriment ;

(d) that there is equal pay for equal work for both men and women ;

(e) that the health and strength of workers, men and women, and the tender age of children are not abused and that citizens are not forced by economic necessity to enter avocations unsuited to their age or strength ;

(f) that children are given opportunities and facilities to develop in a healthy manner and in conditions of freedom and dignity and that childhood and youth are protected against exploitation and against moral and material abandonment.

This is heady and potent stuff. India's Constitution incorporates the vigorous idealism of public virtue and seeks to tame its excesses by institutionalizing them, shearing off irregular revolutionary elites with their willingness to assume irregular prerogatives outside of constitutional authority in the name of "WE, THE PEOPLE OF INDIA". India's bold constitutional move is to bring revolutionary "abnormal" politics into everyday political affairs, and to do so on a continuing basis, by infusing "normal" politics with the vigour of public-virtue politics. That is a daring move : one fraught with danger, and it can backfire. If the vigour of the "abnormal" politics of permanent revolution becomes too strong, it can break out of its constitutional forms and consume the Constitution, manifesting itself in a totalitarian "welfare" despotism in the name of "WE, THE PEOPLE OF INDIA". The sovereignty of the Indian people would become hollow. Thus, India's constitution makers faced another problem : the vigour of permanent revolutionary politics must be constrained to its proper constitutional role, but how ? That constraint is what India's constitution makers sought to provide in the separation of powers and checks and balances, *supra*, and in Part III of the Constitution : "Fundamental Rights",[7] which is buttressed with the check of judicial review by an independent judiciary. Thus confined, permanent revolution is expected to occur in a constitutional context.

An "Essential Feature" of India's Constitution is, therefore, its Fundamental Rights,[8] and they must be vigorously enforced by independent courts.[9] Court enforcement of Fundamental Rights is of paramount importance as a check on legislative power because Fundamental Rights identify substantive areas that are not subject to the public-virtue politics of "permanent revolution". It is most unlikely that a fervent Legislature will act as a check on itself. In a crucially important way, Part III of the Constitution, the fundamental Rights with its check of Judicial Review, provide substantive constitutional constraints and limitations on Part IV, the Directive Principles. Together, they create the "right" kind of politics for India, as foreseen by the constitution makers.

India's constitution makers created a fundamental Rights

framework for human dignity wishin which the State is constitutionally obligated to pursue the altruistic goals of social and economic equality set forth by the Directive Principles. Early in its history, India's Supreme Court was faithful to the vision of the Constitution's founders, holding that a Directive Principle cannot override a Fundamental Right.[10] In case of a conflict between a Directive Principle and a Fundamental Right, it is the former, not the latter, that must give way. Directive Principles must conform, and run subsidiary, to Fundamental Rights, staying within the Fundamental Rights framework.[11]

The Fundamental Rights of Part III are the basic human rights held by all Indians regardless of race, religion, social position or other irrelevant factors. The rights are intended to be inviolable. Mr. Justice Jackson has well summarized the philosophy underlying Fundamental Rights when he commented on the American Bill of Rights in *West Virginia v. Barnette* :[12]

> The very purpose of a Bill of Rights was to withdraw certain subjects from the vicissitudes of political controversy, to place them beyond (the) reach of majorities and officials and to establish them as legal principles to be applied by the courts. One's right to life, liberty, and property, to free speech, a free Press, freedom of worship and assembly, and other fundamental rights may not be submitted to vote ; they depend on the outcome of no election.

It was this sense of constitutionalism that led Carl J. Friedrich to call a constitution's primary objective "that of protecting the individual member of the political community against interference in his personal sphere of genuine autonomy,"[13] and Walter F. Murphy to conclude that "The fundamental value that constitutionalism protects is human dignity."[14] Obviously, Fundamental Rights are a vitally necessary component of India's constitutional plan, as is judicial review by a fully independent judiciary composed of judges of great character, learning, substance and integrity. A main function of the Indian Supreme Court is that it be the final decision-maker on whether a piece of legislation, or executive action, is constitutional. Its primary "client" is the Constitution itself. Recognizing this necessity in his lectures, Dr. Aiyar expressly agreed with President Woodrow

Wilson that "the Courts are the balance-wheel of the Constitution".[15]

It is worth pausing for a moment to note a key aspect of a Fundamental Right. A Fundamental Right differs from an ordinary right in a crucially important way. It ordinarily is paramount to and supersedes conflicting legislation that aims at advancing the public welfare.[16] The difference between two kinds of rights can be seen by considering four hypotheticals beginning with one about a two-way street, say Janpath in New Delhi. Currently, I have a right, so long as I obey traffic regulations, to travel in both directions along Janpath. But, if the proper authorities reasonably believe the public welfare will be advanced and decree a new policy, namely, that Janpath shall have traffic flowing in one direction only, then their decree conflicts with my previous right to travel Janpath in both directions. I say "previous" right because the right I had does not survive the new policy ; it is not paramount to the new public welfare legislation making Janpath one-way. The legislature is paramount in this instance. Indeed, my previous policy right allowing me to travel in either direction along Janpath was based on the previous policy that Janpath be a two-way thoroughfare, and in that sense my previous right was inferior to the public good to be achieved. The policy goal is prior to the right, and achieving the goal is more important than its implementing rights which exist only to serve achievement of the goal.

Suppose a hypothetical nation has 100,000 subjects, a ruler, and an economy in need of economic stimulation.[17] Assume further that all economists agree that the only effective way to stimulate the economy is to give $ 1,000 to each of 10,000 randomly chosen people, rather than $ 100 to all 100,000 people, and the ruler agrees. Clearly, each of the 10,000 persons, randomly chosen, has a policy right to $ 1,000. If default should occur and a randomly chosen person is not paid, he may bring a lawsuit, and a court should order that he be paid $ 1,000. The court's judgment would be based on principle, not policy ; i.e., principle would recognize and implement the scope of policy rights. But, if a similar lawsuit were brought by a person who was not randomly chosen to receive money, then the court, equally acting on principle, should properly dismiss his lawsuit because he has no policy right. He is outside the scope of the economic policy that seeks to advance the public welfare, and the right to receive the money is fully dependent on the scope of the policy. Now change the assumptions and assume that religion is absolutely forbidden in this hypothetical nation ; that the ruler believes, correctly, that his society needs piety, and that the correct amount of piety would be available if only 10,000 of his 100,000 subjects, randomly chosen, were permitted to practise religion, which he decrees. The character of the right to practice religion is a policy right limited to 10,000 subjects only, and has exactly the same kind of character as the right involved when the ruler wanted to stimulate the economy (or my right to travel in either direction along Janpath). In this situation, the right to practise religion is a mere policy right subordinate to achieving the superior public good of having the proper amount of piety in the community.

But, now turn to Fundamental Rights. Suppose the hypothetical ruler becomes enlightened and recognizes that human beings have a right to religion, not in order to achieve any policy goals like piety, but simply because they are human beings, and he decrees the right to religion, on this ground, for all his subjects, except for 1,000, who bring a lawsuit. Assume the ruler correctly believes the overall public welfare will be promoted if these 1,000 subjects are denied a right to religion. Clearly, the courts should order that the 1,000 excluded subjects have an equal human right to religion. Again, the courts will have acted on principle. This right is paramount to, and supersedes, the ruler's decree limiting the right to religion, excluding 1,000 subjects. This right is a Fundamental Human Right, and it is different from an Ordinary Policy Right because of the scope of its underlying reason.

One should compare the Fundamental Right's reason to the reason lying behind the policy right in the hypothetical involving stimulation of the economy. The reason for giving money to only 10,000 subjects in the economic stimulation programme was an "index-dependent" reason. The scope, i.e., the strength, of the reason is both limited and directly related to the number of subjects who will receive the money. Although the strength of the reason is limited, it is as strong for the 10,000th randomly selected person as for the first, but that's it. The reason for giving out the money vanishes at some point and is replaced by a reason for not giving out any more. That is why the person who sued but who was not randomly chosen to receive money lost his lawsuit. The reason for handling out money had vanished.

But, this state of affairs is not true for Fundamental Rights. Their reasons are different. They are based on "index-free", not "index-dependent", reasons. Based on an index-free reason it recognizes a right to religion in all human beings, simply because they are human beings. The reason for the right does not vanish when other human beings appear and claim it. That is why the 1,000 subjects previously excluded from the right to religion by our hypothetical ruler should win their lawsuit. This is not to say that the right to religion in all circumstances cannot be a limited, index-dependent policy-based right. It can be based on an index-dependent reason as the hypothetical about achieving religious piety clearly shows. But, it is to say that the Fundamental Rights identified in Part III of India's Constitution are, by that document, based on index-free, and not index-dependent reasons—reasons that recognize the right as inhering in all human beings simply because they are human beings. As such, the rights are declared by India's Constitution to be "Fundamental", i.e., paramount to and supersede conflicting legislation or executive action that seeks to limit them in order to advance the public's welfare. Viewed in this light, it is easy to see why Fundamental Rights promote human dignity and why India's constitution makers insisted on them (and the check of Judicial Review) to constrain the vigour of "permanent revolution". This perspective also explains why Fundamental Rights were made judicially enforceable, but not the Directive Principles. Clearly, Fundamental Rights are a prime "essential feature" of India's Constitution.

The Power to Amend—A Problem

But, there is a problem. India's entire constitutional balance can be completely upset by the power to amend. If this power is too easily exercisable, it will be exercised too often with a view toward getting rid of either an inconvenient Fundamental Right or a checking judicial decision that stands in the way of the "permanent revolution". Unfortunately, India's Constitution has proved to be easily amendable. For example, the Constitution of the United States is almost 200 years old and has only twenty-six amendments, while about twenty amendments to India's Constitution were enacted between 1971-77.

Basically, under Article 368, India's Constitution can be amended by a two-thirds vote of the members of each House of Parliament present and voting (so long as that number also equals a majority vote of the total membership of each House) plus the assent of the President[18] unless one of a few "entrenched provisions" is involved in which event the amendment must be approved by one-half of the State Legislatures.[19] The Fundamental Rights, found in Part III, Articles 12 to 35 of India's Constitution, are not identified as "entrenched provisions". This has led to use of the amendment process against them which, in turn, has resulted in substantial litigation testing the constitutional role of India's Supreme Court.

Article 13(2) declares that

> The State shall not make any law which taxes away or abridges the rights conferred in this Part [Fundamental Rights] and any law made in contravention of this clause shall, to the extent of the contravention, be void.

In *Shankari Prasad Singh v. Union of India*,[20] Justice Shastri, for a Bench of five judges, delivered the unanimous judgment of the Supreme Court ruling that[21]

> [T]he terms of Art. 368 are perfectly general and empower Parliament to amend the Constitution, without any exception whatever.

Presumably, therefore, Fundamental Rights are not immune from constitutional amendment by Parliament, and the word "law" in Article 13 must refer only to ordinary legislative acts and not to constitutional amendments impairing Fundamental Rights. Implicit in this decision is the view that Article 13 did not qualify the amending power of Article 368.

These views were later reiterated by a majority of the Court in *Sajjan Singh v. Rajasthan*,[22] again with a Bench of five judges, although two judges dissented. Justice Hidayatullah stated that the "Constitution gives so many assurances in Part III that it would be difficult to think that they were the playthings of a special majority."[23] Justice Mudholker was of the view that the word "law" in Article 13 included a constitutional amendment under Article 368 and that, therefore, the Fundamental Rights part was unalterable. In his view, Article 13 qualified the amending power found in Article 368 making the Fundamental Rights part of India's Constitution unamendable.[24]

The concerns of the two dissenting judges came before an eleven-judge Bench in *Golak Nath v. State of Punjab*[25] involving another attack on three constitutional amendments one of which was previously upheld in *Sankari Prasad, supra.* By a vote of six-to-five, the Supreme Court held that India's Parliament had no power "to amend any of the provisions of Part III . . . so as to take away or abridge the fundamental rights enshrined therein".[26] *Golaknath* was decided in 1967, but one of the amendments it would invalidate dated from 1951, another from 1955 and another from 1964. Profound chaos and turmoil in social and economic relations would ensue if the Court ruled that the amendments were void *ab initio*. To avoid such calamities, the Court relied on American cases[27] and adopted the doctrine of prospective overruling which was construed to enable the Court to reverse its prior decisions *supra* ; to continue the validity of the three amendments in issue, and to declare that after judgment the Indian Parliament would have no power to amend or abridge any of the Fundamental Rights.

The majority in *Golaknath* ruled that the word "law" in Article 13(2) included amendments to the Constitution, thereby precluding amendment of the Fundamental Rights. This position required the majority to confront the meaning of amending Article 368. Partially relying on the Article's marginal note[28] and relying in part on its wording,[29] the majority concluded that Article 368, which in its terms is substantively unlimited, was procedural only, setting forth only the procedural steps for amending the Constitution. This exclusively procedural view of Article 368 is based on the assumption that the substantive amending power is located elsewhere,[30] and the majority was forced to identify where.

Somewhat artificially, the majority located the substantive power to amend in Article 245 and 246, when read in conjunction with List I of the Seventh Schedule to the Constitution. Articles 245 and 246 are found in the section entitled "Relations Between the Union and the States", and deal with the distribution of powers between National and State Legislatures. Among other matters, they provide that the national "Parliament has exclusive power to make laws with respect to any of the matters enumerated in List I in the Seventh Schedule".[31] At the end of List I is entry 97 which reads : "Any other matter not enumerated in List II (setting forth areas subject exclusively to State power) or List III (setting forth areas of concurrent State and Parliament power). . . ."[32] Thus, open-ended entry 97 was construed to give Parliament the exclusive substantive power to amend the Constitution without India's Constitution expressly saying so.[33]

After losing two important constitutional cases in 1970[34] and 1971,[35] Mrs. Gandhi dissolved Parliament. The ensuing election brought her Congress Party back into power with a majority large enough to pass constitutional amendments. The first of several amendments, the Twentyfourth, was intended to overrule the *Golaknath* case by adding to Article 13 : "(4) Nothing in this article shall apply to any Amendment of this Constitution made under Article 361," and by adding to Article 368 a new heading ("Power of Parliament to amend the Constitution and procedure therefor) : and two new clauses : "(1) Nothwithstanding anything in this Constitution, Parliament may in exercise of its constituent power amend by way of addition, variation or repeal any provision of this Constitution in accordance with the procedures laid down in this article" and "Nothing in Article 13 shall apply to any amendment under this article."[36]

A Twentyfifth Amendment added a new Article, 31C, providing that Parliamentary laws implementing the Directive Principles in Article 39(b) and (c)[37] could not be deemed void under Article 13 on the ground that they violated rights found in Article 14 (equal protection of the laws) or Article 19 (free speech, assembly, association, travel or practise a profession or carry on an occupation) and continued stating that "no law containing a declaration that it is for giving effect to such policy shall be called in question in any court on the ground that it does not give effect to such policy. . . ." A Twentyninth Amendment sought to establish similar safeguards for Parliamentary laws against their being struck for infringing on Fundamental Rights.

These amendments—and the continuing validity of *Golaknath*—were subjects of decision in *Kesavananda v. State of Kerala.*[38]

This case is much too long and complex to be fully analysed in the space available here. The hearing took sixtyfive working days and there are eleven opinions for a full Bench of thirteen judges. Suffice it to say that the Kerala Land Reforms were defended by reliance on the three new constitutional amendments while petitioners relied on *Golaknath* and an "essential features" limitation which was left open by *Golaknath.*[39] In retrospect it can be seen that *Kesavananda* gave rise to two kinds of issues : (1) whether the amending power of India's Parliament under Article 368 is absolute or qualified by an "essential feature" limitation, and (2) if it is qualified, whether any of the three amendments involved was invalid because of a conflict with one or more "essential features" of the Constitution. The Supreme Court made several holdings, answering that Article 368 is qualified by an "essent al feature" limitation. Only two are identified here. First, a majority[40] held that the amending power in Article 368 is, itself, substantive, extending to all parts of the Constitution and that the word "law" in Article 13 is ambiguous and must be given a meaning that harmonizes with Article 368. Thus, *Golaknath* was overruled without any need to consider the new Twenty-fourth Amendment on this point.

A second crucially important holding involved a majority[41] declaring that although every article of the Indian Constitution was subject to amendment, the "essential features" of the Constitution could not be "abrogated" by amendment. Thus, Parliament's amending power is qualified and is not absolute. India's Constitution can be amended so long as its "essential features" remain the same.[42] Clearly, the "essential features" rationatle can include the Fundamental Rights, Part III of the Constitution, which is all that *Golaknath* protected. But, the "essential features" protection can, of course, cover a wider area. Only time and further Supreme Court decisions will demarcate the actual boundaries of protection.[43] On the other hand, *Golaknath* broadly prohibited any amendment to the Fundamental Rights part whatsoever, but the "essential features" limitation prevents only their "abrogation". Presumably, therefore, it is the "core" of each Fundamental Right, as it is identified by India's Supreme Court, that is immune. Only the core is an "essential feature" and not subject to amendment by Parliament, which may control the unessential periphery.[44]

Viewed in historical context, the Supreme Court's decision appears workable and justifiable. In 1949, the Constituent Assembly believed that it had preserved the sovereignty of India's people and confined "permanent revolution" within a framework of Fundamental Rights, Judicial Review and a scheme of checks and balances which would not easily be upset. It had, it thought, created a high obstacle to easy constitutional amendment by requiring a two-thirds majority of Parliament, reinforced by a majority of State Legislatures, for amending the Constitution. Clearly, the Assembly believed there would be only few amendments over time with each carrying an overwhelmingly broad consensus behind it. But the Constituent Assembly failed to foresee the monumental successes and the tightly disciplined organizational nature of the Congress Party. Its huge successes at the polls and its strict discipline meant that a constitutional amendment can easily occur when only a few important Ministers and high civil servants desire one. Thus, during 1971-77 about twenty amendments were enacted, not to mention that over 100 Acts of Parliament were elevated above the Fundamental Rights during the twenty-month Emergency period.

Rather clearly, the Constitution was not working as intended by the Constituent Assembly. The Constitution was not maintaining the rule of law against an overwhelming government. Hence, it became necessary to restore the Constitution to the position envisioned for it by its Founders. Seen in this perspective, the "essential features" limitation restores the rule of law and the needed balances, ensuring that India's Constitution will be better suited to her contemporary and her future needs. It is not odd that the new constitutional settlement was made by India's judiciary because India has a Constitution guaranteeing Fundamental Rights and institutionalizing "permanent-revolution".[45] In this constitutional situation truly, "The Courts are the balance-wheel of the Constitution."[46]

FOOTNOTES

1. Alladi Krishnaswami Aiyar, *The Constitution and Fundamental Rights*, 5 (1955) (Published by the Srinivasa Sastri Institute of Politics, Mylapore, Madras). Every citizen, whether male or female, who has reached the age of 21 has a right to vote without discrimination.

Dr. Aiyar stated that

"If democracy is to be broad-based and the system of government that is to function is to have the ultimate sanction of the people as a whole, in a country where a large mass of people are illiterate, where the people owning property are few, the introduction of any property or educational qualification for the exercise of the franchise would be a negation of the principles of democracy. If any such qualification were introduced, that would have disenfranchised a large number of depressed and labouring classes."

And, further, he said,

"It cannot, after all, be assumed that a person with a bare elementary education and with a knowledge of the three R's is in a better position to exercise the franchise than a labourer or a cultivator who may be expected to know what his interests are and choose his representatives." *Id.* at p. 7.

2. For a historical account of India's constitutional development, see, M. Ramaswamy, *Constitutional Developments in India*, 1600-1955, 8 Stanford Law Rev. 326 (1956). India's Constitution is a massive document with 395 Articles, 10 Schedules, and multiple Amendments.
3. Preamble, Constitution of India, " . . . The basic theory of our Constitution is that "Pouvoir Constituent" is vested in the people and was exercised, for and on their behalf by the Constituent Assembly for the purpose of framing the Constitution." Shelat and Grover, J.J., in *Kesavananda v. State of Kerala,* AIR 1973 SC 1461 at paragraph 556.
4. Although my statement is different in important respects, the idea of two kinds of politics derives from B. Ackerman, *Discovering the Constitution,* 93 Yale L.J. 1013 (1984).
5. C. Montesquieu, *The Spirit of the Laws,* 21 (R. Neumann, ed. 1949) ("The Politic Greeks, who lived under a popular government, knew no other support than virtue . . . ").
6. Article 37 provides :

   The provisions contained in this Part shall not be enforceable by any court, but the principles therein laid down are nevertheless fundamental in the governance of the country and it shall be the duty of the State to apply these principles in making laws.

   And, see, *In re Kerala Education Bill,* AIR (1958) SC 956.
7. The incorporation of Fundamental Rights, or a Bill of Rights, was a feature which the British Parliament consistently eschewed in the Constitution Acts it enacted for Canada, Australia and India, but India's constitution makers, seeing its necessity and desirability, included Part III on Fundamental Rights.
8. The Fundamental Rights of the Indian Constitution are relatively standard, i.e., freedom of speech, religion, assembly ; equal protection of the law ; etc., but they have a unique feature. The Bill of Rights of the Constitution of the United States broadly declares rights, many in unqualified terms, which have been qualified by court decisions. But, the Indian Constitution declares its Fundamental

Rights and also prescribes their limitations in the Constitution, itself; e.g., Article 25 recognizes the Right to Freedom of Religion but qualifies the Right expressly allowing the State to legislate on "any economic, financial, political or other secular activity which may be associated with religious practice."

9. Article 32, "Remedies for Enforcement of Rights Conferred by this Part" appears in Part III setting forth Fundamental Rights and specifically states that the "right to move the Supreme Court by appropriate proceedings for the enforcement of the rights conferred by this Part is guaranteed," and empowers parliament to give similar jurisdiction to lower courts. Article 13(2) of Part III provides that the "State shall not make any law which takes away or abridges the rights conferred by this Part and any law made in contravention of this clause shall, to the extent of the contravention, be void."
10. *Madras v. Champakam Dorairajan*, AIR 1951 SC 226, 228.
11. *Ibid*, and see, *Quareshi v. Bihar*, AIR 1958 SC 731.
12. 319 U.S. 624 at 638 (1943).
13. C.J. Friedrich, *Constitutions and Constitutionalism in 3 International Encyclopedia of the Social Sciences*, 318, 319 (D. Sills, ed. 1968).
14. W.F. Murphy, *An Ordering of Constitutional Values*, 53 So. Cal. L. Rev. 703, 758 (1980).
15. *Op. cit.*, note 1, at p. 15.
16. Generally, see, R. Dworkin, *Taking Rights Seriously* (1978) (Oxford University Press). Being based on principle all fundamental rights cannot be absolute because one person's fundamental right may conflict with another person's in which event the one based on the principle of greater gravity would prevail.
17. See D.H. Regan, "Glosses on Dworkin: Rights, Principles, and Policies", printed in M. Cohen, *Ronald Dworkin and Contemporary Jurisprudence* (1984) (Pub., Rowman and Allenheld).
18. Article 368 (2).
19. Article 368(2) a, b, c, d, e. The entrenched provisions are the manner of electing the President (Articles 54 and 55); the extent of the executive power of the Union and the States (Articles 73 and 162); the Supreme Court and the State High Courts (Articles 133-147 and 214-231); the distribution of legislative powers between the States and the Union (Articles 245-55); the representation of the States in Parliament [Article 368(2) (d)], and the amending article itself (Article 368).
20. AIR 1951 SC 458 upholding an amendment affecting Fundamental Rights found in Art. 15 (discrimination), Article 19(1) (free speech) and Art. 31 (property).
21. *Id.* at 463.
22. AIR 1965 SC 845.
23. *Id.* at 862.
24. *Id.* at 863-64.
25. AIR 1967 SC 1643.
26. *Id.* at 1669.

27. E.g., *Linkletter v. Walker*, 381 U.S. 618 (1965).
28. "Procedure for Amendment of the Constitution".
29. So far as it is revelant here, Article 368 provides : "An amendment of this Constitution may be initiated only by the introduction of a Bill for the purpose in either House of Parliament and when the Bill is passed in each House by a majority of not less than two-thirds of the members of that House present and voting, it shall be presented to the President for his assent . . . ."
30. The sixth majority judge, Hidayatullah, J., accepted the amendatory process of Article 368 but found it did not reach Fundamental Rights.
31. Article 246 (3).
32. See *Golak Nath* at pp. 1658-59.
33. In *Kesavananda v. State of Kerala*, AIR 1973 SC 1461, at paragraph 635, Hegde and Mukherjea, J.J., commented that "It is difficult to believe that our Constitution makers, who were keenly conscious of the importance of the provision relating to the amendment of the Constitution (Article 368) and debated that question for several days, would have left the important power hidden in entry 97 of List I leaving it to the off-chance of the courts locating that power in that entry."
34. *R.C. Cooper v. Union of India*, AIR 1970 SC 564, holding that Parliament's legislation nationalizing commercial banks violated Art. 31 of the Constitution.
35. *Madhav Rao Jivaji Rao Scindia v. Union of India*, AIR 1971 SC 530, holding unconstitutional government action seeking to deprive Rulers of the Princely States of their privy purses.
36. These provisions are found in the Constitution Act of 1971.
37. The forty-second Amendment of 1976 seeks to broaden this to include all Directive Principles.
38. AIR 1973 SC 1461. This is a vast document reporting eleven opinions from thirteen judges and running to 566 pages. My references to it will be to figures placed in brackets which refer to paragraph numbers found in the *All Indian Reporter*. The petitioner attacked the constitutional validity of the Kerala Land Reforms of 1969 and 1971, and the case initially came before the Constitutional Bench, but was transferred to a Full Bench of thirteen judges.
39. The term "essential features" is used in *Kesavananda* by Raddy, J., at (1171), but Sikri, C.J., uses the term "basic features" (304) ; "essential features, basic elements and fundamental principles" by Shelat and Grover, J.J. (497) ; "basic structure or framework" by Khanna, J. (1437). The idea is similar to the one elaborated in Charles Black, *Structure and Relationship in Constitutional Law* (1969). It takes root in a structural and functional analysis of the Constitution and not in any particular section or article, but differs from Black's analysis in that only "core" essential features are of direct concern to *Kesavananda's* doctrine.
40. Hegde and Mukherjea, J.J. (663- 42 and 640) ; Reddy, J. (1174) ; Ray,

J. (834); Palekar, J. (1279); Khanna, J. (1519-20); Matthew, J. (1595); Beg, J. (1840); Dwivedi, J. (1913-16); Chandrachud, J. (2075-79).

41. Make up of Sikri, C.J., and Reddy and Khanna, J.J., each rendering separate opinions, and Shelat and Grover, J.J., and Hegde and Mukherjea, J.J., with each pair joining in an opinion.

42. The "essential featuers" limitation would apply equally and disqualify an amendment seeking to amend the amending Art. 368 to give Parliament power to amend even the "essential features" of the Constitution. In a sense, this result is similar to that which would be achieved regarding the amending Art. (V) of the Constitution of the United States, stating that "no state, without its consent, shall be deprived of its equal suffrage in the Senate." Rather clearly, if a constitutional amendment sought to amend Art. V and deprive a state of equal senatorial suffrage without its consent, the proposed amendment would, most likely be ruled unconstitutional because it violated an "essential feature" of the U.S. constitution. It has never been suggested that Art. V's prohibition could be avoided by first amending that Article, without a state's consent, and then deprive that state of its equal suffrage in the Senate. It also should be noted that in 1935 the Irish Supreme Court in *The State (Ryan) v. Lennon* [1935] I.R. 170, ruled that the 1922 Constitution could not be amended so as to violate the "Articles of Agreement for a Treaty between Great Britain and Ireland", which was scheduled into the Constitution.

43. In *Kesavananda* it was generally made clear that the Preamble was a significant guide to understanding the Constitution and its essential structures. Sikri, C.J. (15, 89-98, 121, 292); Shelat and Grover, J.J. (523-30, 538-39); Hegde and Mukherjea, J.J. (663-65, 677); Reddy, J. (1164-71). Sikri, C.J., said that "The Constitution should be read in light of the grand and noble vision expressed in the Preamble", (121) and Shelat and Grover, J.J., studied the drafting of the Preamble and concluded that abrogation was impossible; that the Drafting Committee of the Constituent Assembly believed that the Preamble incorporated "the essential features of the new State" and that it has a "transcendental position" in constitutional interpretation (530, 33 and 38).

The Preamble states:

> WE, THE PEOPLE OF INDIA, having solemnly resolved to constitute India into a SOVEREIGN DEMOCRATIC REPUBLIC and to secure to all its citizens;
> JUSTICE, social, economic and political;
> LIBERTY of thought, expression, belief, faith and worship;
> EQUALITY of status and of opportunity, and to promote among them all;
> FRATERNITY, assuring the dignity of the individual and the unity of the nation;
> IN OUR CONSTITUENT ASSEMBLY this Twenty-sixth day of

November 1949 do HEREBY ADOPT, ENACT AND GIVE TO OURSELVES THIS CONSTITUTION.

44. This flexibility might be especially important with respect to the Right to Property. Considered in its political context, it would appear that the *Election case, Indira Gandhi v. Raj Narain*, AIR 1975 SC 2299, accepted and legitimated the "essential features" limitation (and Mrs. Gandhi's continuance as Prime Minister) even though the limitation was not directly in issue, but it was accepted as binding constitutional law by the judges who had dissented in *Kesavananda*. Thus, presumably, the "essential features" limitation is Indian Constitutional Law, and it can be removed only by India's Supreme Court overruling itself or by constitutional amendment which would have to follow a procedure other than that in Article 368 (see note 42, *supra*), which means a return to some type of "abnormal" politics described herein, such as, e.g., a referendum to all the voters ("*We, the People of India*") or perhaps by voters creating a new Constituent Assembly for that purpose. This view appears confirmed by *Minerva Mills v. Union of India*, AIR 1980 SC 1789, which dealt with the 42nd Amendment Act that added two new paragraphs to Article 368. One, Article 368 (4), provided that

> No amendment to this Constitution . . . made or purported to have been made under this Act shall be called in question in any court or on any grounds.

The other, Article 368(5), declared that

> . . . there shall be no limitation whatever on the constitutional power of Parliament to amend . . . or repeal the provisions of this Constitution under this Act.

Thus, the 42nd Amendment Act asserted the supremacy of Parliament not only over India's Supreme Court but also over India's Constitution, itself. On July 31, 1980, the Supreme Court in *Minerva Mills, supra*, held that the two amendments were void because they violated the doctrine laid down in *Kesavnanda* which was followed in the *Election case, supra*. Thus, it seems the matter has been laid to rest—Parliament cannot alter the "basic" or "essential features" of Indian Constitution.

45. "Our Constitution is not a mere political document. It is essentially a social document. It is based on a social philosophy and every social philosophy like every religion has two main features, namely, basic and circumstantial. The former remains constant but the practices associated with it may change . . . . a Constitution like ours contains certain features which are so essential that they cannot be changed or destroyed."

This extract comes from Hegde and Mukherjea, J.J., in *Kesavananda, supra*, at paragraphs 667-69.

46. See note 15, *supra*.

SIX

N.A. PALKHIVALA

STATES ARE NOT VASSALS OF THE UNION*

THE largest experiment ever undertaken in human history in the art of democratic living has been carried on in India since 1950. Never before, and nowhere else, has more than one-seventh of the human race lived together in freedom as a single political entity. The uniqueness of this phenomenon is rendered even more impressive by the fact that till 1950 India was never a united country.

In such a situation it is not only natural but inevitable that differences and disputes should arise between the Centre and the 22 States that constitute the Union, and even between the States *inter se*. The problem must be resolved in a spirit of goodwill and with far-sighted vision.

There is no doubt about the great injustices done by the Centre to the States ; but it must be remembered that the injuries done to the States are, in a sense, self-inflicted. The Centre is nothing but the States in their federal garb : the Parliament and the Central Government consist of none but the elected representatives of the States (barring the handful of nominated members). The real authors of the injustices are the self-centred representatives of the States who, after being elected to Parliament, have betrayed the true interests of the very States which returned them.

The Constitution provides for a co-operative federation of States with a bias in favour of the Centre. Such a bias, within reasonable limits, is necessary, having regard to the conditions

* Seminar on 'Centre-State Relations', Bangalore, August 5-7, 1983. Abridged version, *India Today*, August 31, 1983, printed in *We, The People*. With the kind permission of the author.

prevailing in our country. The essential question is—what are the reasonable limits within which the constitutional bias in favour of the Union should be contained ?

The approach to the problem of Centre-State relations must be governed by the following basic considerations which aim at reconciliation of conflicting viewpoints :

(1) A national consensus should clearly remind the Centre that it has not inherited the Viceroy's mantle of Paramountcy. What is needed at the Centre today is not an authoritarian government but the moral authority to govern. And the Centre would have no moral authority to govern unless it displays a sense of constitutional morality, particularly a sense of justice and fairness towards the States.

(2) We do need a strong Union. But a strong Union is in no way inconsistent with strong States. On the contrary, by definition, a strong Union can only be a Union of strong States.

(3) Where a paramount national interest dictates a line of action, the narrower viewpoint of a State or the parochial attitude of a municipality must not stand in the way.

For instance, the States should be persuaded in the national interest to agree to the substitution of sales tax by additional excise to be levied by the Centre and fairly distributed among the States—thus providing the States with the same growing revenues as they would derive from sales tax after deducting the cost of collection. Similarly, the States should revoke the power granted by them to their municipalities to levy the antiquated octroi, and resources should be raised for the local bodies in more civilized ways. Delays at check-posts range from 30 to 45 per cent of the effective travelling time of commercial vehicles. The 15,000 check-posts where octroi or entry tax is collected in different States result in 15 per cent of fuel consumption being wasted and virtually involve 80,000 trucks being rendered idle.

But these laudable reforms can and should be effected without detriment to the self-respect or the resources position of the States and the municipalities. The Constitution never intended that the Chief Ministers of the States would have to be on a perpetual round of pilgrimages to New Delhi supplicating the Centre for its discretionary bounties.

(4) As far as possible, the grievances of the States should be redressed by building up salutary conventions and traditions which are in conformity with the true spirit of the Constitution, rather than by amending the Constitution. There are good reasons why constitutional amendment should be treated as the option of the last resort :

(*a*) The Constitution is intended not merely to provide for the exigencies of the moment but to endure through a long lapse of years. We should get accustomed to a specious view of the great instrument. The Constitution was meant to impart such a momentum to the living spirit of our national identity that the Union of States may remain indestructible beyond our times, and in the days when our place will know us no more. Therefore, in dealing with a constitution, the wisest principle to act upon is that when it is not necessary to change, it is necessary not to change.

(*b*) If the Constitution is worked in the right spirit, there would be no need to consider any amendment so far as Centre-State relations are concerned. The problem has arisen today in an acute form because over a period of years the Centre has acted in a manner which at best has been contrary to the spirit of the Constitution and at worst has been tantamount to a fraud upon the Constitution. Many people hastily assume that the working of the Constitution has revealed its grave shortcomings, whereas the truth of the matter is that it is a noble Constitution which has been worked in an ignoble spirit.

(*c*) Today a crisis of national identity broods over the country. We are in the throes of our re-birth as a single nation. Emotions are running high in a few States, particularly Punjab. The forces of passion and ignorance are in the ascendant. At such a juncture, to open the door of large-scale constitutional revision may involve a grave danger to the unity and integrity of the country.

Industries and Economic Development

The States would have made far greater progress if the scheme of the Constitution had been respected in the field of economics. There are three significant Entries in the State List: (*a*) Industries, (*b*) Trade and commerce, and (*c*) Production, supply and distribution of goods. The Union List permits Parliament to legislate in respect of "Industries, the control of which by the Union is declared by Parliament by law to be expedient in the public interest." Thus, the basic scheme of the Constitution is that industries and commerce should remain State subjects and should be dealt with primarily by the States; and that it is only those industries, the control of which by the Union is expedient in the public interest, that must be regulated by the Centre.

Parliament passed the Industries (Development and Regulation) Act in 1951, specifying those industries which in the public interest would have to be controlled by the Centre. The Act as originally drafted was fair and reasonable and rightly gave control to the Union over those industries which were vital to national development. However, in course of time, more and more industries were added to the Industries (Development and Regulation) Act till the basic constitutional scheme has now been patently subverted.

Without any amendment to the Constitution, "Industries" has been nefariously transformed into a Union subject and has ceased to be a State subject. Today at least 93 per cent of organised industries, in terms of the value of output, have been brought under the bailiwick of the Union. Even items like razor blades, paper, gum, matchsticks, household electrical appliances, cosmetics, soaps and other toilet requisites, fabrics and footwear, pressure-cookers, cutlery, steel furniture, zip fasteners, hurricane lanterns, bicycles, dry cells, TV sets, agricultural implements—have all been brought under the Centre's control. There can be no doubt that this is an indefensible violation of the Constitution. It is imperative that the States should regain their legitimate powers over industries and commerce.

The true position of the States in commerce and industry, according to the unmistakable mandate of the Constitution, can and should be restored; and for this purpose no amendment of the Constitution is needed. All that is necessary is to delete various items in the First Schedule to the Industries (Development and Regulation) Act. If only industries which are crucial to the national interest were controlled by the Centre and the States were given their rightful jurisdiction over the rest of the field of industry and commerce, those States which have a balanced and pragmatic outlook on economic problems would benefit tremendously. In order that the nation may not suffer as a result of any States not permitting industries to come up, the Centre may reserve to itself the power to start, or license the starting of, industrial units in such States. In other words, the position should be that the Centre may step in where a State will not allow industries to commence or develop, unlike the position today when the Centre has the veto where the States want industries to start or grow.

Over-centralisation has been one of the main reasons for our poor rate of economic growth which is one of the lowest in the world.

President's Rule

Under Article 356, President's Rule can be imposed in a State "if the President, on receipt of a report from the Governor of a State or otherwise, is satisfied that a situation has arisen in which the government of the State cannot be carried on in accordance with the provisions of this Constitution."

This power has been grossly abused and President's Rule has been imposed on the States more than 70 times. All States, except Sikkim, have been given at one time or another doses of this pretentious curative. Several cases where President's Rule has been imposed by the Centre in a partisan spirit for party ends have already passed into history.

The Rajamannar Committee in its Report published in 1971 recommended deletion of Article 356. The other view is that the article would continue to serve a useful purpose if it is invoked *bona fide* in appropriate cases only. It may be better to retain the article while devising some machinery to prevent its misuse.

K. Santhanam, deprecating the imposition of Presidential rule whenever a State Ministry is defeated, observed, "Ordinarily, when a Ministry is defeated and an alternative Ministry cannot be formed, the proper course should be immediate dissolution and re-election so that people of the State would have a chance to decide for themselves. It is only where law and order cannot be maintained and the Legislature cannot function in peace that Presidential rule can be really justified. In the discussions in the Constituent Assembly on Article 356, it was emphasized by many speakers that except in cases of civil disorder, Presidential rule should not be imposed without first a dissolution and general elections."

Appointment of Governors

There has to be a Governor for each State (Article 153). The Governor is appointed by the President (Article 155) and he holds office during the pleasure of the President (Article 156).

According to the judgment of the Supreme Court delivered on May 4, 1979, in *Dr. Raghukul Tilak's case*[1] the relationship of employer and employee does not exist between the Government of India and the Governor, and the Governor's office "is not subordinate or subservient to the Government of India". While this is the true constitutional position, we have systematically devalued various constitutional institutions including the office of the Governor. In practice the Governor has been reduced to virtually the same position as that of the Resident Agent in a Native State in the days of the British raj. Several Governors have debased their high office by lending their services to fulfil the partisan objectives of the political party in power at the Centre.

One of the difficult questions is—how to restore the Governorship to the high status envisaged by the architects of the Constitution. The Rajamannar Committee made the following recommendations :

> "The Governor should be appointed always in consultation with the State Cabinet. The other alternative will be to make the appointment in consultation with a high powered body specially constituted for the purpose.
>
> "The Governor should be rendered ineligible for a second term of office as Governor or any other office under Government. He should not be liable to removal except for proved misbehaviour or incapacity after inquiry by the Supreme Court.
>
> "A specific provision should be inserted in the Constitution

1. A.I.R., 1979, S.C. 1109.

enabling the President to issue Instruments of Instructions to the Governors. The Instruments of Instructions should lay down guidelines indicating the matters in respect of which the Governor should consult the Central Government or in relation to which the Central Government could issue directions to him. Those Instructions should also specify the principles with reference to which the Governor should act as the head of the State including the occasions for the exercise of discretionary powers."

President's Assent to State Bills

A Bill passed by the State Legislature is presented to the Governor and the Governor has to declare "that he assents to the Bill or that he withholds assent therefrom or that he reserves the Bill for the consideration of the President" (Article 200). The President may direct the Governor to return the Bill to the State Legislature with a message requesting reconsideration of the Bill ; and if it is again passed by the State Legislature with or without amendment, it is presented once more to the President for his consideration (Article 201), but in no case is the President bound to give his assent.

The object of the Constitution makers in enacting these provisions was simple and clear. While the constitutionality of any State legislature can always be challenged in a court of law, its wisdom cannot be ; and, further, it is better to prevent a clearly unconstitutional measure from reaching the statute book than to have it struck down later by the court. A Governor is expected by the Constitution to reserve only such Bills for the President's assent as are patently unconstitutional or palpably against the national interest. In practice, Governors have been known to surrender their judgment and act as the deferential subordinates of the Central Government in exercising their extraordinary power. Moreover, the Centre's own record in enacting legislation is not such as to justify the belief that it is superior to the States either in wisdom or in knowledge of constitutional limitations.

The Rajamannar Committee recommended repeal of that provision which permits the Governor to reserve any Bill for the consideration of the President. However, this power may be usefully retained, if its indiscriminate use can be checked by some machinery. e.g., by providing mandatory guidelines in the Instrument of Instructions to the Governor.

Extra-constitutional Authorities

Among the extra-constitutional authorities, the Planning Commission takes the palm. "Economic and social planning" is in the Concurrent List. But no law has been enacted by Parliament in exercise of this power. The Planning Commission is a body without any constitutional or legislative sanction.

The Chaiman of the Fourth Finance Commission in his Supplementary Note to the Report described it as a "quasi-political body",. K. Santhanam observed that the Planning Commission had set up a sort of vertical federation, thus displacing the territorial or horizontal federation established by the Constitution. The Study Team appointed by the Administrative Reforms Commission observed that planning at the hands of the Planning Commission had the result that "the three horizontal layers of administration, represented by the lists of Central, Concurrent and State subjects, have been vertically partitioned into plan and non-plan sectors ; and . . . within the plan world, the compulsions and consequences of planning have tended to unite the three horizontal pieces into a single monolithic chunk from the Centre although operated in respect of Concurrent and State subjects in the States." Dr. K. Subba Rao was of the view that the Planning Commission "functions in violation of the provisions of the Constitution . . . . The Centre through the Planning Commission controlled not only the State sector of the plan but also their implementation." The Rajamannar Committee was of the view that the "Centre is able to impose its will on the States in the formulation and execution of the plans by virtue of the non-statutory grants under Article 282, which are dependent on the absolute discretion of the Centre. It will thus be seen that the process of planning and the activities of the Planning Commission have a very deleterious effect on the autonomy of the States particularly in spheres exclusively allotted to the States by the Constitution."

The abovequoted words of criticism are fully justified. Today there are two types of grants made by the Centre to the State—(i) grants-in-aid of the revenues of the States as recommended by the Finance Commission (Article 275) ; and (ii) discretionary grants by the Central Government (Article 282) which are usually made in accordance with the recommendations of the Planning Commission. Of the total grants disbursed by the Centre to the States, only 30 per cent is as per the recommendations of the Finance Commission, while the remaining 70 per cent represents discretionary grants given to the States on the advice of the Planning Commission.

To remove this distortion of the constitutional scheme, it is necessary that even discretionary grants under Article 282 should be dealt with by a constitutional authority like the Finance Commission, and not by the Planning Commission.

Financial Relations

Any fair-minded and impartial observer can have no doubt that having regard to the growing responsibilities of the States, the distribution of taxes and revenues is very unfair to the States and far too favourable to the Centre.

Taxes on income are levied and collected by the Government of India and distributed between the Union and the States [Article 270(1)]. But the expression "taxes on income" does not include corporation tax [Article 270(4)]. "Corporation tax" means any tax on income which is payable by companies and for which no credit is given to the shareholders who receive dividends from the companies [Article 366(6)]. As a result of the changes made by the Finance Act, 1959, all income-tax paid by limited companies must now be treated as corporation tax, and consequently the States are not entitled to any share of it.

Union duties of excise may be shared between the Union and the States but only "if Parliament by law so provides" (Article 272). The Chairmain of the Fourth Finance Commission referred to the possiblity of making a constitutional amendment placing excise duties on the same footing as income-tax, that is, making excise duties also divisible between the Union and the States.

Even when a tax or duty is compulsorily divisible between the Centre and the States, the Union has the right to levy a surcharge which is excluded from the divisible pool (Article 271). This extraordinary power is exercised in the most ordinary fashion : every annual budget contains the levy of a surcharge on income-tax exclusively for the purposes of the Union.

The Seventh Finance Commission had recommended that 40

per cent of the Central excise duty should be transferred to the States. In the last three years the Centre stopped raising rates of excise on items like petroleum, iron and steel, aluminium and coal, but only raised the prices. The entire benefit of this increase in prices goes to the Centre which is the producer and seller of the goods. According to a recent speech of the West Bengal Finance Minister, by raising prices instead of excise the Centre gathered additional revenues of Rs. 6,500 crores in which the States are not entitled to a share, whereas, if the excise had been increased, Rs. 2,600 crores would have come to the States as per the recommendation of the Seventh Finance Commission.

The States must be given a legal right to a larger share in the tax revenues collected by the Centre, instead of having to rely upon the discretionary largesse of the Union under Article 282.

Inter-State Council and Constitutional Conventions

The formation of an Inter-State Council as envisaged in Article 263 of the Constitution is long overdue. The Conference of the Council of Chief Ministers held on March 20, 1983, on the initiative of the Karnataka Chief Minister, was a significant constitutional development. Active co-operation among the States should be institutionalized and States must solve their inter-State problems by mutual discussion and negotiation. For example, problems regarding electricity, water and rivers should be sorted out by the States themselves without the intervention of the Centre. Imaginative co-operation between the States would be a most fruitful way of counteracting excessive domination by the Centre.

It is a pity that there should be the need for a union of States —as distinct from the Union of States which the Centre is supposed to be—but the States are left with no other alternative under the present set-up.

The ways in which the Centre unduly dominates the States are beyond enumeration and are symptomatic of the Centre's attitude towards its "vassals". Exceptional constitutional powers are used in a routine manner, and standards of constitutional decency are unknown. There is no political will to let healthy conventions grow up to serve as guides to the Centre in its manifold dealings with the States.

An unfailing index to the maturity of a democracy is the

degree of its respect for unwritten conventions. By this criterion of maturity, the Indian democracy must be regarded as being still in its swaddling clothes. Not only have we failed to build up any conventions, but we have thrown to the winds even those norms of decency and decorum in public life which prevailed in India when we became a republic.

Dr. K. Subba Rao wisely observed : "Unless the party that happens to be in power in the Centre develops conventions to shed its party affiliations in the matter of its relations with the States, the federal Government cannot effectively function in our country."

The Only Lasting Solution

Those who are in favour of major constitutional amendments to re-define relations between the Centre and the States must come to terms with one profound truth.

The only satisfactory and lasting solution of the vexed problem is to be found not in the statute book but in the conscience of men in power. The long-suffering States can be given redress not by a change of law but by a change of heart. The ultimate guarantees of a fair deal to the States are the individual conscience of the representatives they return to Parliament and a vigorous and well-informed public opinion.

We must get away from the fallacy of "the legal solubility of all problems". In a Constitution what is left unsaid is as important as what is said. Our constitutional equilibrium can be preserved only by Obedience to the Unenforceable.

The survival of our democracy and the unity and integrity of the nation depend upon the realization that constitutional morality is no less essential than constitutional legality. *Dharama* (Righteousness : sense of public duty or virtue) lives in the hearts of public men : when it dies there, no constitution, no law, no amendment, can save it.

SEVEN

P JAGANMOHAN REDDY

A CONSTITUTION
What It Is And What It Signifies*

LORD Bryce defined a constitution as "a frame of political society, organized through and by law, that is to say, one in which law has established permanent institutions with recognized functions and definite rights." In a general sort of way, we can say that a constitution is a collection of principles according to which the powers of the government, the rights of the governed, and the relations with which the two are adjusted; and where all these are not found in a single document which itself can be altered or amended according to the circumstances from time to time, it may be ascertained from separate laws given special authority as the laws of the constitution; or it may be embodied in one or two fundamental laws while the rest is found in conventions, customs, common law followed and accepted by the people and having the force of law. According to Sir Ivor Jennings (in *Cabinet Government*), a constitution may necessarily rest on acquiescence whether it is established by referendum or by tacit approval or even by force. Perhaps, he has in mind constitutions which have been overridden by strong personalities as evidenced by Napoleon or Mussolini or Hitler, all of whom compelled acquiescence in a change which made them the heads of government with supreme authority. As Strong (in his *Modern Political Constitutions*) observes, "Whatever its form a true constitution will have the following facts very clearly marked: first, how the various agencies are organised; secondly, what power is entrusted to those agencies; and thirdly, in what manner such power is to

* Prof. S. Venkatraman Endowment Lecture 1983—With the kind permission of the author and the Andhra University.

be exercised, ... The objects of a constitution, in short, are to limit the arbitrary action of the government, to guarantee the rights of the governed, and to define the operation of the sovereign power." To this, I would only add as an emphasis that the values of human freedom, the concepts of human rights and the consciousness of the people who are governed insisting on a guarantee of these rights against transgression by the government and an independent agency to determine the *inter se* rights when allegations of such transgression are brought before it, are an equally essential part of the Constitution. Viewed from this angle, there are certain essential elements necessary for a state to be sovereign state. Though the term sovereignty is a highly controversial term, it may for the present be defined in its internal and external aspects, in terms of authority and independence. Internally it means the power over the individuals or associations of individuals within the area of its jurisdiction. Externally it signifies the absolute independence of that state with reference to all other states. The chief agency of a sovereign state is the government or the executive, without which the state cannot function. Government is an organization which is vested with the right to exercise sovereign power inherent or specified d is charged with the maintenance of peace and security of the state both within and without. It must have, broadly speaking, legislative power, executive power and judicial power allocated to the three agencies of the State—Legislative, Executive and Judicial. The legislature is the department of government concerned with the making of laws and in a well-ordered constitution, and in particular where states governed by representative form of government, the power of the Legislature to control the other two departments may be more or less limited or varied according as decided at the time of framing the Costitution.

The executive department is represented by the head of the state or the Prime Minister, including the whole body of public servants, civil and military apart from the Chief Minister and the public servants under his control at the state level. It is charged with the duty of administering the state according to law. The judicial department is charged with the duty to decide upon the application of the existing law to the individual cases, generally laws passed by the Legislature as well as constitutional prescriptions. Such judicial power constitutes an essential facet of governmental power which is by its nature coercive. In cases where the Legislature has no fetters to its legislative power the judges have to merely find, interpret and apply the law. But when power is distributed between a central authority and its constituent parts, the judiciary as the arbiter determines the extent of jurisdiction of each unit. In such a system the judiciary can and frequently does override the enactments of the Legislature, be it of the central authority or of the constituent states. It can also refuse to apply the laws on the ground that it is constitutionally beyond the power of any of these legislatures to enact them. In certain other systems of government the judiciary may not have the power at all. It sometimes comes very near being associated with the executive power or the legislative power both of which may respectively influence or impede its functioning as an independent body. It is, therefore, clear that the composition and relationship of these three departments of government distinguish the nature of the sovereign state. The constitutions of modern states largely in the Western world which may be characterized as nation states are democratic in most cases. In the making of a constitutional state, as Strong observes, "the sense of national unity may at first be concerned rather to establish the independence of the group than to achieve the liberty of its individual members, but ultimately it generates the driving powers for the attainment of popular rights. Similarly democratic political organizations, i.e., political democracy, implies that government depends on the consent of the governed; it impiles the consent or dissent of the people who shall have free right of expression at elections, at meetings, or in the Press, etc. In this sense democracy is a system of government in which majority of adult members of a political community with a franchise have a right to participate through a method of representation which secures that the government is ultimately responsible for its actions to that majority."

(I am not here dealing with, nor have I the time to concern myself with the historical evolution from ancient times of constitutional states. I am concerned only with the nation states which came into existence during the eighteenth, and nineteenth centuries as well as the twentieth century so far.)

In a world of nation states, varying in their ideologies,

connoting different conceptual goals, commitments to their people, and assuring their individual and social well-being, it is not easy to say clearly what the Constitution of each such nation state envisages. By and large a constitution at best is a written instrument embodying a great promise though it often remains unfulfilled. That promise we gather from the key provisions incorporated therein, indicating the aims and aspirations of that society and the importance and weight attached to the individual rights in the scale of values, political, social and economic which the society seeks to uphold. Some nation states treat a constitution as prescribing a government for its people, some treat it as limitation on powers of the government or even on the sovereignty of the people themselves. The world constitutionalism has come to be known in respect of such states as implying a limitation on government and/or the people or implying protection of individual rights. There are Constitutions of states which have an ideology antithetical to constitutionalism and some nations have used them as a document incorporating the ideological manifestos, and as a description of the system of government which any such nation holds as ideal for its people. Even in these cases, the states which have framed for themselves such constitutions in the compelling conditions of the world in which they had to live and work could not afford to ignore individual or human rights simply by adopting constitutionalism. There are also libertarian constitutions which are wedded to representative government, based on adult or universal franchise and insuring individual freedom from too much government. Yet the individual may not be able to assert his rights against the so-called interest of the society which is no other than the interest as envisaged by the majority. In other words, while respect for individual freedom may be apparent, there may be a disparity between intention and effective observance when the individual asserts his rights based on a higher natural law against the majority interest.

Natural Law as a Limitation on Government

Before examining a sample of each of the categories of Constitutions and what they envisage, it is necessary to note the origin of the conceptual innovation intended for the control of government and protection of human rights. The theory was that the human being as well as the Government under which he lived was subject to God's laws. Whether it be according to the Bible or in ancient religions, including Hinduism, human activity was subject to God's laws. The Kings that ruled over them were not above these divine laws. In fact the highest law was only that of God, though this did not prevent the individual to have a free choice. Even where he had these rights he was subject to God's laws. All this however does not imply that there were no norms for individual behaviour, action or outlook. There were values of right and wrong, justice and injustice, legal and illegal acts, good and evil, etc. The equal rights claim of the individual, and the dignity of man were all required to be adhered to under God's laws. Though most of this law at some stage or other was claimed to be revealed it was given to man to develop or discover values by his reason. Most of these values dealt with duties imposed on every society and on every individual. All this came to include the right of conscience, the refusal to commit unjust acts and the right to worship your God in your own way. Examples of refusal to comply with man-made laws, which were contrary to the higher law as envisaged and accepted in that society, are galore. Sophocle's *Antigone* tells us of the midwives resisting Pharaoh's order to kill all male Israelite babies, or King Saul's servants refusing to kill the priests. The Bhagavatha informs us that the order of King Kamsa to kill the child (Sri Krishna) born to Devaki and Vasudev was cleverly undone and the like. These are all examples of orders which were contrary to natural higher law of God and persons imbued with and inspired by these rights have risked their lives to protect others deserving to be protected against unjust orders. Later the Stoics and their juristic successors gave a rational reason for complying with what earlier was regarded as compliance with laws of God, by resorting to the process of interpretation which complies with the law of nature. This ultimately evolved into developing and discovering God's law by the application of right reason. This process ultimately came to be accepted as natural rights, refusal to commit unjust acts and a duty to follow the dictates of conscience.

The rights of the individual, the human rights, which are so integrally embedded in the concepts of natural law and natural rights, are concretized during the seventeenth and eighteenth centuries and are synthesized in the nineteenth and twentieth centuries.

A brief narration of the ideas and thinking that prevailed during this period would help in understanding the basic concepts that influenced the framers of the several Constitutions.

Human Dignity as a Value

The nineteenth century contributed largely to human rights by synthesizing and rationalizing the eighteenth century concept of social contract and projecting rights and freedoms as being a necessary concomitant to good life and good society. These concepts were responsible for the abolition of slavery in many countries and contributed to the international prohibition of the slave trade. This is also the era of several famous thinkers, such as John Stuart Mill, the apostle of liberty, Herbert Spencer, the champion of *laissez faire*—freedom from government interference as a new economic liberty—having for its basis the texts of Adam Smith, the propounder of New Economic Theory, particularly his labour theory. In his classic book, *The Wealh of Nations*, which is almost his only book, Adam Smith said : "It is not from the benevolence of the butcher, the brewer or the baker that we expect our dinner but from their regard to their own interest. We address ourselves not to their humanity but their self-love and never talk to think of our own necessity but of their advantages."

The central moral idea in Mill's ethics, like Immanuel Kant's, was really respect for human beings, the sense that they must be treated with due regard for the dignity that moral responsibility entails and without which moral responsibility is impossible. He thought of the value of personality not as a metaphysical dogma but as something to be realized in the actual condition of a free society. Again Mill's liberalism accepted political and social freedom as in itself good, not because it contributed to a desirable end but because freedom is the indispensable proper condition of a responsible human being. To live one's own life, developing one's own native traits and capacities, is not just a means to happiness ; it really is a substantial part of happiness. The philosophy of Mill and Spencer taken together left the theory of liberalism, according to some critics, in an unintelligible confusion.[1]

Man as Rational Being

Another philosopher who received wide acceptance of his view on these fundamental questions was Immanuel Kant. He defended nothing so firmly as the timeless, unchanging rights of the individual, whoever he may be, whatever the time, whatever his place in society or his personal attributes, provided he is a man, the possessor of reason and as such obliged to respect reason in all other men as they respect it in him. Kant hated inequality. He hated hierarchies, oligarchies, paternalism, no matter how benevolent. He detested emotionalism, disordered enthusiasm, what he called *Schwarmerie*; it is indeed this kind of sentimental rhetoric, as it seemed to him, that marred the outpourings of his contemporary and fellow-Prussian, Johann Gottfried Herder, the father of cultural and ultimately every kind of nationalism in Europe. Many in Germany had welcomed the French Revolution, while Kant never abandoned his faith in it, and its proclamation of the rights of man, even when it degenerated into terrorism and bloodshed, which made most of its original liberal-minded supporters in many lands shy away from it in horror. His strictly political writings are celebrated models of liberal nationalism. Thus while propounding that the ground of my obeying the law is that it orders or should order what any rational man in my situation would command himself to do or not; that states should devote their resources to education, culture, the moral improvement of their citizens, and not to increasing their material power and conquest, he elaborated a famous project for a league of nations and for perpetual peace.[2] To Kant the very notion of an agent entails freedom of the will to act rightly or wrongly, virtuously or viciously and it is not only the "external" factors—physical, chemical, biological, physiological, etc.—that can prevent or destroy freedom, but "internal" psychological ones too. According to Kant's thinking Man's unique property, what distinguishes him from every other entity in the universe as he knows it, is his self-government, his autonomy. Everything else is in the realm of heteronomy, which is the opposite of autonomy, namely, obeying laws that issue from something outside oneself—for example the material world in which causality reigns the realm of the natural sciences. The doctrine that man is an end in himself, and not a means to anything not himself, derives from this view ; since he is the ultimate author of the rules to which he freely submits, to make him submit to something that does not proceed from his own rational nature is to degrace him—to treat him as a child, an animal or an object. To deprive a human being of the power of choice is to do him the greatest imaginable injury. This will be so no matter how benevolent the intention with which it is done. Kant's doctrine is directed against all paternalism, in particular enlightened despotism, like that of his own king, Frederick the Great of Prussia, and against the utilitarian materialism of the leading French thinkers of the day.

Dialectics and Marx

The Industrial Revolution and the scientific developments appeared to have made some of the older philosophers not so relevant to these times. Hegel propounded his philosophy towards the beginning of the nineteenth century. His first eassy on the Constitution of Germany written in 1802 aimed at nothing less than a complete reconstruction of modern thought David Hume had put in doubt the very principle of the system of natural law. Rousseau had virtually relegated religion and morals as matters of sentiment ; and Kant had tried to preserve the autonomy of both science and morals by assigning to each its sphere and by sharpening the contrast between theoretical and practical reason. As against this, Hegel attempted to lay down a bolder principle of synthesis ; though somewhat speculative, it professed to offer an enlarged conception of reason that should overlap and include what had been separated by the analysis of Hume and Kant. This new logic, which purported to systematize a new intellectual method, he termed as Dialectics. By this method he tried to distinguish between the realm of fact and the realm of value and make it a vehicle for understanding the problems of morals and religion. Inasmuch as Hegel lived during the Napoleonic period, and as the wars during that period had left the constitutional systems of all the continental European countries in ruins, it appeared that the major problem at the time could not be solved by a further appeal to abstractions like the rights of man, which had proved so disruptive. It was felt at the time that the French Revolution was destructive and nihilistic and the effort to remake society and human nature was conditioned by caprice. The dialectics of Hegel was adopted by Karl Marx with considerable changes, which became an inherent part of Marxian socialism and communism and the ground for the claim for scientific superiority that Marxism has always made. Hegel's political philosophy was to be found in the classic statement of nationalism in a form which had discarded the individualism and the implicit cosmopolitanism of the rights of man.[3]

Just as Hegel had based his theories on the conditions as they existed in Germany during and after Napoleonic wars, Marx based his political and social theory on the natural revolution. His main thesis is that the ownership of the means of production motivated as it is chiefly by the necessity of creating profits overawed the industrial proletariat which had no power except through the pressure of well-organized masses and obliged to set as its end not political liberty but the miantenance or improvement of its standard of living. The abolition of feudalism as a consequence of the revolution meant for Marx the rise to power of the middle classes and the creating of political system which made its power effective creating ultimately in its most developed form the democratic republic. The next stage, according to him, the coming into being of the proletarian class of workers who would displace this middle class from power, just in the same way as the middle class had displaced the older feudal class ; and since the philosophy of the middle class was in substance a claim to the natural rights of property, a proletarian philosophy must be a socialist claim to the human rights of men without property. Marx then argued that inasmuch as the proletariat lay at the bottom of the social structure, with no class below it to be exploited, a proletarian revolution would not lead to a transfer of the power to exploit but would abolish exploitation. This would be the first step to a society without distinctions of social class and a true beginning of history as a record of full human self-realization. These theories of Marx culminated in his classical work *Das Capital.*

The Marxian Thesis

He took economic materialism for granted without, however, developing it nor did he systematically expound his social philosophy. Marx explains what he attempted to do, in his letter to Weydemeyer, March 5, 1852. In that letter, he said :

> What I did that was new was to prove : (1) that the existence of classes is only bound up with particular historic phases in the development of production ; (2) that the class struggle necessarily leads to the dictatorship of the proletariat ; (3) that this dictatorship itself only constitutes the transition to the abolition of all classes and to a classless society.[4]

According to him, the individual counts mainly through his membership in the class, because his ideas—his moral convictions, his aesthetic preferences, even the kind of reasoning that seemed to him convincing—are in the main a reflection of the ideas generected by the class.[5]

A great deal has been written about Marx's theories, their impact upon society during his life-time and subsequently. One thing is certain that during his life-time neither the communist manifesto nor his dialectic materialism nor his views on the social nature of the individual nor his emphasis on freedom as opposed to welfare, nor his thesis on incentives and motivations, nor his prediction of a proletarian revolution in highly developed industrial states had any effect whetever. The impact of his writings and views was visible more after the Russian Revolution in 1917 than before it. This in effect disproved Marx's theory inasmuch as the revolutions in Russia and China were not the revolutions in states that were industrial but peasant-oriented. I must, however, refer to Marx's emphasis on "freedom" as opposed to "welfare", in judging economic progress. The basic variable underlying traditional welfare economics is utility, or the individual's perception of his own well-being. Marx had little patience for this particular focus of attention even in the rudimentary form in which it had appeared in the contemporary literature. Partly he did not like the crude view of human behaviour that goes with this approach, which "transforms all the various interrelationships of men into the single relationship of utility." Partly he did not like the subjectivism of judging progress by the psychology of pleasure, on which utilitarians were so hooked. But more importantly, Marx remained faithful throughout his long productive life to the case for judging the progress of human condition by the freedom—in the positive sense—that people have. He focused on what they can do and not no what they feel about what they can do. "The metric of utility cannot, in general, coincide with that of freedom."[6]

Marx on Individual Liberty

The revolutions that took place in Russia and China were particularly of Russian and Chinese brand. In the first instance the revolution was led by Lenin and in the second by Mao Tse-tung. Both Russia and China were relatively backward societies and both these leaders authored their respective revolutions by a practical revolutionary strategy, adapting Marxism, creatively in part or a sprinkling of it, to the objective and dynamic situation of their respective societies. Between the two communist states the Chinese Communism seems to be opposed more to the social imperialism of Russia than to the Capitalism of the United States. This, however, must be said in spite of what Marxism is considered to represent, that Marx himself far from being an advocate of totalitarianism was a passionate lover of freedom and an ardent champion of liberty. In the Communist Manifesto, speaking of individuals he said : "A free development of each is the condition of the free development of all." Notwithstanding this, the philosophy founded by him has led to the negation of freedom and the establishment of dictatorship in different parts of the world, mostly due to the circumstances in which the Revolutions in Russia and China manifested themselves.

The Socialist Stance

Socialism in the nineteenth century, by and large, was hostile to human rights though there had been and are socialists who are leading proponents of liberty, like John Stuart Mill and other leading thinkers of the twentieth century in Great Britain and Western Europe. The proponents of Socialism have not all been consistent, nor can there be said to be a specific ideology, inasmuch as the same theorists at different times have held defferent views about the rights of an individual in socialist society or in bourgeois society on the way to socialism. Limitation of space do not permit me to examine these in any detail. But this much is certain that socialism, as the word suggests, emphasizes the society, the group subordinating the individual or allowing his elimination eventually if necessary for the salvation of the group. The masses alone have these rights. The individual welfare should come only after society has been re-ordered, as it is said "the narrow bourgeois horizon of rights" can be left far behind and—in a nod to anachronism—the state would wither away and the individual would be free.[7] In short, the socialist state emphasizes not rights against society but duties to society treating it as a matter of the greatest honour to serve the socialist state. In the twentieth century, the Marxist and Leninist states, for many years, did not recognize the people. They preferred the masses and declared the dictatorship of the proletariat. This naturally excluded rights for all who were not the proletariat. Even for the proletariat only group rights, and even so were only those consistent with socialist purposes, were available. Several of these aspects will be dealt with when I come to examine the Socialist Constitutions, but this much is certain that economic advance and welfare came before political or civil rights and were above liberty. The purpose of government in this view was not merely, or even primarily, as a watchdog but its duty was to act, to intervene, to plan, to promote and direct, and to do whatever was in furtherance of this objective. Even where any brand of socialism spoke of rights, it did not think of it as limitations on government but as obligations upon it not as freedom from government but demands upon it. All that it envisaged was a right to work but not a right to think or assemble or even to be secure.

Long before these rights were articulated and influenced the American and French Revolutions the nobles in England extracted from King John at Runnymede in 1215 A.D. concessions for themselves which limited his powers and circumscribed his authority. These concessions were embodied in the famous Magna Carta—the great charter—which mistakenly is considered to be a charter guaranteeing fundamental rights to life, liberty and equality. No doubt this charter while placing limitations on the monarchy vis-a-vis his nobles and feudal lords contained the seed of constitutionalism. The rights that the nobles extracted for themselves were later available to others, and became the foundations for the establishment of a parliament. The concession in the charter that a free man shall only be punished by the lawful judgment of his peers, or by the law of the land, became the foundation of the Rule of Law and in America gave birth to the concept of due process of law.

After extracting from the King the great charter in the thirteenth century, it took nearly four centuries of constant struggle of one description or other to contain the autarchy of the King vis-a-vis the power of the Parliament. In this battle a king had to forfeit his head, the country had to be kingless as a commonwealth, and even after restoration of the monarchy again had to face strife and turmoil to contain the powers of the King and even of Parliament. The result of these struggles began to manifest in the establishment of individual rights by extracting charters, namely, the Petition of Rights 1628, the Agreement of the People 1647 and the Bill of Rights 1688. No taxation without representation was another assertion of such rights. All these contributed to the evolution of a representative government, the expansion of the sufferage, increased protection of a person accused of crime, establishment of freedom of religion and freedom from religious discrimination.

The United Kingdom is an instance of a Government without a written constitution. It is a country where Parliament is supreme and where the power of the king is only to act constitutionally within the limits prescribed by Parliament and the conventions evolved to ensure such function.

Initially when Parliament was asserting its rights, men of wisdom and foresight began to feel that even in a representative form of government, the institution that represents the electorate —the Parliament—could be despotic, though Thomas Paine thought representative form of government epitomized freedom and signified the conferment of human rights. The rights of man rose out of revolutions—the American Revolution against Great Britain and the French Revolution ageinst Ancient Regime.

Division of Powers in Federal Set-up

James Madison in Federalist No. 47 in support of the above thesis said : "The accumulation of powers, legislative, executive and judicial, in the same hands, whether of one, a few or many, and whether hereditary, self-appointed, or elective may justly be pronounced the very definition of tyranny."

Justice Brandeis in *Mayers v United States,* 272 US 52 293 dealt with this very aspect when he observed that "the doctrine of the separation of powers was adopted by the convention of 1787, not to promote efficiency but to preclude the exercise of arbitrary power. The purpose was, not to avoid friction, but by means of the inevitable friction incident to the distribution of the governmental powers among three departments, to save the people from autocracy."

The French Declaration, too, asserts that "A society in which the guarantee of rights is not assured or the separation of powers is not determined has no constitution at all" (Article 16).

The U.S. Constitution contrived to safeguard human rights against concentration of too much power in the Authority and consequently to diffuse it and distribute it among the constituent parts. Here again James Madison in Federalist No. 57 expounds the reason for this, when he says, "In a single republic, all the power surrendered by the people is submitted to the administration of a single government and the usurpations are guarded against by a division of the government into distinct and separate departments. In the compound republic of America, the power surrendered by the people is first divided between two distinct governments, and then the portion allotted to each subdivided among distinct and separate departments. Hence a double security arises to the rights of the people. The different governments will control each other, at the same time that each will be controlled by itself."

Lord Acton in his lectures on the French Revolution (Figgs and Laurence, eds. 1910) saw Federalism as the only way to reconcile liberty and democracy ; it was a check on democracy, on the majority as on the whole people, and provided "Essential security for freedom in every genuine democracy".

Whatever was thought to be included in the concept of Federalism, there is no escape from the conclusion that where individual liberty, etc., is guaranteed, where division of authority is prescribed between the Union and the States, separation of powers, limitations on Government, an independent judiciary and judicial review are envisaged as the concomitants. Without this independent body to adjudicate between the citizen and the state, between state and state, and between the citizens, the state and central authority, all the rights inherent in the citizen and in the states under a federal constitution are a myth, and give rise to the tyranny and despotism of the central authority which is bound to arrogate to itself all the power and authority not vested in it.

A Bill of Rights

The American Declaration of Independence is a stirring justification for the Revolution brought about by the people of the 13 Colonies to free themselves from the yoke of the British. It also speaks of certain inalienable rights, for example the right to preserve life, the right to preserve liberty, the right to pursue happiness and the right to judgment or belief as it was sometimes called. To say that every man has a certain right is by itself not sufficient. This right is connected in several ways with the laws of nature which correspondingly express duties for each statement of a right implies that every other man has at least a duty not to prevent other's exercise of the right in question. In the limited time available it is not possible to examine how the revolutionaries understood rights in relation to life and liberty nor is it possible to undertake an analysis of this concept or how they are connected with powers, nor again whether they thought that all men were of high calibre or, following Locke and Acquinas, were incapable of seeing the truths of natural law.

The Constitution that was framed by the Convention, however, was essentially to construct a government for the United States that would achieve the ideals that the revolutionaries had extracted from the essence of man as they saw him. Even so the efforts of those at the Convention in forging a blueprint of government was based essentially on a compromise which did not even incorporate a Bill of Rights. As Arthur O. Lovejoy in his *Reflections on Human Nature* (Baltimore, 1961, pp. 46-47) said : "The ablest members of the constitutional convention were well aware that their task—unlike that of the continental congress in 1776—was not to lay down abstract principles of political philosophy, not to rest the system they were constructing simply on the theorems about the natural rights of men or of states, though they postulated such rights."

The original constitution, however, barred *ex post facto* laws and Bills of attainder, by both federal and state governments, and forbade the states to impair contracts. It also limited the power to suspend the privilege of *habeas corpus*, prescribed local, jury trial in federal criminal cases, and established procedures and penalties in trials for treason and impeachment proceedings. The desire to secure citizens of another state against prejudice was one of the purposes of establishing the federal judiciary and the clause in Article IV required states to respect the privileges and immunities of citizens of other states. Even so a glaring omission to guarantee equality of all men is the most surprising, particularly when some of the early constitutions of the states did so declare though some of them in spite of it practised slavery. In reality this omission does not appear to be so significant when it is noted that there was no equality between freemen and slaves, propertied classes and propertyless classes, between men and women. This omission of a Bill of Rights was ascribed to the belief of the framers that as the powers granted to the Federal Government were limited it could hardly impinge on individual rights. But as a price of the ratification of the Constitution the Bill of Rights had to be incorporated therein as an amendment. By and large the problem faced by the framers was not so much of political ethics but of practical psychology—a need not so much to preach about what the Americans ought to do as to predict successfully what they would do.

Though the citizen was protected against every act of the Government which sought to transgress his rights, there was nothing in the Constitution nor was there any suggestion that he could lay a claim on the government to contribute to his economic and social welfare. No doubt the Constitution in its preamble and Article I, Section 8 had ordained promotion of the general welfare and had empowered the Congress to collect taxes to provide for it. Even so at the time when the Constitution was framed the framers never envisaged that the purpose of the Constitution was to provide the citizen with food or work or social security. It however took a century and a half for this power of taxation to become the principal means for turning the United States into a Welfare State. The obligation to provide or promote education was contained in some of the state constitutions but the federal government was not enjoined to do so. It also did not provide for the suspension of the Constitution or declaration of an emergency or even in an emergency to rule by decree, nor does it declare unlike the Constitutions of the USSR, China or the Universal Declaration of Human Rights and the preamble to the International Covenant, the duties of the citizens, nor did it make the exercise of these rights contingent on the performance of duties. There is however a provision to suspend the writ of *habeas corpus* in an emergency.

The French Revolution and Declaration had perhaps greater influence in the spread of human rights and ideas of representative government, throughout the world. The principles laid down in the first French Constitution and the Declaration of the Rights of Man and the Citizen owed much to the American Declaration of Independence as well as to Virginia Declaration of Rights. What was implicit in the Anglo-American concept of the presumption of innocence of the accused was declared specifically in Article IX of the French Constitution. It was only in *Coffin v. United States*, 156 U.S. 432 (1895) that the U.S. Supreme Court held that the presumption of innocence was part of the common law of evidence. No constitutional provisions were referred to, nor did the judgment say that the Constitution had made this presumption implicit in criminal trials. The French Constitution was more advanced than the U.S. Constitution in several ways, for instance, when it enunciated that "Liberty consists in the power to do anything that does not injure another," that "every citizen may speak, write and publish freely but he is responsible for the abuse of this liberty in cases determined by the law" (Article XI), that "the law has the right to forbid only such actions as are injurious to society," that "all citizens are equally eligible to all public dignities, places, employments, according to their capacities and without other distinction than their virtues and their talents" and that "taxes should be equally apportioned among all the citizens according to their means" (Articles IV, V, VI, VIII). It also provided for public relief for the poor and free public education—"Economic and Social Rights"—not known in the early years of the American Constitution.

In spite of the significant contribution to the cause of human freedom and economic liberty in the nineteenth century, there was also resistance to this movement of human rights which began with Napoleon, the Congress of Vienna and the efforts of the great powers dedicated to legitimacy rather than to sovereignty of the people, or to furtherance of individual rights. The nineteenth century gave rise to nationalism and imperialism and planted in the new soil, as in Latin America, the seeds of representative government, though, as it turned out, they fell on rocky soil and did not take root or flourish in many of those places. During the period of the First World War—1914 to 1918— and subsequently till until the beginning of the Second World War, old autocracies such as in Russia, Germany, Austro-Hungarian Empire, Italy, Spain, Rumania, Greece, etc., were shattered, and various other countries gave way to new regimes as in Russia. Where autocracies had initially given way to democracies they in turn gave way to new autocracies which were the worst of tyrannies as in Germany, Italy and Spain.

As already noticed the first constitution in the modern sense and that too a written one was established for the United States two centuries ago. This imposed limitation on government and contained a Bill of Rights. The French Rights of Man had a close likeness to the U.S. Bill of Rights. They served as models for the authors of modern constitutions as also the Universal Declaration of Human Rights.

Today almost every one of the 150 or more states has a constitution which is its basic document and as it were its birth certificate and contained at best promises that remain unfulfilled. I have already indicated that a Constitution indicates what its society aspires to, how individual rights are treated and the kind of political system, the social values and the status of the said rights. There are countries whose constitutions are antithetical to constitutionalism in the sense they do not constitute a government with limited powers or provide protection of individual rights and freedoms. They indicate, by incorporating ideological manifestos, the system of government they have. The governments ignore or disregard human rights—though they may pretend to uphold them and describe their system equally as democratic" —a term which has a different meaning from that attributed to it by Western democracies, and which is therefore likely to cause confusion.

Constitutional Types : Limited Powers

As the constitutions of many nations which are born after the Second World War serve only as symbols of their statehood and of their independence, it is not possible to describe the features of every one of them nor the condition of rights incorporated therein. These constitutions however can be grouped broadly into three categories : the Western democratic-libertarian constitutions, the Socialist-Communist constitutions, and the others. It is the first two that demonstrate the ideological division, and differences in attitude to human rights—sometimes quite sharp. The "other" category is in the third world—comprising states which were under colonial rule and those which were not, and those which gained independence after the Second World War. Some of them have followed the western democratic model with emphasis on human rights and representative system of government, and others Eastern socialism with dictatorship of the Communist Party such as Poland, East Germany, Czechoslovakia, etc.

Again Constitutions have been described as written, unwritten, unitary or federal, flexible or rigid, democratic or otherwise, parliamentary or non-parliamentary. As I said earlier, the crux of the democratic representative government, whether federal or unitary, depends on the status of the judiciary, that is, whether it is independent or controlled. The United Kingdom, as I have earlier pointed out, has a unitary constitution and a Parliament which is sovereign. It was once said that the sovereignty of the Parliament is so wide that it could do anything except make a man a woman or a woman a man. On this assumption, critics have commented that there are no guaranteed fundamental rights as are found in the written constitution of the United States and in similar ones. As such these freedoms can be taken away by a Parliament which is despotic. I have refuted this assumption in my judgment in *Kesavananda Bharati's* case [(1973) 4 SCC p. 225]. I said at page 620 : Constitutions have been variously described as rigid or flexible, controlled or uncontrolled, but without going into these concepts it is clear if the state is considered as a society to which certain indefinite but not unlimited powers are attributed then there is no difficulty in holding that the exercise of state power can be limited (A.L. Goodhart ; *English Law and the Moral Law*, p. 54). Even in a unitary state like the United Kingdom where it is believed that the Queen in Parliament is supreme, Professor A.L. Goodhart in the book referred to above points out that this is as misleading as the statement that the Queen's consent is necessary. After referring to Dicey, Coke and Blackstone, for the view that parliamentary government is a type of absolute despotism, he says, "Such a conclusion must be in conflict not only with our sense of what is fitting, but also with our recognition of what happens in fact. The answer is, I believe, that the people as a whole, and Parliament itself, recognize that under the unwritten Constitution, there are certain established principles which limit the scope of Parliament. It is true that the courts cannot enforce these principles as they can under the federal system in the United States, but this does not mean that these principles are any the less binding and effective. For that matter some of them receive greater protection today in England than they do in the United States. These basic principles are, I believe, four in number" (A.L. Goodhart, p. 55). Then he narrates what these four principles are : First that no man is above the law ; second, that those who govern Great Britain do so in a representative capacity and are subject to change but "an immortal government tends to be an immoral government"; third, freedom of speech or thought and assembly are essential parts of any Constitution which provides that people govern themselves because without them self-government becomes impossible ; and fourth, which is a basic part of the English Constitution is the independence of the judiciary and it is inconceivable that Parliament should regard itself as free to abolish the principle which has been accepted as a corner-stone of freedom ever since the Act of Settlement in 1701. Professor Goodhart then concludes :

> "It is therefore, I believe, true to say that it is as wrong in theory as it is in fact to suggest that the British Constitution is a form of enlightened despotism. Those who exercise power in the name of the State are bound by the law, and there are certain definite principles which limit the exercise of the power."

The history of the British shows that they are brought up on struggle and conflict against the King and/or Parliament, for the establishment of their rights, for freedom of speech and Press, and for the establishment of independent judiciary. They will never tolerate the use of parliamentary power, to trample upon or transgress their cherished rights, though theoretically it is omnipotent. On this view I agree with Prof. Goodhart when he says that the British Constitution is not a form of enlightened despotism. Any attempt to make a law to trample upon the cherished rights would be opposed and those that attempt it will be thrown out. Political leaders are well aware of this power of the people.

The United States has incorporated within its Constitution a well-developed human rights doctrine and institutions for protecting them. It has a written constitution, which is difficult to abrogate, replace, suspend or change. There are safeguards against too strong a government by separation of powers, checks and balances and federalism. It has a representative government as a basic right. It has incorporated a Bill of political civil rights. All these elements envisaged are authoritatively interpreted in the light of the due process clause and the power of judicial review by an independent judiciary whose decision has finality. Each of these elements has contributed to the growth of the human rights. The abolition of slavery was followed by civil war and the civil war amendments—the thirteenth, the fourteenth and the fifteenth amendments—brought radical change in the concept of federalism. These amendments have given nation-wide applicability to individual rights subjecting the actions of all the states—North and South—to federal constitutional limitations and to scrutiny by the Federal Judiciary and to Congressional regulation. Some have seen these as a modification which almost makes it a new constitution. This is rather far-fetched. This change, however, enhanced the content of human rights and extended the means for protecting them. Slavery was abolished, equal protection of laws for all was ordained. The Sixteenth Amendment authorized progressive income-tax. This reflected a philosophy of distributing burdens on citizens according to their capacity. It made it possible to transform the United States into a Welfare State and thus provide for economic and social rights. Seventeenth Amendment made it necessary for direct election of Senators which thus conferred on citizens the right to participate in government. Nineteenth Amendment provided that the right to vote shall not be denied on account of sex or race.

The establishment of an independent judiciary enabled it to develop the general principles of the Constitution and to arbitrate on political controversy. This has saved the United States from the need for more frequent and radical change or the need for extra constitutional government, from emergency suspension of the Constitution or of particular rights, both of which have plagued human rights in other countries. As I said earlier, there is no provision in the Constitution for any of these. Though Presidential power has expanded greatly, any high-handed exercises having deleterious effects on individual rights are periodically rectified by Congress or contained by the courts, e.g., legislation to control the President's resort to use of armed forces abroad or to make international agreements on his own authority, or the court's protection of the President's power from Congressional invasion such as, for instance, his power to appoint officials [*Buckly v. Valeo, 224 U.S. 1 (1976)*]. In the case of President Richard Nixon, the Congress and the courts played a convincingly-decisive role that led to his downfall. This has restored the faith in the importance of the separation of powers. Federalism is another innovation which has been used for taking positive action to promote and protect individual rights. It has increased the security of individual rights against invasion by the states and inexorably also against invasion by the federal government.

The direct election of the President and the Senators by adult citizens without regard to sex or race has enabled them to exercise a universal right on the basis of "one man one vote". The innovation of Judicial Review by Chief Justice Marshall is a unique contribution to the United States constitutionalism. Individual rights are now its principal beneficiary. It is also significant to mention that in the amendment process the citizens are concerned directly and the state legislators have also an important role to play. This has helped prevent any attempt to tinker with the Constitution indulged by Congress or the President by means of a legislative measure whether by simple or specified higher majority. Any temptation to suspend, amend or abrogate the Constitution to the detriment of individual rights or freedom is thus made almost impossible. These are a few main features of the American Constitution. It is not possible to spell out on this occasion in any greater detail.

French Constitutional Experiments

The French Constitution evolved by the people of France, conscious of their individual human and natural rights, and influenced by the Rights of Man, has been abrogated due to the tyranny and violence which prevailed by a counter revolution by which Napoleon Bonaparte became the dictator and emperor. After the Congress of Vienna, and the defeat of Napoleon at Waterloo, the French had a second Constitution which again was set aside when Louis Napoleon made himself the head of the State, overthrowing the Second Republic. After the humiliating defeat suffered by the French in Franco-Prussian War, Louis Napoleon was overthrown, the Third Republic came into being. France had its third Constitution. This constitution was the result of a compromise between the monarchists and the republicans. The French in the course of the eighty years preceding the Third Republic had experimented in constitution making. The third Constitution of France had, as Strong says (at page 148-149), "experimented amazingly in constitution-making, a branch of practical politics in which the world had come to look upon Frenchmen as pre-eminent craftsmen, who, to quote one of their own authorities, had a custom to conceive a constitution as a philosophical work in which everything is deduced from a principle, as a work of art of which the order and symmetry must be perfect ; as a scientific machine of which the plan is so exact, the steel so fine and firm that the very smallest hitch is impossible. In the exercise of this political ingenuity the French had contrived to devise no fewer than a dozen constitutions in the space of less than a century. But the circumstances in which the Third Republic was constituted after the French disaster in the Franco-German War were such as to drive French statesmen away from this tradition of the complete document and to found a new regime on three separate laws passed by July 1875."

The general effect of the three laws of 1875, which were the basis of the third Constitution, was to establish a legislature, of two Houses, that is, the Senate and the Chamber of Deputies. If an amendment was to be made a joint session of the two Chambers had to be called, and when so joined, it became the National Assembly. Such a joint session could be convened if either Chamber, by an absolute majority, decided upon it. When so constituted the National Assembly had full power to amend the Constitution as it might decide, except that, by a law of 1884, the abolition of the Republic could not be the subject of a proposal for revision. In fact, the National Assembly under the Third Republic made very few changes in the Constitution during the sixtyfive years of existence.

The situation in which the French constituted the Fourth Republic was very different from that which saw the birth of the Third. It is true that both were conceived in the aftermath of invasion and enemy occupation, but the French people faced in 1946 the effects of a war, or rather of two wars, far more universal and devastating than that of 1870-71. At all events, in 1946, nobody questioned that a republic was the only acceptable form of government. The point at issue concerned rather the nature of the executive and the limitation of the powers of the President. Most of the institutions of the Third Republic were revived, though under other names. Thus the new Constitution speaks of Parliament (le Parlement) and says that it is composed of the National Assembly (former Chamber of Deputies and not, as before, the two Chambers in joint session) and the Council of the Republic (the former Senate).

The method of amendment is set out in a lengthy chapter containing six Articles (82-87). The initiative in this matter lies with the National Assembly, but any proposal for revision has to be examined by a small standing constitutional committee made up of the President and elected members of each Chamber, and presided over by the President of the Republic, whose business it is to examine the constitutionality of the proposal and to seek the agreement of the Council of the Republic. If the proposed amendment is passed, on second reading, by a two-thirds majority in the National Assembly or by a three-fifths majority in each of the Chambers, then, within eight days of its adoption by Parliament, it must be promulgated by the President of the Republic. But if it is adopted only by an absolute majority in each Chamber which is less than the proportions mentioned above it must be submitted to a referendum. The amendment is then adopted only if there is a favourable vote of a majority of the people voting.

Beyond these limitations there are certain other restrictions. For example, any proposed amendment touching the existence of the Council of the Republic cannot be accomplished without the consent of the Council itself or by recourse to a referendum. And the last Article of the section of the Constitution dealing with revision, as I said, states categorically that the republican form of government cannot be the subject of a proposal for revision.

After General De Gaulle became the President of the French Republic the Constitution was again amended to affect its power structure. By this, a Presidential system was introduced which was a combination of the American Presidential system and the British

Parliamentary system. This is yet another occasion when France changed its Constitution. The Referendum process is more often resorted to and even in elections to representative assembly there are two stages to complete the process of constituting the Chamber of Deputies. All this is to ensure that there is a definite and positive mandate from the people, as against a mere marginal vote, to administer the state.

It has been seen that though the American Constitution has been amended with great caution, the Constitution in its basic or essential aspects survives and views on constitutionalism are adjusted to changing times. On the other hand, as I have pointed out earlier, the French Constitution has been abrogated and replaced several times by other French Constitutions, so much so, it is said, that when a Frenchman went to a bookshop and asked for a copy of the French Constitution the book-seller told him, "Sir, we do not sell periodic literature here".

The German Experience

As a result of the Austro-Prussian War and Franco-Prussian War, the German Empire was proclaimed in 1871. This lasted till the closing days of the First World War. Under the Empire of 1871, federalism of a unique type came into being with the hereditary King of Prussia becoming the hereditary Emperor of Germany. The Prussians under this state were dominant in the two houses of the Imperial Legislature. The real legislative power did not vest in the people represented in the Reichstag but lay in the Upper House, Bundesrat, where the envoys of the Constituent states sat and in which Prussia had a predominating influence. This German Empire was neither truly federal nor truly democratic.

After the First World War, the Weimar Republic came into existence with federalism which prescribed in the lists the powers of the units (see Articles 6, 7 and 12). While the Reichstag represented the people, the Reichstat (Upper House) was still made up of envoys of the state governments but its powers were greatly diminished. The creation of the Supreme Court as the interpreter of the Constitution introduced a real element of federalism. An amendment of the Constitution can be effected without a referendum by ordinary legislative method under certain restrictions regarding majorities in the Chambers, but either the Upper House or the people might bring the machinery of referendum into operation under restrictions of time and percentage of numbers respectively. It is these provisions which enabled Adolf Hitler after becoming its Chancellor constitutionally to override and destroy the Weimer Constitution. The humiliation of the defeat in the First World War for which he found many scapegoats and his demagoguery enabled him to make himself the dictator and convert the state into a unitary one.

In view of this, after the defeat of Hitler in the Second World War, occupying powers concerned themselves with the kind of constitution Germany should have so that they could restore to the Germans the political power to run their state. While Russia out of the four occupying powers wanted a strong federal government at the centre lest it leave the road open to a Bismark or a Hitler who would make national unity his rallying cry, the other three powers, being in a hurry, acted independently of the USSR. The first draft of a constitution for a federation of eleven German states which was prepared by experts was submitted to the German Constituent Assembly at Bonn and the new Republic was inaugurated in September 1949. The Republic has two legislative chambers, Lower House (Bundestag) and an Upper House, the Federal Council (Bundesrat)—with a President, elected by absolute majorities of both Houses to which he is responsible through a Cabinet of Ministers. This Constitution, technically known as the basic law, is the constitution under which Western Germany has been governed since 1949. An amendment to the basic law could only be made by a law which expressly alters or adds to the text of the basic law and requires two-thirds majority in both Houses for its adoption, although there is no reference in it to the use of the referendum. One significant feature of this basic law is that no proposal for amendment could be admitted to affect the (a) organization of the Federation into Lander, (b) the basic cooperation of the Lander in legislation, or (c) the basic principles laid down in the Constitution concerning human rights and (d) the democratic social and federal character of the Republic.

The British Dominions

While dealing with Western democratic libertarian constitutions it is necessary to mention variations of this type, namely, the type adopted for the British dominions—the British Colonial Empire comprising those territories over which England ruled but which became self-governing dominions long prior to the First and Second World Wars. Dominion status was granted to some of these territories by an Act of Parliament of the United Kingdom. These dominions were Canada, Australia, Union of South Africa, Southern Ireland, New Zealand and Newfoundland. This was necessitated by and was in response to a growing sense of nationhood among these dominions. The Irih State of Southern Ireland was created as a result of civil war between North and South Ireland and Britain, by a treaty between Great Britain and Southern Ireland in 1922, which was ratified by the British Parliament and the Irish Constituent Assembly. Each of the self-governing Dominions had a Governor-General and was either unitary or federal as the case may be. In 1931, the Imperial Parliament gave effect to certain resolutions passed by the Imperial Conference held in the year 1926 by an Act known as the Statute of Westminster, and these Dominions were declared to be free and associated as Members of the British Commonwealth of Nations. The Constitutions of these Dominions were democratic and libertarian, based on the freedom of the individual and representative form of parliamentary government similar to that in the United Kingdom. There was of course, as I said, some Dominions which were federal in character and to that extent were influenced by the federalism of the United States.

In all these countries the established political civil rights and liberties are generally protected. There is essential equality under law and equal opportunity as well as some tendencies to equalize and distribute wealth more justly.

Many of this category of states provide social services and welfare. There is individual choice of profession, occupation and vocational work. These were free from governmental compulsion. Even among the states, which are socialist in outlook, there is a basic reluctance to sacrifice the individual even for the greater good of all except in times of war or emergency. Though there is an extensive governmental intervention in the economy, yet there is a deep reluctance to sacrifice the present for the future or to sacrifice important rights of living persons for uncertain benefits to unborn generations. In these states there is political opposition, there is more than one party and the suffrage is essentially universal. As the people are politically aware, the government has also to be responsible and accountable to them. In all these countries, as already stated, the judiciary is independent and justice is largely un-influenced by political considerations. The concern for human rights evinced by the people of these libertarian states is the bastion upon wh ch representative democracy survives in those countries.

Socialist Constitutions

The next category of constitutions are those of socialist-communist states. These states have an aspiration to maximize economic welfare of all. Their philosophy is that the means of production shall be owned by the state, that they should have economic planning, public ownership of public utilities, or principal industries, and of financial institutions. They permit limited individual economic enterprise and accumulation of private property. Socialism and democracy cannot be compared, for their response to questions about society is different. Even Hitler's National Socialism or Nazism had certain things in common with socialism in that there was planning and regulation for the benefit of the State, that the individual had little or no rights and that the government and leadership were not representative of or accountable to the people. Even among the socialists there have been libertarian socialists such as those in Great Britain, Western Europe, Sweden, Israel and also in India. In all these countries both human rights and socialist ideology flourish. Marxist-Leninist socialism, such as in the Soviet Union and the People's Republic of China and Castro's Cuba, is all a category by itself. It is ideologically anti-thetical to Western democracy, including emphasis on individual rights. Under the Chinese Constitution of 1978, Marxism and Leninism is also associated with Mao Tsetung's thought as "guiding ideology of the People's Republic of China".

There are large similarities in doctrine, and in the condition of human rights in the Soviet Union and Communist China. There are also significant differences between them, but in practice these are not easily ascertainable as to which of tbem is ideological and which national. The 1954 Constitution of the People's Republic of China followed the 1936 Soviet Constitution closely, but later on the falling out of these two giants, and the hostility between them, caused China in 1975 to reject Soviet

"Deviations" and to re-assert revolutionary dedication and ideological purity in its Constitution. The reference to the paragraphs proclaiming friendships for the USSR and the People's democracies was deleted. The Constitutions of the Soviet Union and China have nothing in common with Thomas Paine's ideology or constitutions. They were not ordained or established by the people as the contract with, and the condition of the government they establish. It is not a case of constitution first and government coming into existence later under it. It is a case of establishment of government first and the Constitution coming later.[8]

However, the recent communist constitutions claim the authority from the people, though earlier the Soviet Constitution proclaimed a dictatorship of the Proletariat. In 1961 however following the response to prevailing doctrines of sovereignty of the people, being in consonance with national unity and patriotism which was aroused during the war, the USSR declared in the Constitution of 1977 that the dictatorship of proletariat had fulfilled its historic mission and the Soviet Union is now a State "of the whole people". The preamble states "the aims of the dictatorship of the proletariat having been fulfilled, the Soviet State has become a state of the whole people." Article 2 provides that "All power in the USSR belongs to the people," while still retaining references to the "working people" (see Articles 1, 50). In the 1975 Chinese Constitution, perhaps to show what in its view was deviationism of the USSR, China introduced a reference to the dictatorship of the proletariat in Articles 1, 12, 13, even while declaring that power "belongs to the people" (Article 3). Article 6 of the Soviet Constitution states that the communist party is the "leading and guiding force of Soviet Society and the nucleus of its political system, of all states organization and public organizations."

Article 2 states that the Soviet Constitution provides that the people exercise state power through Soviets of People's Deputies. There is a pyramid of workers' representation which is termed democratic centralism with an obligation of lower bodies to observe the decisions of higher ones (Article 3). Article 5 provides that the major matters of state shall be submitted to nation-wide discussion and put to a popular vote (Referendum). Under the 1936 USSR Constitution it was provided that "He who does not work neither shall he eat" and "from each according to his ability and to each according to his work" (Article 12). But in 1977 USSR Constitution, the provision which says that he who does not work shall not eat has been omitted though the second may still be implied. Article 14 says that socially useful work and its results determine a person's status in society. The individual rights are listed as basic rights, freedoms and duties of citizens beginning with economic rights (from Articles 40-49); e.g., that the citizens of the USSR have a right to work (Article 40), the "right to rest and leisure", to health protection, to maintenance in old age, sickness and disabilities (Articles 41-43); right to housing and education (Articles 44-45); right to enjoy cultural benefits (Article 46) and in accordance with the aims of building communism the freedom of scientific, technical and artistic work (Article 47); the right to take part in the management and administration of State and public affairs; to submit proposals for including the activity of public bodies and to criticize their shortcomings (Articles 48, 49). The Soviet Constitution also proclaims civil and political rights and freedoms. Article 50 guarantees freedom of speech, of the Press and of association, etc. These are all subject to the interest of the people and the need to strengthen and develop the socialist system (Article 51). The right to associate in public organizations that promote their political activities, etc., is again subject to the need for building communism. Article 52 gurantees freedom of conscience, i.e., the right to profess any religion and to conduct religious worship or atheistic propaganda. In the USSR the Church is separated from the State and the Schools from the Church. Again the individuality of the person is guaranteed and no one may be arrested except by a court decision or on warrant of a procurator (Article 54). Similarly Article 55 guarantees inviolability of the home which no one without lawful grounds can enter against his will. Article 56 states that the privacy of citizens, their correspondence, telephone conversation, telegraphic communication is protected by law. All State bodies, public organizations and officials are enjoined by Article 57 to respect the individual and protect the rights and freedoms of citizens. Citizens of the USSR have a right to lodge complaints against the actions of official, state bodies and public bodies and the actions of officials that contravene the law or exceed their powers and infringe the rights of the citizens may be appealed against in the court in the manner prescribed by law (Article 58).

In so far as the administration of justice is concerned, Article 155 says, judges and people's assessors are independent and subject only to the law ; that justice is administered in the USSR on the principle of equality of citizens before the law and the court (Article 156) ; that proceedings in all courts shall be open to the public and hearings *in camera* are allowed only in cases provided for by law with observance of all rules of judicial procedure (Article 157) ; that a defendant in the criminal action is guaranteed the right to legal assistance (Article 158) ; and that no one may be adjudged guilty of a crime and subject to punishment as a criminal except by the sentence of a court and in conformity with the law (Article 160) ; and that in cases provided for by legislation citizens shall be given legal assistance free of charge (Article 161).

Unenforceable Freedoms in Socialist Countries

All these rights and freedoms proclaimed in the USSR Constitution are impressive, but there is no mention about prohibition of slavery or servitude, torture, or cruelty, inhuman or degrading treatment or punishment, arbitrary arrests, detention or exile or the freedom of movement and residence within one's country and the right to leave one's country and to return. There are no legal prohibitions ordained by the people upon its government. These provisions are mere ideological declaration by the government to the world. It does not state what the government is required to do or provide. An example relating to the guarantees of freedom of speech and Press by the Soviet Constitution is subject to a qualification which, as a practical matter, destroys those freedoms. The qualification, in effect, means that anyone who says anything or publishes anything that would harm the Soviet Union can be published. What will harm the Soviet Union ? The answer is : Anything the people in power fear would interfere with them or their policies. During the 1930s the theories of a Russian agronomist, Trofim Denisovich Lysenko, came into prominence. He believed, wrongly, that the characteristics plants acquired while growing could be inherited. His theories proved disastrous to Soviet agriculture, yet because his beliefs fitted in with Russian political thinking it became virtually impossible for scientists to disagree with him in public—or even, for the most part, in private. Those who did lost funds, jobs and sometimes their lives. Because there is no tradition of free speech and free Press in the Soviet Union, this one relatively simple matter—free and informed discussion of genetics—was severely restricted, to the great detriment of the Russian people and of their leaders as well. It is because of the egregious error in the theory of Lysenko which was not allowed to be criticized or commented upon in the Soviet Union, the renowned genetist, J.B.S. Haldane, Fellow of the Royal Society, resigned in protest from the Communist Party. Another instance is that while Article 54 provides that no one may be arrested except by a decision of court or on the warrant of procurator, there is no requirement that the court decision or the procurator's warrant should be consistent with some constitutional or other human rights standard. Again the procurator general, who is charged with assuring that officials comply with the Soviet Law, can presumably demand compliance with constitutional promises as well, which is expressly provided for under the Chinese Constitution of 1978. As Louis Henkin in his book *The Rights of Man Today* (Westview Press/Bowlder Colorado) has rightly observed in respect of some of these provisions, at page 66:

> For the Western observer, what is missing from the Soviet Constitution and the Soviet system is the assurance that the Constitution will be honoured at the highest levels of government. Although the Constitution is headed 'fundamental law' and declares that it shall have 'supreme legal force' (Article 173), to the Western observer it seems not to be law at all, surely not higher law. The Constitution, it is stated, 'provides the basis' and 'all laws and other acts of state bodies shall be promulgated . . . in conformity with it' and the author asks, but what basis is there for confidence that laws will in fact conform to it? (The Constitution, moreover, can be amended by the legislature—the Supreme Soviet—by a two-thirds vote (Article 174) and the Supreme Soviet has long been essentially a rubber stamp for its Presidium (Articles 119-23.) There is no judicial review to enforce the Constitution against the principal policy-makers, or even against others when these do not wish it. The procurator general, who might enforce the Constitution against officialdom, cannot enforce it against the Supreme Soviet—

> to which he is accountable (Article 108). The procurator general himself is also the chief prosecutor and there is apparently no remedy against his abuse of the criminal process. When the Constitution promises that there will be 'legality', that things will be done according to law, there is no assurance against law that is itself oppressive, and no resource if the law is or becomes inadequate, or is repealed.

This comparison between the United States Constitution and the USSR Constitution may be comparing the unlike. While the first amendment to the U.S. Constitution prohibits the government from doing something and is only negative, Articles 39 to 58 of the USSR Constitution of 1977 are not a legal prohibition ordained upon the government. They are a mere statement of various freedoms declared by the Soviet Constitution. There is no recourse if the legislature enacts a law that is prejudicial to the several freedoms. It fails to assure that they are guaranteed. All rights embodied in the aforesaid constitutional provisions are subject to law, which law is not subject to any restriction. The judiciary itself is not independent in that judges who are appointed by the Supreme Soviet are equally responsible to it. This apart, Article 121(5) states that the Presidium of the Supreme Soviet shall interpret the laws of the USSR. Similar provisions in the Constitution of the People's Republic of China are also ideological declarations (Articles 44-59 lay down the fundamental rights and duties of citizens). All these declared rights are subject to the socialist system being safeguarded and it is enjoined to check counter-revolutionary activities, punish all traitors, counter-revolutionaries, new-born elements and other bad elements (Article 18). These rights consequently are enjoyed by the people only by the political sufferance and grace of the government. The courts and the procurator, under the 1978 Constitution, are responsible to National People's Congress, the highest organ of State power, and the National People's Congress which makes laws can also amend the Constitution (Articles 20, 22-42 and 43).

In this category can be included East Germany, Czechoslovakia, Poland, Romania, Albania, Yugoslavia and Hungary—all communist states or satellites of Soviet Russia following similar patterns of government where the Communist Party is dominant and individual rights or individual freedoms are subject to the interest of the state as determined by higher executive and must yield to it at any time or at all times. Some of the new states which obtained independence after the Second World War also fall into this category such as Castro's Cuba, Vietnam, etc. Even in countries where Marxist, Leninist (Stalinist-Marxist) or Marxist-Leninist-Maoist principles are said to be adopted as basis of their respective constitutions, in recent decades even these had to respond to a changed world, particularly to the Western ideas of freedom which have great popular appeal or are propagated by a strong international movement or which are given great political importance by virtue of the United Nations Declaration or International Covenants regarding human rights. These countries are at least compelled to adopt individual rights, they are also impelled to join the International Human Rights movement and to assume International Human Rights obligations by adhering to international agreements. Though these were denied initially positive support, as the communist bloc abstained from voting in 1948 on the Universal Declaration of Human Rights, they have now been accepted by it. In 1973 the Soviet Union subscribed to the International Covenant on Economic, Social and Cultural Rights and the covenant on civil and Political Rights and at the Helsinki Conference in 1975 on Security and Cooperation in Europe the Soviet Union and its allies accepted the Human Rights as a "Principle guiding relations between participating States" and declared expressly that they "will act in conformity with" the Universal Declaration and will comply with the International Human Rights Covenants by which they may be bound. Though these were accepted, the question is whether there has been an unreserved implementation of the aforesaid covenants or only a grudging, modest and half-hearted implementation by insistence on their own interpretation of the documents including the derogation provisions and "loopholes".

The other category of states known as the Third World does not furnish any distinct ideological objective unless it be a development in a developing country. The Third World includes states spread over all the geographical areas of the world, some very old like Egypt, some modern but established as those in Latin America, and many newborn. A few are rich and some very poor. Almost all the Third World states have or had constitutions containing a Bill of Rights. Most of these were drafted after World War II on the model of the U.S. Bill of Rights, the French Declaration of the Rights of Man, the Universal Declaration of Human Rights, and/or the European convention on Human Rights. Many constitutions have special features necessitated by local history or other local circumstances. Constitutions of older societies reflect the established order, the legal system, the traditions and assumptions based on social values which are taken for granted and are not specifically affirmed in the Constitution. Constitutions framed for the new or radically transformed socialists perforce articulate an ideological or other selected values. Some of the main features of all these constitutions are the right to vote, conferred on all adults of and above a particular age irrespective of sex or race. Some states make voting compulsory at least for literate citizens such as Brazil (1969, Article 147), Guatemala (1965, Article 19). Our Constitution (Indian) prohibits discrimination on grounds of race, religion, caste, sex or place of birth (Article 15), guarantees freedom of conscience, free profession and propagation of religion (Article 25), freedom to manage religious affairs (Article 26), cultural and educational rights (Article 29) and the right of minorities to establish and administer educational institutions (Article 30) and provides for special representation for the underprivileged and the "ex-untouchables" (Articles 330 to 334). In Part IV of the Constitution, Articles 36 to 51 set out the Directive Principles of State Policy which however are not enforceable by any court but are fundamental in the governance of the country, and it shall be the duty of the state to apply these principles in making laws (Article 31). Cyprus provides proportional representation for the Greeks and Turky with a built-in veto (1960, Articles 62, 78). Pakistan reserved a certain number of seats for women for a number of years (1973, Articles 51, 4). Many Constitutions provide for only one party, e.g., Tanzania (Article 3, 1965). The Federal Republic of Germany outlaws parties which seek to impair or abolish the free democratic basic order or to endanger the existence of the Federal Republic of Germany (1949, Article 21, Clause 2, amended from time to time). Several Latin American countries explicitly outlaw communist party (Guatemala, Article 27). Most Constitutions promise freedom of opinion, speech, Press, and provide often for punishment for abuse and some provide such freedoms only so long as they are not hostile to the socialist system (Romania, 1952, Article 29). They also generally provide for freedom of religion. It is interesting to see that Malaysia controls the propagation of other religions among Muslims (1957, Article 11, Clause 4). Zaire forbids names of saints as a religious practice. These Constitutions generally also proclaim freedom from slavery and forced labour but some permit forced labour for reasons or purposes specified by law (El Salvador, 1962, Article 155). There are variations on the aforesaid aspects in different countries. Equality is now universally proclaimed but in Liberia only blacks can be citizens.

These states came into being after the Second World War, some of which were erstwhile colonial possessions of the British, the Americans, the French or the Dutch and they attained independence as a result of the effort of their peoples. States like India, Pakistan, Burma, Bangladesh, Malaysia, Indonesia, the Philippines, and some of the African countries like Kenya, Zimbabwe, Libya, etc., adopted what may be regarded as the libertarian Western type of democracy, though some of them liked to describe themselves as socialist.

In all these countries which were socially and economically backward a great deal of leeway had to be made to bring them to the status of a modern state and to relieve their peoples from abject poverty and backwardness. This being the object some of these new states in their attempt to modernize their society and develop their economy were concerned more with economic and social planning for the future rather than with the prevailing conditions of life and individual freedoms.

At this stage I wish to refer to what has been said by Louis Henkin—in a terse statement giving a panorama of civil, political, economic and social rights. He says (at pages 81-82) :

> "Criminal procedure widely promises the rights with which we are familiar. Some states outlaw trials *in absentia* (Uruguay, 1967, Article 21). Some provide the right 'to a defence' (of the 1936 Soviet Constitution, Article 111); some also specify the right to counsel (Egypt, Article 67). Capital punishment is outlawed in many states : some preclude capital punishment for women or for persons over

> a given age (Guatemala, Article 54). In some states, there is also a maximum prison sentence [Venezuela, Article 60(7)]. Search and Seizure is barred in some states during night hours (Guatemala, Article 57). Some extend a privilege not to testify against blood relatives (Bolivia, 1967, Article 14)."

Economic and social rights are variously worded. In Uruguay every person has a right to a decent home (Article 45) ; in Paraguay to a home standing on its own land (1967, Article 83). In a number of Constitutions, the state is obligated to provide work and welfare (Denmark, Article 75) ; some add "in so far as economic development and its financial resources permit" (Turkey, 1961, Article 53). Some socialist constitutions severely restrict private enterprise ; some encourge it (Malta, 1964, Article 19). Some combat intemperance (India, Article 47). Most provide a right to universal education (Cuba, 1975, Article 50) ; (Guatemala, Article 94). Italy specifies a right to "institute legal proceedings for the protection of their own rights and legitimate interests" (1947, Article 24, cf. Article 57 of the 1977 USSR Constitution). Mexico promises free access to the courts (Article 17). Ecuador provides that the state must protect a child from the moment of conception (1967, Article 30).

Particular variations apart, the proliferation of Constitutions and Bills of Rights doubtless responds to widespread and prevailing conceptions—at least slogans—of "Constitutionalism", "democracy", "popular sovereignty" however defined (or undefined), and to a *Zeitgeist* of aspiration and an ideal of progress. The constitutions originally provided both domestic and international legitimacy and in many instances were a condition of decolonization or statehood. But especially as ideology of development becomes stronger, constitutions have been condemned by some as unrealistic and inappropriate Western impositions, undesirable and dangerous even, because they put brakes on governments that, they say, are rather in need of accelerators.

Many of them had little patience with individual rights where they considered these to be obstacles especially to the so-called economic and social rights. In only few cases, like the Tanzania of Julius Nyerere and India, is attention given to individual rights and an effort is made to build institutions and evolve policies that will protect individual rights and freedoms. In the case of Tanzania, this is being done in the revolutionary context and in a single-party socialist state. There have been books on the constitution, judicial review and fundamental freedoms in Anglophonic Independent Africa, which can be usefully studied. States like Pakistan, Burma, Bangladesh have all given the go-bye to democracy, liberalism and have all become dictatorships. They are governed by Military Rulers.

As I said although there is a virtual universal lip-service paid to democracy, the system that is followed in some of these countries is essentially a one-party system, often a one-man government without any meaningful political opposition, and dissent is viewed as akin to treason. In many states however there are a few effective limitations on government. In some the rights are not higher laws, there is no independent judiciary, nor a judiciary which has the power to give protection to freedoms and rights, nor are there traditions for respecting individual rights which permeate the people, nor is there any independent or alert Press free from censorship to preserve these rights. Instances where there are reports of massacres such as in Burundi, the elimination of masses of communists in Indonesia, liquidations of many millions in Cambodia, are not lacking. The most serious obstacle to human rights is the provision for suspending a constitution by declaring emergency which would empower the government to trample upon individual rights without any accountability.

The provisions for declaration of emergency, suspension of the Constitution and derogation of the rights in times of emergency, which are the very antithesis of a representative democratic free government, abound in many of the constitutions. Take the case of the Republic of South Africa, under whose Terrorism Act anyone can be detained if the police has "reason to believe" that he is a terrorist or he has withheld from South African police any information relating to terrorists (Section 6, Act 83 of 1967). The State of Columbia has been without emergency rule only for two out of about thirtyfive years. Often an emergency can be declared by an executive fiat which can then rule by its own decree. As a consequence of the declaration of emergency, Press censorship and individual detention, mostly unreviewable, is enforced and can be extended for an indefinite period. In Indonesia the report of the government itself shows that 50,000 political prisoners were detained, most of them without trial. There have been authoritative reports of detention and torture in Brazil and Chile, in the middle of 1970. Independent judicial review with a view to protecting individual rights during emergency rule is not possible when the Constitution bars such review. In fact Emergency rule tends to end judicial independence.

Emergency in India

Nearer home in India the effect of the declaration of emergency and consequent suppression of freedom, the terror it inflicted upon the people of this country and the trauma caused to national dignity and pride is very fresh in our minds. I find it necessary to dwell on the several aspects of the manner in which the Constitution has been dealt with, to ascertain what is envisaged and what is not, and to point out how attempts were made, to use the words of an eminent jurist, to deface and defile it (our constitution—Defaced and Defiled—N.A. Palkhivala, Macmillan 1974). The power to declare an emergency and issue ordinance is an inheritance from the colonial past. The British during their rule of India had always insisted on such a power. When the Governor-General under the Government of India Act promulgated an ordinance constituting a special tribunal it was contended that the provision prohibiting an appeal from its judgment was invalid as the emergency proclaimed was not justified. The Privy Council in the case of *Bhagat Singh v. The King Emperor* (58 I.A. 169), held that the judgment of the Governor-General could not be upset on the ground that no state of emergency existed and the ordinance with all that followed was illegal, and completely without foundation on the very face of it, and therefore decided that it would be idle to allow an appeal to be argued. The Government of India Act 1935 was also to the same effect, that is to say, that the Governor-General could promulgate ordinances in an emergency for any of the provinces or parts of a province (Section 102). Unfortunately the framers of our Constitution, notwithstanding their bitter experience under such power, were overawed by the holocaust that followed the partition of India and made provisions for declaration of an emergency and for legislation by ordinance.

Before I deal with the emergency powers under our Constitution it is necessary to notice the attempts made to erode the independence of the judiciary and the impact of such attempts during the emergency.

Amending Power of Indian Parliament

Ever since *Golaknath v. State of Punjab* (AIR 1967 SC 1643), where a majority of the Supreme Court Judges, includ ng Chief Justice Subba Rao, held that the fundamental rights enshrined in Part III of the Constitution could not by virtue of Article 13(2) be taken away, or abridged by an amendment under Article 368, attempts were made to nullify that judgment. The executive felt that Parliament was supreme and could under Article 368 amend any part of the Constitution, abrogate or take away any of the provisions. In fact, it could also abrogate the entire Constitution and replace another one instead. To give effect to this, Parliament enacted several amendments on the plea that as a result of this judgment socio-economic legislation could not be enacted. Thereafter, two judgments of the Supreme Court again irked the government, namely, *R.C. Cooper v. The Union of India* (AIR 1970 SC 564), which upheld the challenge to the Bank Nationalisation Act, and the *Privy Purses case*, *Madhava Rao v. Union of India* (AIR 1971 SC 530), which set aside the abolition of Privy Purses guaranteed by the Constitution. All these three cases resulted in the twentyfourth and twentyfifth amendments. By the former, the judgment in Golaknath's case was sought to be overcome by enacting that Article 13(2) shall not apply to constitutional amendments, which in effect empowered Parliament to take away or abridge all or any of the Fundamental Rights and to confer generally on Parliament an unfettered power to alter or take away the whole or any part of the Constitution. By twentyfifth Amendment, Article 31(2) was amended to provide that the acquisition of anyone's property can be made on payment of an "amount" instead of "compensation". This amendment also inserted Article 31C which had a wide sweep. Under this provision no law giving effect to the policy of the state towards securing the principles specified in Clause (b) or Clause (c) of Article 39 shall be deemed to be void on the ground that it is inconsistent with, or takes away or abridges any of the rights conferred by Article 14, Article 19, or Article 31 ; and "no law containing a declaration that it is for giving effect to such a policy shall be called in question in any court on the ground that it does not give effect to such policy." In other words the amendment attempted to give a blank charter to Parliament and all the State Legislatures and empowered them to override the constitutional mandate regarding human rights. There are many more implications arising out of Article 31C.

Kesavananda---A Historic Judgment

This has been done in *Kesavananda Bharati v. the State of Kerala* (AIR 1973 SC 1461) to which judgment I was a party. It has made history on more than one aspect. Firstly, the majority overruled *Golaknath's case*, and secondly, it held that Parliament, in the exercise of its amending power, cannot alter the basic structure or framework of the Constitution. In other words Article 368 cannot be pressed into service to destroy the basic structure of the Constitution. In this view, Parliament cannot extend its amending power, as was sought to be effected by the twentyfourth Amendment, nor could it oust the jurisdiction of the court as was sought to be done by Article 31C.

After this judgment three senior judges who were with the majority were superseded and the fourth judge who was the next senior and who held in favour of the government was appointed as Chief Justice. The floodgates of governmental and official propaganda against the judiciary were opened. The Law Minister and another Minister openly declared on May 2, 1973, in Parliament that the judges should be committed judges. The latter further declared unabashedly that the government was motivated by the consideration that the Chief Justice should be one who would "help" the government and whose political philosophy "would be the most suitable" from the executive point of view. A great deal of controversy was aroused in the country. The government and its votaries, the so-called radicals whose plan was to enter the government as supporters of the party in power forming the government and capture it from within, constantly and tenaciously denigrated judges whose judgment limited the power of Parliament, while the members of the Bar in all the High Courts in the country and those who cherished freedom and individual rights supported the judgment as it built a "bulwark" against usurpation of power for establishment of a dictatorship or the conversion of India into a hereditary monarchy.[9]

While this controversy was going on, the Allahabad High Court in an enquiry on an election petition unseated the Prime Minister on June 12, 1975 and held her guilty of corrupt practices. On June 25, Emergency was declared without first obtaining the approval of the Cabinet. The country was stunned and it went dead. Newspapers could not be printed, censorship was drastic. Parliament passed within hours an amendment to the Constitution reversing the judgment of the Allahabad High Court. The Representation of the People Act was amended, removing the corrupt practices of which the Prime Minister was held guilty from being offences and with retrospective effect, declaring that these offences did not ever exist. People were detained without trial and even without furnishing them with grounds of detention.

Article 22 of our Constitution, though it regulates preventive detention, leaves the power open for laws to be made, such as the Maintenance of Internal Security Act of 1971, which laws authorize the detention of anyone the government "believes . . . is acting in a manner prejudicial to the State". The law has gone to the extent of even exempting the detaining authority from giving even the grounds of detention. Articles 352-360 of our Constitution enact emergency provisions and leave it to the satisfaction of the President to declare emergency where the security of India or any part of the territory is threatened whether by war or external aggression or internal disturbances. A proclamation however can be made before the actual occurrence of war or any such aggression or disturbance provided the President is satisfied that there is imminent danger thereof. Neither the Supreme Court nor any other court has the jurisdiction to entertain any question as to the satisfaction of the President on any ground regarding the validity of either the declaration made by proclamation by the President or the continued operation of such proclamation (Article 352). Article 358 suspends provisions of Article 19 during emergency and Article 359 empowers the President by order to declare that the right to move any court for the enforcement of such of the rights conferred by Part III as may be mentioned in the order and all proceedings pending in any court for the enforcement of the rights so mentioned shall remain suspended for the period during which the proclamation is in force or for such shorter period as may be stated in the order.

Habeas Corpus Case

I do not propose to examine in detail the niceties of the impact of these emergency provisions except to say that these provisions vest the government with draconian powers and the citizen as : has been held in the *Habeas Corpus case* (*ADM*, *Jabalpur v. Shivakant Shukla*, AIR 1976 SC 1207), by a majority of four judges of the Constitution Bench of the Supreme Court, has no right to move the court even if the law under which a person has been detained is a void law and his detention is illegal. The Attorney-General of the time had the temerity to even submit that if the life of a person was being taken away illegally the Supreme Court had no power to stop it. The conscience of the court is supposed to have been also suspended along with the suspension of the rights of the people. The majority of the court gladly accepted this position. It was to the lasting credit of Khanna, J., that he alone dissented without any regard to the personal consequences his decision would inflict upon him, in that, though he was the next senior to the Chief Justice he would be superseded if he took a view opposed to the government. Notwithstanding the jeopardy to which he was subject he took the view which the legal world and the citizens of this country have hailed as the only correct view. Indeed for taking this view he was superseded and consequently he resigned. If it was not for the *Kesavananda Bharati's case* which made the destruction of the basic structure of the Constitution impermissible, we do not know what the history of this country would have been.

One has only to notice that two of the senior judges in the *Habeas Corpus case* who formed the majority expressed hope and gave certificates to the executive that it will not abuse the emergency powers, when the petitioner's counsel submitted that power without judicial restraint will be abused. While rejecting the contention one of them said that he understood that "the care and concern bestowed by the state authorities upon the welfare of detenues who are well housed, wellfed and well-treated is almost maternal" (page 1319). The other judge while noting "the fear expressed by counsel after counsel that the executive may whip and strip and starve the detenue and if this was their judgment, even shoot him down" said that "such misdeeds have not tarnished the record of free India," and that he has a "diamond-bright, diamond-hard hope that such things will never come to pass" (page 1349). While these encomiums were being paid to the executive by these two learned judges, Rajan, an engineering student in Kerala, was being continuously tortured with iron and wooden rollers by the police who ultimately murdered him. There was again the case of Smt. Snehalatha Reddy who was also tortured in Bangalore but not murdered. She died as a result of the treatment meted out to her. When subsequently many cases of similar terrorism, torture and inhuman treatment of the detenues came to light after the Emergency, the hopes of the aforesaid two judges, which could have been best described as naive as well as those of the Chief Justice and another judge, were completely belied. Seervai describes the *Habeas Corpus case* and *Rajan's case* as part of Indian history, just as the trial of the Seven Bishops is a part of English history, the trial of Dred Scott is a part of American history and the trial of Dreyfus is a part of French history. (See H.M. Seervai, *The Emergency, Furture Safeguards and the Habeas Corpus Case : A Criticism*, Tripathi, Bombay, p. 2.) The people however decided to vote out a government responsible for creating such situations which, it was assumed, would help perpetuate itself in power.

Attempts to undo Kesavananda

It may also be mentioned that soon after the emergency was declared an abortive attempt was made by the then Attorney-General who argued the *Habeas Corpus case* to have the *Kesavananda Bharati case* reconsidered. A thirteen-judge Bench was constituted. Most of the judges who sat in *Kesavananda Bharati case* had either retired or resigned on supersession. Only Justice Khanna of the judges who formed the majority was there and among those who had conceded plenary and omni-sovereign powers to Parliament and who were on the Bench were the Chief Justice Ray, Beg, Chandrachud and Mathew, J.J. It was hoped that the Bench would overrule the earlier decision, but those who entertained such an idea were in for great disappointment. The matter was heard for two days, on November 10 and 11, 1975, but on the third day Chief Justice Ray as suddenly as he had constituted it dissolved the Bench, perhaps because his brother judges might have told him that the Bench could not hear it as there was no *lis* which made it necessary to constitute a Bench and hear it. I assume that this was the reason for the dissolution because if I remember right it was perhaps due to the continual questioning of the Attorney-General by a few judges as to how the question referred fell for decision and whether a Bench referred the matter to the Chief Justice to constitute a larger Bench. On the third day, it would appear the Chief Justice said that the arguments were going haywire and dissolved it. What is however on record is interesting to notice particularly the question whether *Kesavananda* impeded socio-economic legislation and in what way it was a hindrance to progress. According to Seervai's *Constitutional Law of India* (2nd edn., Vol. II, p. 1532 and 1536). Mr. Justice Khanna and Mr. Justice Untwalia asked the Attorney-General the following questions :

> Has this theory of basic structure impeded or come in the way of legislating any socio-economic measure ? And the answer was categorically in the negative. Mr. Justice Untwalia asked the following question :
> "Is there any example where the Parliament wanted to amend the Constitution in the public interest and has been prevented by Kesavananda's doctrine ?"

And again the answer was in the negative. In fact, the Attorney-General wanted to say that the real point was, not whether *Kesavananda's case* had prevented any amendment of the Constitution in the public interest but that the Parliament did not know where it stood in the matter of amendments since the doctrine of basic structure was incapable of precise definition. That this submission has no leg to stand on is apparent if one were to ask, is the term primary or secondary capable of a precise definition ? Are the concepts of natural justice, reasonableness, negligence, determinable precisely ? If not, would it follow that these concepts should not be given effect to ? It is unthinkable to hold that just because a concept or a term has no precise definition that concept or term has no basis in law. It is exactly where there is imprecision that the courts are called on to determine creatively their meaning and import.

Again another attempt was made after the 1980 election which brought back to power the party responsible for the 42nd Amendment to have *Kesavananda* overruled, but this attempt also failed : that was in *Minerva Mills Ltd. v. Union of India* (AIR 1980 SC 1789). It may be mentioned that Clause 5 of Article 368 was amended by the 42nd Amendment to confer on Parliament the power to amend the Constitution without any limitation whatever. The majority consisting of Chandrachud, C.J., Gupta, Untwalia and Kailasam, J.J. (Bhagwati, J., dissenting) held that Section 55 of the Amending Act which added Clauses (4) and (5) to Article 368 confers on Parliament a vast and undefined power to amend the Constitution so as to distort it out of recognition. Since the Constitution conferred only a limited amending power on Parliament as held in *Kesavananda Bharati's case*, Parliament cannot, under the exercise of that limited power, enlarge that very power into an absolute power. Hence Section 55 of the Amendment Act was held to be beyond the amending power of Parliament and void since it removed the limitations on the power of Parliament so as to confer a power to damage or destroy the basic or essential features or basic structure of the Constitution. So, till today, every attempt has been made to get the *Kesavananda Bharati's case* overruled, but without success. I dare say further attempts will be made to have it overruled as more than anything else this case has become a red rag to the Executive bull, not because it has been a hindrance to the implementation of schemes for social reform but it is needed for asserting authoritarian power. I say that this conclusion is justified as otherwise why is omni-sovereign power necessary when the Constitution is flexible enough to provide for social justice and establish a Welfare State. In fact, some of the Directive Principles are very clear on this. As one British Jurist, Sir Ivor Jennings (in his book *Some Characteristics of the Indian Constitution*) pointed out, "the ghosts of Sidney and Beatrice Webb stalk through the pages of the Indian Constitution." The impact of the fabian socialists on some of the important Constitution-makers was very deep and it is very clear to us. The Constitution, however, does not speak the doctrinaire language ; its concern is for the promotion of social, economic and political justice, about which the Preamble is very eloquent.

In a speech delivered at Poona University on October 28, 1982, on "Judiciary : Attacks and Survival", Justice Tulzapurker of the Supreme Court (published in AIR, February 1983, Journal Section) expressed his views on this aspect thus : "I fail to understand why in spite of all this, such criticism should be persistently voiced that the Judiciary comes in the way of socio-economic measures or hampers justice being reached to the common man, the toiling masses and the weaker sections of the community. I am really surprised that the Tenth Law Commission presided over by Justice K.K. Mathew should include in its latest Questionnaire the following question : 'Have the judgments of the Supreme Court regarding compensations payable upon the abolition of feudal rights brought to nought the process of social reforms ?' Much water has flown down the Ganges since those judgments were rendered by the Supreme Court and the current settled view has been that the Legislative measures will not be illegal or void on that count unless the compensation provided for is illusory. Besides I fail to appreciate the relevance of the question in the context of the 44th Amendment whereby the provisions dealing with the right to property as a Fundamental Right have been deleted from the Constitution. The criticism that the Judiciary is proving a road-block to social and economic progress or constitutes a hurdle in reaching justice to the common man, in my view, is a myth which has been exploded long since. I suggest that this bogey, which is being raised again and again, deserved to be buried six fathoms deep. The politicians should not pass the buck of their own failure in reaching the benefits of socio-economic measures to the common man on to the judiciary." I had also voiced similar views during the Emergency in my Sir Alladi Lectures in this University in December 1975.

It thus appears that, in spite of there being no impediment for the legislative or the executive to carry out any socio-economic measures, to continue to indulge in the criticism that the judiciary has impeded or is impeding such legislation or that the basic structure concept by its very imprecise nature would hinder all progressive amendments to the Constitution, would only expose the hollowness of the criticism and the deliberate political campaign intended to weaken and demoralize the judiciary with a view to conceal governmental insincerity and inefficiency in the matter of solving the vital problems of the country. If so people are entitled to ask, why is it the party in power wants such unlimited power given to Parliament ? Are they not entitled to draw the inference by its persistence in having *Kesavananda* undone and to hold that the objective of vesting Parliament with unlimited power is not to effect socio-economic measures, which it can do without any impediment but is probably with a view to abrogating the Constitution, taking away the Fundamental rights and enabling persons who want to rule to be vested with dictatorial powers ? The people are however becoming slowly awake and alert to this kind of propaganda and motivation.

Presidential Form : Toying with an Idea

Yet another attempt to alter the structure of the representative democracy was toyed with, namely, the adoption of the French type of Presidential system adopted by De Gaulle in 1968, but evidently for the present such an attempt is given up. It may be pertinent to notice that the framers of the Indian Constitution considered and rejected the American Presidential form in favour of the Parliamentary system with which we were already familiar. Some thought the American Presidential system was not working as well as the British because the Chief Executive is separated from the Legislature (Munshi). Yet others thought that in fact democracy cannot afford to take the risk of a perpetual cleavage between the Legislative and the executive wing (Alladi). The whole exercise in now again suggesting a Presidential form of government seems to be that the executive will not be responsible to the legislature. It is not perhaps realized that this system also has its own drawbacks and fetters. The way in which a President lobbies the members of the Congress and the Senate to get through the measures proposed by him including the budget, the nominations for high offices, etc., makes him dependent on the members of these Houses.

Bane of Defections

A defector under the Parliamentary system will equally be so under the Presidential system and will function with greater efficacy in that he can extract his own price for his vote in the legislative bodies. Whatever be the system, the outlook, temperament and ethos of our political leaders—that they cannot brook dissent, they are authoritarian in temperament, and if they are confronted with any obstacle they want to remove it rather than devise ways and means to get over it—has to be taken into account. For instance as soon as a court holds against any measure of the executive, it immediately amends the Constitution as if it is a Rent Control Act. This would not have however been possible but for another element, namely, the illiteracy of the electorate, which due to sheer hero-worship acts like sheep and does not vote for a party or its policies but instead votes for the individual who leads it. In spite of this outlook of the electorate generally it is to its credit that at no time has it voted more than 50 per cent in favour of the party in power except perhaps on one occasion during Pandit Nehru's regime. Invariably the vote in favour of the party in power did not exceed 45 per cent of the votes polled. It is remarkable that it is the system of election which gives massive majority with a minority of votes. This is also responsible for our Parliamentary system creating frustration and has thus prevented strong opposition to grow—an opposition which is a concomitant for the efficient working of democracy. The third impediment is the ruling party's anxiety to perpetuate itself in power by hook or by crook, in furtherance of which they have resorted to getting persons elected on one ticket to change over to another party by offering them sops. In other words, the elected representative by corrupt means is easily persuaded without the slightest compunction to change over, and as it were to kick the electorate in its face for expressing their confidence in him. Though he ceases to represent the majority of voters of his constituency no one so far has challenged these defections in a court, as the credentials of such a representative to represent the electorate have ceased and he no longer represents the electorate. Though the Government of whatever hue, when in power, is for obvious reasons reluctant to bring an anti-defection measure. I am sure if any defection is challenged there is hope of the court declaring such a representative to be disqualified, and unseating him. By a resort to defections in order to remain in power, an indigenous type of dictatorship has also been developed which I term as the dictatorship of a simulant democracy. On two or three occasions the electorate has no doubt asserted itself to the surprise of the party in power which was thrown out. More of such actions by the electorate is required to throw out, not only the party but the corrupt and defecting representatives. Once this is done the representatives who offer themselves will perforce be from persons of character, integrity, public spirit and patriotic, lest any other with lesser traits and attributes may be rejected. Till this discernment, assertiveness and insistence on good men representing them becomes ingrained in the electorate, and becomes part of its outlook, we must expect our democracy to go on in this rickety fashion.

Maneka Gandhi Case

In so far as the extent of the judicial power is concerned, a bright feature was discernible in the judgment of the Supreme Court, in *Maneka Gandhi v. Union of India* (AIR 1978 SC 597). In this case the court almost equated procedure according to law to the American concept of due process. This has opened up for the court a wide vista of enquiry into every act of the government where individual freedom and other rights are alleged to be infringed or be likely to be infringed, in order to determine whether any such act violates the guaranteed Fundamental Rights and well-established freedoms of the individual. There are certain observations which show that it is not the view of the court that a right, which is not specifically mentioned by name, can never be a fundamental right within Article 19(2), or again the observation relating to ownership of property and what goddess Lakshmi symbolizes are to be considered pertinent. It is said "these unenumerated rights which are part of the rights of man and an integral part of his personality, his get-up and his very existence, though may not be specifically enumerated in the Constitution would nonetheless be recognized as the freedom of locomotion in and out of the country has been recognized." While interpreting Article 21, it is again said, "The principle of reasonableness which legally as well as philosophically is an essential element of equality or non-arbitrariness pervades Article 14 like a brooding omnipresence and the procedure contemplated by Article 21 must answer the test of reasonableness in order to conform with Article 14."

Another bright feature and progressive trend is the innovation of the Supreme Court in entertaining "public interest" cases even on letters of the concerned parties who are too poor to come to the Court or persons interested in the determination of an enquiry into injustice arising out of or in respect of an unconstitutional act. The only difficulty in this is the great burden which the Supreme Court will have to bear because of an on-rush of letters and petitions—many of which may or may not deserve to be considered or enquired into. It is also not right that letters addressed to particular Judges should be heard only by a Bench of which he is a member. Certain ground norms have to be evolved whereby all such letters should be sent to the Registrar for being placed before the Chief Justice of India for appropriate orders. It is the Chief Justice of India who has the jurisdiction to constitute Benches and therefore it is to him these petitions must be sent. Such public interest petitions may also be entertained by High Courts thus sharing the burden of the Supreme Court as suggested by the Bar Association of the Supreme Court recently. The criticism that the Judiciary does not help the poor in India is greatly blunted by this innovation.

Judges Surrender Autonomy

As against this progressive trend, there are two judgments, one regarding transfer of High Court Judges without their consent (*S.H. Sheth v. Union of India, 1977, SC 2328*) and another in what is known as *Judges' Case* (S.P. Gupta v. the President of India, AIR 1982 SC 148). In the first case the judgment of the Gujarat High Court which held that before a Judge of the High Court can be transferred his consent should be obtained was reversed by the Supreme Court which held that the consent of the Judge need not be obtained before he is transferred. This case arose out of a good number of transfers of Judges and Chief Justices of the High Courts during the Emergency, which action it was alleged was intended as a punitive measure against Judges who gave judgments against the Executive or otherwise incurred the wrath of the Executive. In the second case the Supreme Court, by a majority, handed over as it were on a platter, a declaration that the Executive has the power to override the views of the Chief Justice of a High Court as well as the Chief Justice of India in the appointment of Judges to the High Courts and to the Supreme Court of India. Till this decision was rendered, the views of the Chief Justice of India were being given primacy.[10] Thus the latter judgment has spread gloom and do not forebode well for the judicial independence which is so much the cherished objective of our Constitution. If Judges can be transferred by an executive fiat which has the primacy and if the Executive can also appoint them overruling the views of the Chief Justices so as to accord with the philosophy of the late Mohan Kumaramangalam which he enunciated on behalf of the government in defence of the supersession of judges, is it not a matter for concern and gloom ? No wonder the Chief Justice of India is suggesting a panel to be set up for recommending names of persons to be appointed as Judges so as to take away the unlimited power which the Supreme Court conceded to the Executive. This is intended to restore the confidence in the independence of the Judiciary. These matters being of great importance should, on an appropriate occasion, be considered by a Full Court or at any rate by a larger Bench of the Supreme Court.

Basic Values

If I may sum up my views on what a Constitution is and should envisage, it is that these questions depend on social conditions and attitudes. The cry of power to the people has dangerous portents. History has warned us against this. Lord Acton alluding to the episode of the Greek Commander of the battle of Argimisea (406 B.C.) being tried by the people as a whole and executed says, "The fate of every democracy, of every government based on the sovereignty of the people, depends on the choice it makes between these opposite principles : absolute power on the one hand, and on the other the restraints of legality and the authority of tradition. It must stand or fall according to its choice, whether to give the supremacy to the law or to the will of the people ; whether to constitute a moral association maintained by duty, or a physical one kept together by force." The respect and regard for the freedom of the individual, for the rule of law, and for human rights, reflects to a substantial extent in the Constitution and the Bill of Rights which a State adopts. This in turn depends upon whether the society for which a constitution is framed has achieved a measure of consciousness where its electorate not only has the prescience to elect proper representatives but also to compel them to fulfil the mandate given by it. In democracies where the franchise has been given in dosages over periods under pressure of its people, its functioning and accountability is sensitive to and conforms with its will as represented by the majority for which it has voted. In constitutions such as ours in India where irrespective of the immaturity of the electorate to understand issues, or notwithstanding the superstition, communalism, casteism, parochialism or regionalism and illiteracy prevalent in it, universal adult franchise is suddenly conferred, elections are won by a party and its leaders by throwing dust into its eyes. This state of affairs will continue till the electorate gets wise, becomes conscious of its rights, its duties, and its power—a stage which takes a long time to reach. In the meanwhile the ineptness of the electorate leads to corruption, inefficiency and callousness on the part of the party which it elects and which continues to exploit all the aforesaid features to win successive elections and to acquire a monopoly of power. The progressive increase in the consciousness and realization of its power at the polls by the electorate for choosing representatives who can influence the government to be accountable depends on increase in literacy by implementing the directives in Article 45 of the Constitution, a Press, free from censorship, on a desire to mete out political justice and on the society's commitment to traditions, values and attitudes. If these necessary concomitants are desired, they are provided for in the Constitution and are guaranteed. In this context it must also be noted that one of the most important elements which flow from the aforesaid guarantees is the right of dissent.

Dissent is a part of human nature and personality. Whenever two persons have to live together or do anything dissent raises its head. Dissent is a way of life in the family—the husband, the wife, the sons and daughters, all exhibit this trait in dealing with each other. Sometimes and perhaps often this makes life worthwhile, and living together with it makes it interesting. If you have no dissent in the family, life together wlll become a bore and insipid. Similarly dissent is an inseparable part of people and public life, particularly in a democracy. Representatives of the people and political leaders who administer the government or are in opposition have to learn to live with it rather than treat those who dissent as hostile and unfriendly. Unless we learn to tolerate it in public life as we tolerate it in our domestic life, our democracy will not function smoothly or effectively.

No doubt the nature of the relationship of the individual with others is the concern of each society and its government. When Constitutions, laws, institutions and social forces are inadequate to sustain a commitment to human rights, one can say that the society has failed. The hope for individual rights would then depend on forces beyond and abvoe the nation-state system. In all such situations the attitudes and values of large majority of individuals in a society, their determination to assert their rights and freedom against their government or a coterie or the caucus of the ruling party, will determine the kind of Constitution that suits it. If what they envisage is not obtainable from the Constitution because of the power structure that has been designed, then individual rights and the right of dissent are reduced to nothing. The strength of decisive public opinion and the determination to get the opinion accepted by placing limitation if necessary on the power of the government—these in a large measure will determine the quality of the government they desire and deserve. There is however the danger of the electors electing a leader who is likely to be a despot and when they do this they do not remain free for long, but the despotism is of their own making. It is, therefore, necessary for checks and balances to be built into a Constitution, to avoid such a contingency, which makes men use their liberty in such a way as to thereafter become slaves. The incorporation of a Bill of Rights or Fundamental Rights as in our Constitution, limiting the powers of the Executive and the Legislature, and the creation of an Independent Judiciary, is the only way of ensuring the survival of basic human rights and freedoms which the state should be powerless to take away. It is for this reason neither the American Constitution nor ours attempts to propound an ideology as its goal, though our Constitution seems to have been influenced by persons conversant with fabian socialism which is epitomized in the Directive Principles of State policy. The wisdom of the framers was in not laying a clear-cut political or public ideology or a politicized national interest. The Constitution neither incorporates nor projects a political manifesto. What the Constitution propounds as I have shown are values and freedoms which help the people to debate and choose without the fear of losing them altogether.

In the ultimate analysis it is the abiding consciousness and faith of the people in freedom and liberty, in their cherished rights and social values, in their desire to establish a Welfare State where the disadvantaged are no less entitled to justice, and in the freedom to choose as leaders men and women of character, integrity and a reasonable level of competence—it is in them that lie the safest and strongest foundations of a truly constitutional government.

FOOTNOTES

1. See generally, *History of Political Theory* by George Sabine and Thornson, pp. 641 to 644.
2. See *Liberty, Equality-Property and the Constitution*, P. Jaganmohan Reddy, Calcutta University, 1982, p. 48.
3. Ibid., 570-595.
4. *A History of Political Theory*, by Sabine and Thornson, p. 692.
5. I have in Sir Ashutosh Mukherjee Lectures on *Liberty, Equality, Property and the Constitution* (Calcutta University Press) dealt with these aspects in Lecture II, pp. 41-62.
6. "From Marx since his Death", by Professor Amartya Sen, Drummon Professor of Political Economy at Oxford University, *The Statesman*, March 14, 1983.
7. "In the opinion of Marxism, the liberation of the individual is impossible until the mass has been liberated." J. Stalin, "Anarchism or Socialism". I Sochienua (Collected works) (1946) 295-296 quoted in the *Soviet Legal System.*

   (Hazard Butler and Magged, 3rd ed., 1977) 84.

   Marx suggested that only in "Higher phase of Communist Society can the narrow bourgeois horizon of rights be left far behind all". Will society inscribe these now famous words on its learner? Marx, *The Critique of Gotha Programme* (1933) 31.
8. For Paine "Government has no right to make itself a Party" to the making of the Constitution; the Communist Constitutions were effectively granted by the Government to the people though later were formally called on to approve them.
9. See, an analysis of this case and the views expressed by David Gwynn 'Migran in "The Indian Essential Features" case', *International and Comparative Law Quarterly*, Vol. 30, 1981, pp. 307-337.
10. Compare the deep respect which Sardar Vallabhbhai Patel had for the Constitution and the value it embodied as seen from the book *Sardar's Letters—Mostly Unknown*, Post-Centenary, Vol. III, (Ed.) G.M. Nandurkar, Sardar Vallabhbhai Patel Smarak Bhavan, Ahmedabad. In it is mentioned that the Madras Chief Minister, Kumaraswamy Raja, was frothing at the mouth because the Chief Justice of India had rejected his nominee for appointment to the High Court, who was also supported by the Chief Justice of Madras, and

recommended someone else instead. Kumaraswamy Raja said in the letter, "The procedure of the Chief Justice of India himself suggesting the names is unusual and novel. It is also not in accordance with the instructions issued by the Government of India."

Not content with that, he proceeded to propound the doctrine of committed judges. Legal competence is not enough. The judges must also have a "sympathy with the State Governments", endeavours for the maintenance of social justice, peace and stability."

The Sardar gave him short shrift. "The Chief Justice can very well retort that, if all that he is expected to do is to register his approval to the proposal made by the State Government, it is quite pointless for him to be consulted and certainly the Constitution would not have provided for a mere formality to be observed. I do not think we can contest the right of the Chief Justice to make suggestions if he feels that a particular person would be suitable in preference to one already suggested by you, even though with the concurrence of the Chief Justice and the Governor."

The draft letter he sent to the Chief Minister for recording his views, which the C.M. gratefully accepted, omitted the commitment doctrine and cited, among "other factors", a capacity to hold the scales even.

From this it is evident that the Chief Justice of India was given great prominence and, in fact, even a suggestion of a name other than that recommended by both the Chief Justice of the State and the Chief Minister, was considered to be in order. This is because the Sardar had deeply respected the Constitution and the values it embodies.

* This is the first Prof. S. Venkataraman Endowment Lecture delivered by the author and published by Andhra University in August, 1983.

EIGHT

RAJEEV DHAVAN

REFORM OF THE INDIAN CONSTITUTION*

A Prefatory Comment

Constitutional reform has played a very important part in Indian "establishment" politics. From the middle of the nineteenth century to the present century, Indian "establishment" politics has produced many proposals for the creation, sustenance and reform of various constitutional structures.

In this context, the word "establishment" has been taken to include those people who possess power under the existing constitutional set-up or those who want and have a reasonable expectation of possessing power in the existing constitutional set-up or any alternative constitutional set-up which has a reasonably good chance of emerging. Those who have "power" are taken, in this context, to include those who make decisions in any particular set-up and those who have access to and influence over those who make decisions or over the processes by which decisions are made.

Over the past hundred years, the "establishment" in India has constantly publicized and dramatized its quest for an appropriate constitutional set-up. Even though the many proposals put forward by the "establishment" have been much publicized, there has, in fact, not always been controversy about the proposals that were put forward and accepted. This apparent lack of controversy may imply at least two possible conclusions. The first possible conclusion is the possibility that there was a consensus in the "establishment" as to its normative expectations about the present constitutional set-up or about the alternative possibilities that might exist. It is highly likely that such a consensus did not exist or was, or is even possible. The second possible conclusion is that the "establishment" was not really too worried about the actual constitutional set-up that had emerged or was going to emerge as long as, it paid some lip-service to certain liberal democratic presuppositions and was flexible enough to accommodate the aspirations of the "establishment". The emphasis on paying lip-service to certain liberal democratic notions was necessary partly because it was—and, to some extent is—part of the "establishment" mileau and partly because it was useful as a negotiating ploy—whether symbolic or otherwise—to satisfy the British that India would retain the liberal democratic traditions which the "establishment" in Britain believed in. This would also assure the perpetuation and continuance of certain trends in foreign relations. The emphasis on flexibility was necessay because a flexible structure would not only reproduce the existing social *status quo* but also permit accommodating changes in the event of the existing *status quo* becoming vulnerable to the claims of other "power aspiring" members within the existing or emerging "establishment".

By and large, the "establishment" in India discussed their predilections about constitutional matters (i.e., the formal distribution of power) amongst themselves. This is hardly surprising. Any "establishment" anywhere in the world tries to settle these questions within itself unless it becomes absolutely necessary for the "establishment" to extend the discussion to a constituency outside the "establishment". Sometimes it becomes necessary for the "establishment"—or part of an "establishment"—in any country take a discussion on constitutional matters outside the "establishment". This may arise because of pressures from within or without the "establishment" or other external pressures. The "masses"—as they are sometimes called in India—were involved in the "freedom" movement. But, this was done on the basis that constitutional matters would be discussed by the the leaders and not within the movement as a whole. Since then—and perhaps as a result of patterns set during the "freedom" movement—constitutional discussion has remained a privilege and responsibility of the "establishment".

In India, most social and political institutions suffer the

advantage of survival. The Indian social system is both rigid and flexible. It is rigid because the social system is designed on the basis of status notions which are fairly rigid and which cannot be upset or changed easily. At the same time, the social system is also flexible because its stability does not depend on the continuance of any particular legal or political system. Thus, social factors preponderate to dominate any formal legal or political structure which is created. The fact that a parliamentary system was superimposed on India's polity really meant that those who had social power had to change their *modus operandi.* The norms of the new legal and constitutional order were not instrumental in evolving any significant changes in the social *status quo.* Any changes that occurred in the social *status quo* were not really induced as a result of the institution of the new legal and constitutional order which has remained, by and large, malleable in the hands of those who possess social power. This does not mean that social changes have not occurred in India. Considerable social changes have taken place. The pressure of population, urban demographic shifts in the population whether due to economic or political reasons, the inequity of the existing social *status quo* and the latent possibilities of the growth of opportunism and varying kinds of expectation in the Indian people have all led to various changes. As it happens, this has not really led to any significant changes in the constitutional and legal system which has been internally re-adapted for dealing with these differential demands.

While the constitutional and legal system is susceptible to an adaptable incrementalism, it is not really capable of inducing changes in the social *status quo* on its own. If India decides to abandon its fate to this adaptative incrementalism, it must be prepared to compromise its conscience by accepting the continuance of glaring inequalities. The word "glaring" is not intended to indulge the dramatic. It is merely to make a realistic description of what actually exists. Even if the "establishment" decides to treat the question as a management rather than a moral question, it would be forced to accept that even as a management question, the problems of India have already exceeded dangerous levels. At a certain point, the distrust and discontentment engendered by the existing state of affairs will make things impossible to manage. Looked at as a moral question, the persistence of these inequalities make it quite clear that the quaint oddities through which these inequalities are expressed can no longer really be treated as cultural relics which must be preserved and enioyed for their own sake as part of "the wonder that was India".

The real difficulty lies in the fact that any legal or constitutional move which is based on paradigms on which the constitutional and legal system has hitherto been based are not likely to be effective. In the past, the social *status quo* has proved to be much too strong against any of these moves. It is this and the continuing belief in the moral untenability of the existing social *status quo* that has necessitated the need to look for alternative paradigms on the basis of which changes can be made.

In this paper, we have divided the area of inquiry into five distinct areas each of which is dealt with separately. These areas are as follows :

(*i*) Perceptions of Constitutional Development in India ;
(*ii*) Political Mobilization-Participation, Accountability and Responsibility ;
(*iii*) The Regional Distribution of Power ;
(*iv*) Rights and Duties in the Indian Legal System ;
(*v*) Dispute Settlement in India.

Each of these areas is discussed in the sections that follow.

The discussion in the sections that follow proceeds on a basis that is quite different from the one on which the "establishment" has viewed legal and constitutional reform. The manner in which the "establishment" has viewed constitutional and legal reform has been discussed only by way of juxtaposition in order to emphasize the differences that exist between the pattern that has been evolved in this paper and the pattern or patterns that have been suggested and evolved by the "establishment". The views of the "establishment" have been expressed in various documents which have been listed in the Appendix to this paper. Even if these documents do not always contain what the "establishment" has wanted to say, they do contain what the "establishment" has managed to say.

I. Perceptions of Constitutional Development in India

People perceive constitutional developments for all kinds of purposes and in all kinds of ways. Some people may perceive a particular form of constitutional development simply in order to get themselves into a position of power or to sustain the position of power which they have. Some people may want to create certain constitutional structures to camouflage their attempt to obtain or retain power. Some people may ganuinely believe that the society in which they live will be benefited by their obtaining or retaining power. Some people may take the view that although the projected or existing constitutional structure is theoretically open to the possibility of someone else coming into power, it is almost certain that these other persons will not get into power. Some people may take the view that what is important is not that one or another group of people capture power but that a system be created so that whoever does get into power is chosen from a small range of competing alternatives. It is very rare—in fact, it is virtually impossible—to find people who create constitutional structures for their own sake. And those that do are often motivated to follow through a certain "idea" with a crusading tenacity.

The people responsible for planning India's constitutional development in the nineteenth and twentieth centuries were motivated by all kinds of considerations. The Indian leaders were anxious to evolve a system whereby Indians could govern themselves. They knew that this would, in effect, mean that power would pass from the British to a small Indian group. Nobody in those days had any doubt that the power that would come as a result of "freedom" would pass on to this small elite. Very few people took the view that this was necessarily a bad thing. Of course, not everyone who formed part of this elite would obtain the gifts of power. And so, throughout the "freedom" movement we find all kinds of disputes about how people would be selected for office. Sometimes these disputes take the form of controversies about the strategies that ought to be followed in order to achieve "freedom". Sometimes the disputes are about the constitutional structures that should be set up. The latter controversies are very rare. This may have been partly because of the strategic reason that the movement had to show itself off as being a cohesive movement. This was also because the movement was not wholly concerned about the constitutional structure. This is probably because the people who were part of the "freedom" movement were aware that any liberal democratic structure would be able to accommodate the political wants, desires and expectations of a large number of the elite.

It is important to bear this in mind while reading the formal expressions of the constitutional expectations of those who were in charge of the "freedom" movement. These formal expressions contain the usual liberal democratic inclusions which were prevalent at the time. These—as the documents mentioned in the Appendix make clear—also contain some of the "anti-democratic" reservations which were prevalent at the time. There is a reference to the property vote in some of these documents.

But these various documents also display an affinity to the idea of accommodating a large part of the elite which were a part of the freedom movement. Thus, quotas of communal representation are a part and parcel of these documents. It is significant to note that these "testaments" of constitutional expectation proceeded from Indians and not the British. The "testaments" that we have chosen were not really negotiatory proposals of what the leaders could realistically expect to achieve. They were expressions of what the elite wanted.

The idea of accommodation (accommodating various sectors of the elite) is a very important component of liberal democracy. For that reason, the fact that it was imported into the constitutional perceptions of the leaders of the "freedom" movement is hardly surprising. After all, notions of "separation of powers" and "federalism" can be seen both as "rational" and "efficient" distributions of power (for it is claimed that they are at least that) as well as devices which pay lip-service to the idea of accommodation. But the idea of "accommodation" was also an important mechanism for the management of the "freedom" movement. The participants of the movement impliedly told themselves that there would be room for every body at various levels. Certain professional groups—like lawyers—were not very sure about their position. They prepared various schemes to make sure that their position was not ignored. Apart from these special reservations which were made for certain classes of people (usually, communal groups and "backward" classes) and a few professional groups, the basis for the constitutional perceptions underlying many constitutional proposals was to create a structure that would accommodate as many people as possible.

It was assumed that the structure would be efficacious but no real thought was given to that subject. It was also assumed that the structure was going to be fair because a large number of people were going to be accommodated in the name of a larger number of people within a structure which, at least theoretically, invited everyone's participation. These attitudes are quite apparent in the famous debate on the "Motion on the Draft Constitution" in the winter of 1948. In particular Ambedkar's introductory speech in which he explained why he had chosen the individual rather than the group as his starting point merits and repays study.

The idea of "accommodation" was a very important idea. On the one hand it led to the creation of Pakistan ; on the other it led to creation of a strange political morality in India. Everybody assumed that the Constitution was created only as a "free for all" to be exploited by various elite groups. In other words, while in other liberal democracies elite groups evolve various mechanisms in order to discipline the distribution of power, Indian elites having entrenched themselves in what seemed like a comfortable position seemed to have ignored the need for the continuous operation of a political morality to monitor the distribution of the spoils of the system. As it happened this also suited those members of the elite who wanted to use the 'free for all' system. It also helped various elites to create new alliances and accommodate new pressures and the rise of new elites.

It is not being suggested that constitutional development should not concern itself with the mechanics of how people and groups obtain and preserve power. It is only important to note two important aspects of perceptions of constitutional development in India. The first is that the idea of "accommodation" was a very important part of decision making. In this process of accommodation, the needs, aspirations and wants of a large number of people were completely overlooked. The second is that the overall goals of Indian constitutional development were not really discussed for a very long time. The discussion on the latter emerges in a concrete shape only during the Constituent Assembly debates. And even at this juncture the negotiations over the idea of accommodation were so significant that the discussion on the overall goals often breaks into an unconvincing rhetoric. As a result an important teleological dimension has always been missing from perceptions of constitutional development. India's constitutional elite have often tried to fill this uncomfortable gap by relying on hortatory tactics.

We need to reassess our perceptions of constitutional development. Constitutional development is not just concerned with power sharing. It is also concerned with basic issues of what a society wants and needs and why. After 1947, the "establishment" in India has declared a commitment to certain equalitarian goals on the basis of plans to create an industrial base and promote re-distribution of wealth and opportunity. These plans have, more often than not, accommodated political and social pressures with a resilience which has jeopardized the viability of the plans. In order to preserve this resilience, no real alternative constitutional perceptions have emerged.

II. Political Mobilization-Participation, Accountability and Responsibility

(i)

People dominate other people for all kinds of reasons. The weapons used for this process of domination are very varied. They range from a direct and unabashed use of force to a range of more subtle forms of domination. In one sense the state represents a form of domination. It is interesting to see how this form of domination is explained or justified. The classical form of explanation found in religious literature and works of political theory is that this process of domination became necessary because it was impossible to govern society on any other basis. In religious works such a breakdown in society is explained on various bases and in various ways. Governments are set up as part of a pattern of restoration. In works of political theory such a notion of breakdown is described more directly. The level of "remedial" restoration depends on the extent of the breakdown. This kind of explanation is not just peculiar to the techniques of arguments used by the Western contractualists. It is an explanation which has also been used in the Chapters 59 and 67 of the *Shanti Parva* of the Mahabharata.

The upshot of this notion of breakdown is the creation of certain kinds of justification for the existence of government. Both of these justifications seek to try to show that the purpose of government is for the benefit of the people. The *first* of these justifications lies in what may be called a broad concept of "trusteeship". The underlying idea is that government is contained within the conspectus of a "trust". The purpose of government is to ensure that this trust is discharged. The purpose of this "trust" concept is to legitimize the notion of government in terms other than those which suggest that the function of government is to permit the domination of one person or group of people by another person or group of people. There is, of course, a considerable amount of disputation as to the origins of this "trust". The explanations range from the idea of divine right to theories of an imaginary notional "trust" based on some concept of need or inevitability. There is also some disputation as to the kind of action that may have to be taken if there was a "breach of trust". Some theories did not counsel any kind of action ; other theories suggested—as was suggested in a significant passage in the *Anusasana Parva* of the Mahabharata (Chapter 61 sl. 31-33)—that in the event of such a breach of "trust" the king should be "slain like a mad dog". A particular difficulty with "trust" theories was that in a large number of cases the system of restraint that was imposed and envisaged was a moral one. Remedial action was not really envisaged except as an extremely marginal expression of oppression and revulsion. Needless to say, even this was not always conceded. The essential point is that having reposed the "trust" in an all-powerful state, there was really no logical or structural method by which a breach of trust could be controlled or monitored. Any system of correction that could be used could only be devised by the ruler as a magnanimous gesture or an exercise in management.

The *second* justification that was offered for the existence of government was that the government acted in the name of the people. This was a different argument from the "trust" argument. Under the "trust" argument the people were just beneficiaries under the system of government. Further, under the "trust" argument it was not really necessary that the people should be the makers or the beneficiaries of the "trust". We shall call this alternative justification the "agency" concept. This argument takes the position that the government is an agent of the people. It has to act on their behalf. The nature of the agency and the manner in which it has arisen has given rise to a great number of controversies. The controversies have been concerned with the relationship between the people and their agents. One set of these controversies relates to the manner in which the agents are selected. Various kinds of structural alternatives have been put forward. Most selection procedures have in fact resulted in certain social and economic elites being chosen as the agents. In fact, theories have also been evolved to suggest that the purpose of the selection is, in fact, to choose between "competing elites". The second set of these controversies relates to the manner in which the agents can be controlled. There are various attitudes to this process of control. Some of these are consciously worked out ; some of the attitudes have been unthinkingly worked out resulting in what can be called "government by default". The "no control" or "little control" position has been explained and justified in various ways. In this context, one argument is the time argument. This argument has been based on the idea that the agents must be given some latitude over a certain period of time. This argument has been further justified on the basis that the agent cannot be treated as a delegate whose efficiency can be interfered with whenever the delegators want to interfere with it. Other arguments have also been made on the basis of the notion of efficiency. Constant interference with the work of agents will make government impossible. The "extended" control view is defended on various grounds. There is the fear of the accumulation of power. This fear is even more pronounced in the minds of those elite who are not in power. They feel that if there is little control of the elite in power then it would be impossible for the non-governing elite to obtain any kind of power.

Over the years it has become quite apparent that a system based on the "agency" concept cannot really be continued on the basis of a "no control" or a "little control" position. This concern has not always solely arisen out of a desire to give the people a greater control over their rulers. Management considerations have also played a very important part in sustaining the movement away from a "no control" or "little control" position. The people have been asked to participate in the control of their agents because it is one way the anxieties of the people can also be given expression while at the same time assisting elites to control the proclivities of their internal and external competitors. Economic and technological changes have ensured that these anxieties, frustrations, wants and needs of the people cannot be totally ignored. Nor are the elite always prepared to provide solutions for all that the people want. Indeed, if that were possible, no government would be necessary. And so, many agencies have been created to give the people greater control over the agents who govern for the people and in their name.

Both these models of government, namely, the "trust" model and the "agency" model, are really top-down models. This is certainly true of the "trust" model. It is also true of the "agency" model because the "agency" model—and the democratic system that it is based on—is really a way in which the power of any elite or group of elites can be "legitimated" by using the idea of "agency" and the apparatus of democratic structures. The real question is whether it might be better to try and devise a model which starts building itself from below rather than one which is either imposed from above or one which "legitimates" the continuation of a particular dominant position in society? In this sense the problem lies in trying to create a new model which is based on the notion of participation both as an end in itself and as a *modus operandi*. The notion of accountability which relies on the concept of "agency" is subordinated to the notion of participation. The participation envisaged under this kind of set-up is a direct form of participation to the exclusion—wherever possible—of structures based on accountability through the "agency" principle.

The notion of participation operates on two bases. At one level it urges a quest for structures of government which are more participatory than those envisaged by the notions of "trust" and "agency". At another level the idea of participation serves as a principle of evaluation. All this rests on the presupposition that participation is necessarily a good thing. Management versions of participation invariably vary from the kind of participation which is being considered here. Even where the structure of management sponsored participation has been similar to the structure used by non-management or direct forms of participation, the dominant ideological motivation supporting each of these structures is quite radically different.

(ii)

In India the dominant style of government has been based on the "trust" model. In ancient times the implications of the "trust" model were explored in great depth. Alongside the "agency" model was also operated in some republics but it is not wholly clear as to how successfully the "agency" model operated. It is also not clear as to whether the "agency" model was really no more than an arbitrary way in which variations of the "trust" model were operated. The "agency" model often operated against considerable internal and external hostility. Both the "trust" and "agency" models were often used to cloak an arbitrary assumption of power for the purpose of domination.

Indian rulers—no less modern leaders as their medieval and ancient counterparts—used the vehicle of the "trust" concept to denote, justify or rationalize—as the case may be—their role in government, the idea being that the rulers were entitled to rule and they should be trusted on the basis that they can be relied upon to rule properly. The people were, and are, often invited to participate in the activities of the "trustee" elite. But this participation did not and does not take place on the basis of the choice of the participant. The participation of the people was often invited on a stage that was already set out for them. An interesting example of this is the "freedom" movement. People were given the choice of either being inspired to participate on a particular basis or not participating at all. This is not just in cases where the "freedom" movement was itself lost in a state of controversy or indecision about the strategy that ought to be followed. It arises more poignantly in the case of certain other social movements which were, in various ways, not permitted to choose forms of expression or pursue demands which did not align with—or were approved by—the custodians of the "freedom" movement.

When the Constitution was framed the genuine participatory alternatives were really ignored. Instead a modality of operation that was chosen was that of trying to continue the "trustee" system by using the apparatus of the "agency" system. This was done in this way. It was generally agreed by the elite that they had a right to rule. The idea was to create a very broad-based government in which many of these elite could be given the right to rule. The best form of government through which this could be done is a collegiate form of government in the parliamentary style. This style of government was adopted. Along with it the apparatus of the "agency" model was also operated.

Under this system the "trustees" styled themselves as such on the basis of certain notions of "status". Since India is run on the basis of status rather than agency notions, the induction of a "trustee" into the government usually meant the induction of a large number of status relations and relationships which were part of the "trustee's" entourage. This bred what lawyers would call corruption. It also provided a method of building a system of social and political alliances.

The big pressure on this "trustee-agency" system—trustee in fact and agency in style—did not come from people demanding that the "agency" apparatus should be made to work in an agency way. The real threat to the "trustee-status" system came because of a swell in the size of self-styled "trustees". Many people came forward and wanted to be regarded as "trustees". There was nothing wrong with this self-declaratory process as an expression of individual personality. The only real difficulty that it created was that the political and administrative system could not give all these people the power and prestige that they wanted. It certainly could not accommodate all these people along with their status relationships. This is where the problems began to surface. The self-styled political "trustees" realized that there was one position that they could achieve with considerable alacrity. They could use the "agency" structure to put themselves into some kind of position of power. And so, a lot of members of various Legislatures and Councils found themselves elected into office. They could now pose as both "agents" and "trustees". This made the position even more difficult. The difficulty arose because there were a lot of "trustees" who were looking for power. This is because they believed that they were fit to rule. Any doubts in that area were cleared by the fact that they had been cleared through the agency structure. This resulted in what can be called a run on the political system. The "trustees" had increased. They wanted power. They decided to get this power by whatever manoeuvres that were available to them. Their task was made considerably easier because the "agency" structure of the parliamentary system did not lay down very clear rules as to how it was to be operated. It depended in its operation on the existence of an institutional morality. Indian "trustees" broke the back of this institutional morality. In fact, they even used the "agency" structure to their advantage whenever they needed to do so.

The number of "trustees" in India is increasing. India is one of the few countries where all the politicians—with very few exceptions—are self-styled "trustees". They do not really want agency support even though they need it from time to time when there is need to indulge in a show of strength. It is also important to remember that politicians are not the only self-styled trustees in India. Administrators and others are also either trustees or part of some trustee's entourage.

One of Mrs. Gandhi's major planks during the Emergency was to reform the "trusteeship" system. She did *not* want to create an "agency" system. Nor did she want to create a participatory system. What she want to do was to reduce the number of "trustees". This the existing "trustees" did not like. As soon as Mrs. Gandhi talked about the creation of a presidential system, many "trustees" realized that this would reduce the opportunities of power which they had. By a series of clever moves they decided to oppose this move. At the same time, some "trustees" joined Mrs. Gandhi's government while others either waited for the chance to join or oppose a government which had reduced the possibilities of their getting into power. The tussle for power continues and will continue.

This account of the working of the "trusteeship" model in India would suggest that India is not really a democracy even in the sense of being based on the notions of "agency". The "agency" facade is both a window dressing and a legitimating device to help fill the credibility gap in the event of the "trustees" not being what they claim to be. Equally, the experiments in "local democracy" are not really exercises in participatory democracy. On the one hand they are vehicles of management control, and on the other they fall into the general pattern of "trusteeship" government in India. It gives an opportunity for government by local "trustees". It also gives regional and national "trustees" the opportunity to use these experiments in local participation to exercise their patronage by giving people in their entourage the opportunity to exploit local opportunities. All kinds of further relationships as well as flimsy alliances are built up on this basis.

All this may sound very severe. There are some people who at least operate "agency" principles. Equally, there are also examples of various social movements which have used the participatory principle effectively. But these are few. India is in a position where it is burdened by an ever increasing number of "trustees". The institutional means of removing and dealing with these "trustees" are very a few. A proper participatory movement may have to by-pass the "trustees". There may not be that much room left for negotiations.

III. The Regional Distribution of Power

The geographic distribution of power becomes necessary for a number of reasons. The first is that those in power of a large regional unit find it very difficult to devise ways and means to govern the system. They have to devise schemes in order to make this control more effective. In order to make this control viable they can use all kinds of methods of control. A very simple method would be to keep the area under control through the use of force. The problem that this creates is that in order to sustain this force over a period of time those in power have to rely upon the medium of a group of trusted people. This is not always possible. And so, those in power have to resort to all kinds of other methods in trying to make sure that there is no social and political entropy in ensuring the continuance of central control over the whole region.

In his *Arthasastra*, Kautilya suggests a large number of fair and foul measures as to how this control can be imposed.[1] These methods were not always approved by other elites in India. Professor R.C. Maujamdar describes the divergent lines of thinking as follows :

> "Kautilya and the author of Ch. 107 of the *Shanti Parva* of the Mahabharata represents two distinct schools of political thought. The former was in favour of a strong monarchy and regarded the republican states as the chief centres of opposition to his policy. Here he recomended their destruction by all means fair or foul of which a lucid account is given in the *Arthasastra*. The other school was in favour of democratic forms of government and was anxious to preserve them from the dangers to which they are naturally exposed. The chief of these were disunion and dissension and lack of secrecy. Hence they recommended forbearance and toleration

and the formation of small cabinets of select leaders."[2]

This is one basic decision that has to be made with every federal structure. The basic decision is about whether local "republics" will be protected or not. The Indian Constitution was designed to make sure that Kautilya's attitude was not overlooked. The Constitution contains various mechanisms to ensure that the government had a range of "fair" and "foul" constitutional means in order to protect the power of the centre. Apart from fiscal provisions and the existence of some all India cadre bureaucracy there were also provisions for political interference with the smaller geographic units that formed part of the Union. The most significant of these provisions is the provision which permits the Union to impose President's Rule in the states. This power has been used indiscriminately by various governments.[3] Various proposals put forward by Mrs. Gandhi in the famous Forty-second Amendment were calculated to increase the range of mechanisms of political control by the Union on the States.

The issue as to whether one should tolerate local "republics" raises many issues. Kautilya's attitude seems to openly put forward the view that the centre should have control because that is a good thing in itself. This is not surprising. Kautilya's work was probably advice to kings who wanted to know how they could retain their power. Kautilya devised a policy which enabled the king to obtain what he wanted. And so, if the local "republic" was tolerated it was not because Kautilya thought "local democracy" was necessarily a good thing. The toleration of local "republics" was evolved on the basis of a management device of allowing people to do whatever they like because disturbing them would make them more difficult to control.

While much of what Kautilya said still holds, *mutatis mutandis*, in modern times, modern governments do not justify the retention of central control as being an end in itself. They argue that central control is necessary to achieve certain ends. In the main, these ends are twofold in nature. The first is the viability of the political unit as a whole and the second is the achievement and sustenance of the social and economic betterment of the people.

If one assumes that the division of the world into various viable political units is a good thing, then it is not wrong to evolve policies to sustain the viability of these units. There are only two major reservations to this. The first is that the attempt to maintain the viability of the unit must not defeat the overall perspective that governments are for the betterment of all. This leads to the second reservation which is that the elite in power must not use the excuse of the viability of the unit as a cloak to preserve the viability of their own power.

The viability of the political geographic unit must, indubitably, be linked to the advancement of the people in that unit. Many governments spend so much time, energy and resources in keeping the unit together—whether for their own purposes or other purposes—that they ignore the social and economic arguments that are also advanced to support the need for a centralized federalism.

Let us, however, look at the attempts to achieve the goals of social and economic advancement. One of the arguments that is made is that policy decisions have to be made centrally so that the resources—human and others—are distributed in the best possible manner. This argument is, to some extent, based on the false assumption that planning is a theoretical exercise which can be worked out centrally. Policy decisions at this level involve two very difficult components. The first of these components consists of the range of choices that ought to be made to further the social and economic advancement of the people. This is a choice that has to be made by the people because they are the beneficiaries and also victims of any planning endeavours. The choice is not just a moral choice. It has strategic implications which may affect the viability of the plan. The second component is a pragmatic version of the first component. A plan has a feasibility component. Whatever is planned must, to some extent, be regarded as feasible and acceptable. If this does not happen the plan will not succeed. *The central argument that is being put forword is this : for both pragmatic and ethical reasons there has to be a participatory input even at the policy-making stage.*

This argument is even more poignant when we consider the implemental strategy of a plan. At the implemental level, there is, on the one hand, the need to evolve adaptive mechanisms whereby a plan can be moderated to local conditions. On the other there is a great danger that this process of adaptation may distort and disturb inputs of the plan. The line between adaption and distortion is very thin. It is therefore necessary to evolve plans in which the distortion or abuse element is minimized. To begin with, this can be achieved only by taking a realistic view of the feasibility of the plan. This argument needs to be explored further. It is by no means being suggested that a good plan should be abandoned simply because the chances of its success are low due to the presence of some vested interests who will almost certainly, distort the plan to serve their own advantage. Any instrumental plan faces all kinds of difficulties. No plan can succeed unless it is able to marshal resources to meet these difficulties. These resources cannot just consist of the use of sledge-hammer techniques to compel compliance with the plan. In fact, even to sustain sledge-hammer techniques the participation of the beneficiaries of the plan is necessary and desirable. The central thrust of all this is that planning and participation far from being antithetical to each other are in effect important mutual support mechanisms. In most countries the participatory input into planning is overlooked. It is replaced by various mechanisms ranging from the hortatory to the "tough"—which are not a substitute for it.

This participatory input need not take place on a geographic basis. This latter point was very effectively made by Mr. Derek Senor in his dissent to the Royal Commission on Local Government in England (1969) :

> "The right view in my approach is to analyse functional and democratic needs in relation to patterns of settlement, activity and community structure in which a motor-age society organised itself. This analysis points out to a general need to define units in terms of potential service and community hinterlands of major centres for the functions associated with planning, transportation and development in terms of the accessibility and population size for the personal services. In a few parts of the country the units so defined coincide and all criteria can be satisfied by a single all-purpose authority. Elsewhere a two-tier level structure is indicated as the only means of reconciling functional effectiveness and local democracy."[4]

No doubt, India is not in the "motor-age", nor is planning in

India concerned only with the distribution of personal services. The need to rely solely on certain patterns of geographic decentralization at certain levels for certain purposes may be even more necessary in India. There is a need to experiment. Some of these experiments have been discussed. The Reports on the Community Development Scheme and National Extension Services (1958), the Report of the Committee on Panchayat Raj (1978) and the various reports of the Administrative Reforms Commission are examples of the exploration of experimental alternatives. But all these experiments seemed to be committed to a particular view of centralism which augurs against the grain, the sentiment behind these experimental ideas.

Quite apart from the pragmatic considerations of making plans more effective, it is an important value consideration to experiment in more direct forms of democracy. This is argued on the basis that one of the central elements of a democracy is to give people a direct participatory role in respect of the decisions that are made about them. In India, this is not always possible. Experiments in direct democracy create and sustain elite structures rather than elite participation. But this does not mean that these experiments in direct democracy should be abandoned. It only means that a combination of correction devices have to be designed from above and below in order to ensure that direct democracy is participatory in nature. We need, of course, to be constantly aware of the danger of correctional devices swallowing the whole concept of participation.

Finally, the distribution of power between the Centre and the States should not take place on such a rigid structural basis that participatory experiments in planning, decision making as well as local democracy may be difficult to sustain.

IV. Rights and Duties in the Indian Legal System

(i)

Indian constitutional experts tend to think of rights in a rather peculiar way. They seem to believe that the rights and responsibilities of the Indian people can be elicited from the Fundamental Rights Chapters of the Indian Constitution (read with the Directive Principles of State Policy). They also seem to believe that the real disagreements about the protection of rights and duties arise because there are sharp differences as to what should be contained in the Fundamental Rights part of the Constitution and in the Directive Principles of State Policy. Some of these constitutional experts tend to feel that if better methods of "access" to the protection of rights were made available, the problem of the maintenance of rights and responsibilities would be solved. The provision of Fundamental Rights cannot by itself be used to maintain a comprehensive system of rights and duties. In real terms the technique used in the Indian Constitution consists of ear-marking certain fundamental rights for preferential enforcement by direct access to certain higher courts. We will call this the "preferred rights technique". This technique represents a very minor part of the strategy in maintaining rights and duties. It consists of protecting a small range of rights for the benefit of those who can afford the resource and motivation of exploiting the procedure which have been laid down. It is directed to deal with complaints against the "state" after some action has occurred or is imminent.

The problem of the protection of rights and responsibilities is a much larger problem. It consists of trying to adjust a large number of claims that exist in any society. It stems from a realization that these rights and responsibilities cannot just be maintained by the judiciary. Nor can they be maintained by other governmental institutional means. People invariably discover that they have to use various institutional and non-institutional means in order to exploit their rights. It is society, and not just the state, that is involved in the maintenance of rights and duties.

Let us begin by distinguishing between a "claim" and a "legal right". By "claim" we mean any want or expectation whether it is recognized by the legal system or not. The legal system operates on the notion of a "pre-existing" right. This means that, at least theoretically, the legal system recognizes only a certain kind of "designated" right which is known to ante-date a claim that is made. This means that every kind of claim will not be recognized. There is a considerable dispute amongst jurists and philosophers as to what a designated right is or ought to consist of. One view is that a "designated" right is one that is designated by the State. This view has been criticized on the basis that it gives the State the arbitrary position of determining what rights it wants to protect and what rights it does not want to protect.

Quite apart from the fact that the State may be susceptible to influence as to the kind of rights it ought to protect, those that link rights with the state seem to think that it is illogical to think that we should define a "legal" right as something which exists independent of the state when we know that the main purpose of "designating" the right is to ensure that the state will enforce that right.

In the "common law" world, those that support a wider notion of a "legal right" seem to institutionally locate the maintenance of this wider notion of a "legal right" in the hands of the judiciary. The judiciary is regarded as being in a crucial position. The theory is that although the judiciary is bound to accept and validate the rights which have been "designated" by various political processes in a society, they have a further power to absorb these "politically designated rights" into a wider notion of rights. The judiciary, according to this line of argument, has the power to indulge a process of "re-designation" and recognize a wider range of theory. The viability of this approach depends very greatly on the position of the judiciary. If the judiciary is in a political position to "re-designate" "politically designated" rights, it might be successful in this endeavour. Quite apart from the question as to whether the judiciary has the political muscle and the training and background to be in charge of this process of "re-designation", the assumption that the judiciary should be the "trustee" of this endeavour may leave a lot to be desired. To begin with, the basis of the working of the judiciary, which decides matters according to law, is the notion of a "pre-existing" right. The notion of a "pre-existnig" right need not be abandoned in the sense that the process of "re-designation" can be linked up to the wider notion of right which could also be treated as "pre-existing". However, what is central to the operation of the judiciary is the idea a "pre-existing right". The function of the judiciary is not supposed to negotiate a decision between two parties. The function of the judiciary is to decide matters according to certain "designated" (and, according to another line of approach, "re-designated") standards. The judiciary can either accept the political "designation" process or concentrate on creating a "re-designation" process. What it cannot do as long as it is a judiciary is to abandon its role of a decision-making authority which decides according to "pre-existing" standards.

If the judiciary decides to give up, wholly or in part, its adherence to politically designated standards, it must devise alternatives of its own.

Where can, and should, these alternatives come from ? One approach is to suggest that the judiciary should evolve principles as it goes along. If these principles are *ad hoc* and arbitrary, there is a danger in the judiciary abandoning its function as a judiciary. It is this danger that is overlooked by judges and jurists who put forward the view that judges should decide according to the "needs" that arise before them. To say that judges must respond to needs is unexceptional. The real problems arise in relation to unifying judicial concepts of "needs" in such a way that the judge is still deciding according to standards. An alternative approach is to argue that these standards are not just *ad hoc* or arbitrary responses to "needs" or any other kind of existential situation, however it may be described. These standards are supposed to represent "rational" principles.

There are some difficulties with the idea of using "rational" principles as standards pointing to the existence of pre-existing rights. The first difficulty is that in its operational practice, this approach militates against the idea of deciding according to clear "pre-existing" standards. The reason for this is that these rational principles—and the logical methodology which guides their enunciation and fromulation—are very general. Even if certain basic principles can be universalized, there is considerable room for disagreement on the emphasis and weight that we may give to the operation of certain principles. This is borne out empirically. So, in the long run the reliance on "rational" principles as providing standards may result in fact in creating a model of "decision making by controversy". The fact that the controversies are loosely channelled in a particular direction does not wholly alter the basic premises on which the model will, and will be expected to, operate.

Quite apart from judicial decision making, it can be, and has been, argued that all governments should proceed on the basis of a certain commitment to certain values. This is not just a commitment that one expects from the judiciary. Therefore, the political designation of rights is also supposed to be guided by a need to maintain certain rights and responsibilities. In fact, the task of "political" institutions and processes is much more difficult because they have to create and maintain certain standards in the face of all kinds of pressures.

The real question then becomes what is the role of the judiciary as a corrective to the perceptions of the political institutions and processes ? Its correctional task must be conditioned by its own social and political position. In another context, the present writer has argued that the correctional role should be limited.[5] It was argued that judges were bureaucrats who had to decide according to "instructions" (i.e., "law" received from politically active institutions and process). In the discharge of their bureaucratic function, they had to sensitively respond to their "instructions" (which also form part of a system of the maintenance of rights and responsibilities). It is the concept of discretion which really gives judges and other bureaucrats the opportunity to evolve or complete the system of rights and duties that exists or ought to exist. It is, however, important to note that the correctional role that ought to be given to the judiciary, in preference to political institutions and processes, cannot be determined on the basis of some unanswerable logic. It is a political question. This political question can be answered only by considering what rights and responsibilities ought to be maintained in any society, and which institution in that particular society is best suited to maintain these rights and responsibilities. It may well transpire that institutions and processes other than the judiciary and judicial processes are better equipped to maintain certain or all rights and duties.

One of the central arguments in this paper is a commitment to the idea that the purpose of any concept of rights and duties is to prevent the exploitation of one person or group by another person or group. This is not based on the notion that all people are equal but on the idea that every person or group has the right to pursue their creativity. No principle of priority needs to be given, as a preliminary starting measure, to one kind of creativity over any other kind of creativity. This paper also argues that the commitment to achieve these purposes cannot be located in any one institution or in a single legal system of rights and duties. Accordingly, strategies such as those of politically "designated" rights, judicially "re-designated" rights, "re-defined" rights are really partial strategies. Sometimes these strategies may be effective ; sometimes they may not. Sometimes no governmental institutional strategy may suffice. Sometimes a combination of many kinds of strategies may have to be devised.

The strategy of chcosing a strategy is not always easy. It is important to distinguish between "policies" and "strategies". A policy is a formulation of what ought to be done. A strategy is a plan of what is going to be done. The distinction is not a distinction between a "plan" or its "implementation". "Policy" is used here as representing a suggestion of the hypothesis that ought to be pursued. The "strategy" contains both the "plan" and its "implementation". It is consistent with both the theme of "non-exploitation" and the theme of "creativity" that while "policies" can emerge from people at the "top" of whatever hierarchical machinery that may exist, "strategies" can emerge only at the "grass-root" level at which people live.

(ii)

Let us turn to the manner in which rights and responsibilites are maintained in India. In order to do this we need to explore three ways in which rights are perceived in India. The *first* way in which people and groups perceive their rights is through the notion of "*status*". Many people view their rights as entitlement arising out of "status". Status is a very important notion in Indian society. It is acquired in various ways—traditional or otherwise. It gives the person who holds this status certain rights and certain responsibilities. The *second* way to explore the manner in which rights are perceived in India is the notion of *need*. People see "rights" as an entitlement to certain kinds of needs. They perceive their needs in various ways and argue that it is their right that their needs should be fulfilled. The *third* way in which rights are perceived is that they are seen as providing *opportunities*. The purpose behind this notion of opportunity is that rights are anabling provisions which would give people the opportunity to do what they want to do. The notion of opportunity has been used in various ways. Some people have used the concept of opportunity to exploit the resources of the country ; others have used the notion of opportunity to perserve their status. Some people have used the notion of opportunity to fulfil their needs. The notion of opportunity has not been used very radically to support the themes of "non-exploitation" and "creativity" which have been mentioned earlier.

Now, let us see how these three perceptions of rights have been accommodated in the Indian legal system. We will concern ourselves with the modern twentieth century Indian legal system while not ignoring the elements of historical continuity wherever this is necessary. The system of law that was superimposed by the British did not really cater to the notions of "status" or the notion of "need". It was primarily concerned with providing opportunities and it designed a legal system which circumscribed the kinds of opportunities it would entertain and encourage. Amongst their priorities were the opportunities created through the ownership of property and the opportunities created through self-assumed transactional relations. The opportunity of creative expression was permitted to those who had property and advantagious transactional relations. The rest could pursue their creativity to the limited extent to which this could be permitted. It was assumed that the permissible limits to all this were determined by the overall strategy of devising a viable system which would preserve only certain kinds of opportunities for certain people. What was important, therefore, was the system by which these opportunities could be maintained. A complicated range of techniques was used to maintain this system. All kinds of laws were also used in order to render this management function possible. People were told in various ways—the law being only one way—that order was a good thing. Psychological techniques like the insistence on the preservation of a code of morality were also used. One of the biggest threats to the system was the fact that many of the "opportunity" enabling norms were so widely drafted that people could have used these opportunity enabling norms for purposes other than those for which these norms were really intended. In order to deal with this, two strategies were used. *Firstly*, a vast scheme of codification to ensure that the purpose behind some of these "opportunity" enabling norms could not be easily misunderstood. The *second* strategy was to make the exploitation of certain opportunities so difficult to attain that it would be impossible for a large number of people to attain them. This was either done by the direct methods of disenfranchisement or a more subtle use of creating social and economic stumbling blocks. As people became more conscious of their rights (i.e., opportunities) the methods of disenfranchisement became more and more subtle.

The British were still faced with insistent demands arising as a result of people perceiving their rights in relation to notions of status and need. Those in a position of status wanted to retain their status and the advantages of their status. Those in need pressed for the fulfilment of their need. The British responded to these kinds of rights in various ways. They realized that these kinds of rights cannot be ignored. The legal system was designed in such a way that some status rights were afforded protection. One of the ways in which this was done was by expressly accepting that rights emanating from certain customs and personal laws would be validated. In addition, to this there was also an attempt to draw a new kind of relationship between perceptions of rights as *status* and perceptions of rights as *opportunities.* Woven into the fabric of many personal laws was the idea that many status relationships notions could, in fact, be partly or wholly treated as transactional relations. This is certainly true of the manner in which notions of "trust" (in the strict sense in which it is used in English doctrines of equity) were introduced in the Hindu law relating to the joint family and religious endowments. Various people posesssing status rights were forced to use opportunity rights techniques and processes in order to maintain their status. A study of various personal laws shows how various status notions have been agitated through opportunity rights notions. This was not done successfully. A glaring example of this is the manner in which the Hindu view of marriage as giving rise to some status rights has been agitated in modern India through an opportunity based system of laws. The result has been disastrous. The disaster has been described very effectively by Professor Derrett in his *The Death of a Marriage Law* (1978).

Need-based rights were also given some attention by the British. The most glaring example of need were dealt with as a matter of priority by the administration and through the use of various legal and social techniques. Otherwise the underlying strategy of the legal system has been to encourage people to satisfy their needs through the opportunity-based system.

A lot of people began to use the opportunity-based system. This was done for all kinds of reasons. Some used the opportunity-based system to preserve their status. Some used the system to satisfy what they conceived to be their needs and some to exploit the system for whatever advantages that they could get. This led to a tremendous overload of the system. This also resulted to some curious results. Judges and administrations invented all kinds of techniques to attempt this gigantic operation of using an opportunity-based system to accommodate status rights and need rights.

After the British left, much of the pattern of rights and duties which were part of the British legal system was retained. The Constitution added to the rights system. The chapter on Fundamental Rights was opportunity based as well as status based. Need-based rights relating to positive discrimination were located in the Fundamental Rights chapter while other need-based perceptions were included as aspiratory assumptions and goals in the chapter on Directive Principles in the Constitution. Much constitutional interpretation of "fundamental rights" has depended on how judges viewed rights. Some judges were tolerant to status rights. They even read certain opportunity rights as status rights. Some judges went to the other extreme of reading status rights as opportunity rights. Still others sought to reform status rights on the basis of need or, in some other cases, opportunity notions.

Meanwhile, the government declared an attack on status rights and, to some extent, certain kinds of opportunity rights. Some of the attacks were purely declaratory. Some of the attacks on status rights were not to eliminate the notion of status rights. Much rather it was to adapt or create new status rights for those in power. Similarly, need-based programmes—such as land reform legislation—were often attacked, to support "status" rights as well as certain kinds of opportunity rights. A large amount of need-based legislation has suffered at the hands of status and opportunity notions. Opportunity here is being used in the sense of providing opportunities to some to exploit others. The basic social strategy of people in India is to continue to create status *niches* as long as it is secure to do so. As soon as these *niches* become insecure people use opportunity-based vehicles to either convert the existing status into a new status or to "free-wheel" the existing status into opportunity sectors. Need-based strategies suffer considerably because the prevalent system of rights and duties does not really accommodate them. This is partly because the need-based strategies are themselves half-hearted—or even devious—strategies. It is also because people with status rights and opportunity rights can manipulate the implementation of need-based strategies to their advantage.

One of the central problems as regards the maintenance of rights and duties in the Indian legal system is that the current legal system cannot be used by everyone for creative purposes. In fact, the system cannot even be used to implement "need"-based strategies. It cannot be used to prevent exploitation. It is dominated by notions of status rights. Where the system is opportunity based those in power have made sure that the opportunities provided by the system are controlled in various ways. People are either denied access to these opportunities or the opportunities themselves are defined in such a way that they can be used only to support certain status rights and opportunity rights.

But there has also been a breakdown in the notion of legality. This is *not* because of the pressure of needs. The breakdown has occurred because those with the advantages of status rights and opportunity rights find that legality stands in the way of their getting what they wanted. The result is that legality is really no more than a guideline which is noticed in its non-observance. The attitude to legality is one of convenience. Many people have been forced to seek their opportunities outside the legal system. Some have left the country. There are vast and powerful demographic movements within India. Those that seek to fulfil their rights outside the legal system are not just the needy. People with "status" rights and "opportunity" rights also exploit non-legal and illegal opportunities to preserve, sustain and expand their rights. Some of the people with "status" rights and "opportunity" rights defend the legal and administrative system because they will be more seriously affected by a breakdown in the system. Others shift in and out of the protection and use the system whenever it is convenient.

At the same time, there are also social movements involving those who are fighting for their "need"-based rights. Such movements try to use the system as well as travel in and out of it. In the long run, it is in the growth of social movements which are not geared to the achievement of "status" and opportunity" rights (the latter in the narrow sense) that the future of Indian society lies. The problems of India are such that social movements based on needs are not a bad thing. But, the concept of need is not enough. The ultimate aim of all movements concerned with the maintenance of rights and responsibilities must be to go beyond the notion of need.

V. Dispute Settlement in India

Before we go any further we need to analyse the concept of a "legal" dispute.

People quarrel about all kinds of things. Sometimes these quarrels are resolved with the same ease with which they were created. Sometimes these quarrels explode or jell into serious disputes. The persistence of these disputes does not just create problems for the disputants. It also creates problems for others. And so, the disputants and others—sometimes, others even against the will of disputants—often create dispute settlement machinery to deal with disputes that arise around them or in the society in which they live. The dispute settlement machinery can be of various types. It may simply seek to get the parties involved to try and resolve their differences. It may be an *ad hoc* machinery—awaking to resolve disputes as they arise. It may be a formal dispute settlement machinery set up either by certain people, groups or institutions. The term "formal" is defined later. It may be set up by an institution which claims to be the "state" or "government" of that society. The machinery may follow a very flexible approach and procedure. Alternatively it may lay down very strict requirements as to how a dispute is to be dealt with by the machinery in question. It may even accept only certain kind of disputes to constitute the kind of disputes which that machinery will deal with.

There is a vast amount of academic disputation as to the distinction between a "legal" dispute and a "non-legal" dispute. It could, of course, be argued that those concerned with the problems of society should not really concern themselves with splitting hairs in an effort to discover the distinction between "legal" and "non-legal" disputes. According to this line of reasoning, society has an interest in, and concern for, all disputes even though it may not be able to intervene in all of them. Therefore, the really significant distinction is not between "legal" disputes and "non-legal" disputes but between "serious" disputes which attract societal intervention and "non-serious" disputes which do not. Another way to explore the latter distinction is to distinguish between "self-contained" disputes and "spillover" disputes. The former are contained in their resolution by the disputants (perhaps, with the help of their immediate accessories); the latter have to be resolved by persons, groups and institutions other than the disputants (and perhaps, their immediate accessories).

In fact, society may not organize its dispute settlement machinery on this basis. It often creates formal dispute settlement machinery which resolves particular kinds of disputes to the exclusion of all others. It is not that this formal dispute settlement machinery deals with "serious" or "spillover" disputes. Those in charge of a society decide which disputes should be singled out for resolution through its formal dispute settlement machinery. In doing this, those in charge of society may be motivated by all kinds of varied considerations. They may designate dispute about certain matters (certain "rights") because they feel that these rights "deserve" to be dealt with that particular dispute settlement machinery. They might select these rights for resolution through that particular process out of a concern for the consolidation and continuance of their own status or power. They might select these rights as part of a management technique to facilitate the control of society. Some rights may be selected simply as a symbolic gesture in the knowledge that such rights would or could not be enforced. All kinds of motivations guide the selection of the rights which are designated for the resolution of the formal dispute settlement machinery.

At this stage, it might be possible to devise some kind of method for distinguishing a "legal" dispute from a "non-legal" one. One possible line of distinction is on the basis of the institutions which are responsible for dispute settlement. A "legal" dispute, according to this distinction, is one which is decided by a certain designated institution or process. A second possible line of distinction is to define a "legal" dispute as one which is concerned with some particular designated "right". The fundamental presupposition in both lines of reasoning is to correlate the definition of a "legal" dispute with a certain kind of process of designation.

The concept of designation plays a very vital role in determining the nature of a dispute in a society. A dispute which can be identified by this process of designation, i.e., (i) is the dispute about a designated right ? (ii) is the dispute resolved (or intended for resolution) by certain designated institutions and processes ?) is called a "legal" dispute.

There is, of course, nothing special about a "legal" dispute other than the fact that it can be identified by this process of designation. A "legal" dispute is not *per se* socially or ethically more important than a "non-legal" dispute. The word "legal" is not intended to attribute a magical quality that is lacking in other disputes other than the attribute of designation. We have already indicated that those responsible for this process of designation may be motivated by all kinds of considerations. The "legal" dispute which is a product of this process of designation cannot automatically win a further evaluative status of being the most worthy or deserving of disputes. It is also important to note that this designation process is not just the product of the rise of a centralized system of authority (i.e., the state) in society. Various groups may use a process of designation to varied extents and for various purposes. Thus, a group of people may use a process of designation to identify disputes other than those which are identified by any designating process set up by or linked to any centralized authority. There may not be any centralized authority. It is a moot question as to whether the title "legal" should be limited only to disputes associated with the state designating processes or whether it should be extended to disputes identified by other designating processes whether the state tolerates them or not ? In fact, the title "legal" has been given by some only to such disputes which are identified by the state designating processes. On this basis the distinguishing feature of a "legal" dispute lies in its relationship to and with state designating processes.

The view taken here is that the concept of a "legal" dispute in its widest sense means any dispute which is identified by any designating process. We will call a "legal" dispute in this sense a "formal" dispute. The concept of a "legal" dispute in its narrow sense means a "formal" dispute which is identified by reference to state designating processes. We shall call this kind of a "legal" dispute (i.e., a "legal" dispute in the narrow sense) an "officialized" dispute.

"Officialized" disputes (OD) may be related to "non-officialized" disputes (NOD, i.e., those "formal" disputes which are not identified by state designating processes (SDP)) in various ways :

I. The SDP may explicitly recognize the existence of some NOD and even make available (or insist on) the use of some OD machinery for the resolution of these NOD (We will call this relational category NOD-I).

II. The SDP may explicitly recognize the existence of some NOD leaving the latter to operate in their own sphere (We will call this relational category NOD-II).

III. The SDP may implicitly recognize the existence of some NOD which operate in their own sphere (We will call this relational category NOD-III).

IV. The SDP may either recognize or not recognize some NOD—the latter operating in their own sphere without any connection to either OD or SDP (We will call this relational category NOD-IV).

V. The SDP may be antithetical to some NOD—regarding the latter as "illegal", according to the former's normative standards (We will call this category NOD-V).

"Informal disputes" (ID) fall in a residuary category of their own. They are informal in the sense that neither the right sought to be vindicated nor the institution or process through which it is vindicated can be identified through any consistent process of designation—state or otherwise. There is a shadowy distinction between an ID and a mere quarrel. While a dispute involves conflicting or inconsistent claims in relation to an opportunity, a mere quarrel is not structured in this way.

Apart from the typologies we have created above, there is another theme which we need to explore in relation to the nature of disputes. This relates to the manner in which "rights" are designated in any dispute structure. We have already indicated that a designation process may either identify the "right" to be vindicated or the institution or process by which this right is to be vindicated, or both. Sometimes the emphasis may be on the nature of the right to be vindicated. Sometimes the dispute settlement methods may take a very flexible view of the notion of the "right" which is to be vindicated. Some dispute settlement methods may entertain any claim as long as it attracks the attention of certain designated processes or institutions. Dispute settlement methods which adhere very strictly to the notion of a pre-existing designated "right" as part of the *modus operandi* of that particular dispute settlement method can be said to be dispute settlement methods which decide disputes according to the rule of law. The central theoretical idea behind "rule of law" dispute settlement (RLDS) is that the right in dispute is deemed to have been recognized as subsisting at the time that the dispute occurred. The dispute in this case relates to whether a particular claim agitated through the dispute settlement method falls within the specified designated right or not ? Thus, RLDS takes place on the basis of already existing norms. Many methods of dispute settlement do not try—or even pretend to try—to resolve disputes on the basis of already existing norms. Dispute settlement which proceeds without an overt reference to already existing norms may be called "Non rule of law dispute settlement" (NRLDS). The emphasis in NRLDS may be on the wishes of the disputants or some goals to be achieved rather than existing norms.

Bearing these various distinctions in mind, let us look at dispute settlement in India.

(i)

India has a very large number of co-existing, though not necessarily cooperating, dispute settlement methods to deal with all kinds of disputes ranging from ID to OD and all the various varieties of NOD. The fact that such a wide range exists is often overlooked. Instead considerable emphasis is given by the government, lawyers, judges and academics to the OD system.

The OD system is given prominence for various reasons. *Firstly*, the OD system is very closely linked to the SDP. It helps to sustain, evolve and transmit certain values and norms which are part of the SDP. To this extent there is a very close relationship between the OD system and the SDP. The closeness of this relationship is not always highlighted because it is often assumed that there are a lot of conflicts between the OD system and governmental institutions (other than the judiciary) responsible for monitoring the SDP. There is no doubt that these conflicts exist. They exist as a natural concomitant to any OD system which permits the judiciary to invalidate the norms which are designated as valid by various branches of the SDP. But, despite these conflicts, it is important to note that the OD system survives and is sustained by a steady diet of normative guidelines which emerge from institutions and processes (other than the judiciary) which are part of the SDP. The government uses the OD system to preserve and sustain the kind of laws which they want to preserve.

Secondly, the OD systems is supported by those people, groups and institutions who feel that they can use the OD system to their advantage. These advantages can arise for various reasons. The norms of the OD system may be such that they can be used by some people, groups and institutions to their advantage to the exclusion of other people, groups and institutions. Apart from the advantages of the norms used by the OD system, the OD system may operate in such a way as to give preferential "access" to certain people, groups and institutions. The notion of "access" here is a very wide notion. It does not just concern itself with "resource access" (i.e., having the material resources to reach the OD system) but also with "motivational access" (i.e., having the personal and social motivation to reach and exploit the OD system).

Thirdly, the OD system is supported by professional lawyers and judges who not only support themselves through the OD system but also use their position within the OD system to create and sustain a social role and position for themselves. Inevitably, lawyers and judges often take the position that although they must accept the norms that arise out of the SDP, they have an independent critical attitude to the rights and duties of the people. This had led them to notionally evolve various kinds of fundamentalist philosophies and approaches (FPA) which are calculated to state their commitment to a range of values beyond the values that underlie the norms which are designated for application in the OD system. It is not always easy to react to these fundamentalist philosophies and approaches. A cynical attitude might suggest that much that is contained in these FPA is really rhetoric. A more benign attitude would be that such FPA are well meant and can be used by the OD system in its dispute settlement programme. This does, however, raise the question as to how effective the use of these FPA can be. Logically, the operation of these FPA may be severely limited by the persistence of the norms which have been designated for use by the OD system. Sometimes the FPA may play a very dominant role ; sometimes it may not. A lot really depends on the social position, prestige and status of those responsible for creating and sustaining the FPA. Despite the protestations of jurists like Ronald Dworkin, in his *Taking Rights Seriously* (1977), the FPA is not always created on the basis of rationalistic and universal principles. It is hardly surprising that much of the FPA derives sustenance from the norms which have been designated for use by the OD system. The FPA also derives considerable sustenance from the social backgrounds, wants and expectations of those who create and sustain the FPA. In India, it is uncommon for lawyers and judges to make a lot of social and political capital of their FPA. Since India became independent there has been a sustained volume of such declaratory exhortations. Many of these declarations are treated with a pinch of salt by persons other than lawyers and judges. The existence of these FPA do not even fundamentally influence the decision. Lawyers' dedication to their FPA is often belied by their own litigating practice whereby their talents are sold to only a few people. The manner in which judges use the FPA defies prediction and analysis. It has been shown that the Supreme Court of India has not really used its overtly declared FPA as a consistent guide to its decision making.

But let us return to India's OD system. It has run into a lot of trouble. One of the reasons for this is that there is a very wide gap between the manner in which the OD system is supposed to be used and the manner in which the OD system is actually used. India's OD system is theoretically based on what we earlier described as "rule of law" notions. To adapt the phraseology we used earlier, the OD system is theoretically a RLDS system. A RLDS system operates on the morality that people want and desire their disputes to be decided according to the rule of certain designated norms. The operational morality of the FLDS system requires those who use the system to carefully determine whether a designated right is, or is not, in dispute. A dispute arises only when there is a dispute as to the existence or interpretation of a designated right. A central feature of the OD system as it actually works in India is that litigants and their lawyers are not really concerned with whether they really have a "right" or not. They take the view that the OD system can be used to support any claims which they might want to put forward. They are not really concerned with whether the claim can be supported on the basis of an existing "right". They work on the assumption that, somehow or other, techniques can be evolved to fit any claim into some designated "right" or the other. This is not all. Lawyers and their litigants do not just use the OD system to get decisions according to law. They are *only* interested in results—whether interim or final. They are not interested in how the result is reached or whether the result is fair or just. Consequently, the OD system is exploited to achieve interim and other results. The operational morality which guides the use of the OD system is a "free for all" approach. This "free for all" approach has two important consequences. The first consequence is that this operational morality eats into the RLDS notions which are supposed to guide the working of the OD system. The system acquires certain *ad hoc* characteristics which makes the system unwieldy, arbitrary and unpredictable. This corrodes the concept of a designated "right". The second consequence is that there is a large volume of cases that make their way into the OD system. Everyone plays the system. The institution of cases towers over their disposal. Arrears of cases that are pending before the OD system increase. Cases have been known to have been pending for many, many years.

Now, how do we deal with this kind of OD system which only services a few people because a large number of people do not have "resource" and "motivational access" to the OD system and which has itself got clogged and distorted because the operational morality that has guided its use has destroyed the RLDS notions which are supposed to be the heart of the system? The government has reacted to this in various ways. The government's major reaction has been a mechanical reaction. It has been to make the OD system larger and more resourceful. The major move in this regard has been to create more judges in the hope that more judges will at least be able to deal with the increasing arrears of cases which have still to be cleared by the OD system. In addition there has also been some kind of attempt to reduce the number of cases that come to the higher courts in the hope that this might reduce the cases that are added to the docket of the higher courts and at the same time sustain a pattern of decision making in lower courts. Both these strategies have failed. The increase of judges has been matched by an ever increasing spiral of increasing arrears of cases. The increased number of judges has also meant that the courts which house this increased number of judges also lose a coherent institutional viability. The attempt to control the volume of cases which go to the higher courts has also failed. This is partly because lawyers and litigants invariably re-agitate cases through the hierarchy. At the same time, the courts have always been willing to accommodate this re-agitational strategy partly because it gives them more prominence.

The government has tried to respond to the problems of the OD in some other ways as well. One of these consists of an attempt to deal with the problem of "resource access". Several proposals have been made to provide legal aid. At a national level these proposals have been made in the Krishna Iyer Report : *Processual Justice to the People* (1973). Justice Krishna Iyer and Justice Bhagwati are both Supreme Court Judges. (The latter now the Chief Justice.) They have also tried to sustain a programme of legal aid as a constitutional right. Various proposals have also been made at state levels. The *Bhagwati-Krishna Iyer Report* also proposes that the government spread legal education and help to deal with problems of "motivational access". The governments of the Union and of various states have not been very forthright or generous in supporting various legal aid schemes. These moves to deal with the problems of "access" have a lot of limitations. To begin with they do not deal with the fundamental problem of "motivational access". The OD—or for that matter, any—system can be effective only if people use it. What stands in the way of its effective use is not just the problem of "resource access". Even after resources have been provided there is still the problem of "motivational access". People must be aware of their rights and be able and willing to pursue them. "Motivational access" is not easy to come by. *It may just transpire that the move to provide "motivational access" should come from below rather than above.* In addition to the problems of "access"—"resource" and "motivational"—the major underlying assumption behind these various legal aid proposals is that the RLDS basis of the OD system is necessarily a good thing. We have already indicated that there is very wide gap between the morality underlying a RLDS system and the operational morality which guides the use of India's OD system. In such a situation is there any point in injecting resources into a system in the knowledge that these increased resources will only increase the incidence of abuse of the system ?

An alternative strategy of reform has been to try and create links between OD systems and NOD systems. The *Report on Nyaya Panchayats* (1962) seemed to press for what we have earlier categorized as NOD-I. A policy of non-interference has also been launched in respect of categories NOD-II, NOD-III and NOD-IV. Not surprisingly, NOD-V are also tolerated—by a process of compromise and default. Tribunals have also been created in order to produce state-sponsored variations of NOD-I and to expand the OD on an NRLDS basis. Some very difficult problems have arisen out of the relationships between the OD and NOD systems. There has been a tendency to incorporate NOD systems as part of the OD system. This is done for two reasons—first, there is an assumption that NOD systems may be unjust because they may reproduce the inequities of the social order without creating ground-level correctional techniques to root out these inequities ; second, a desire to control NOD systems and the groups who run them. The absence of correctional techniques in NOD systems may, indeed, attract the intervention of the OD system. At the same time, we should readily assume that the NOD systems do not have, and cannot develop, their own correctional techniques. There is a big danger that OD systems may totally assimilate NOD systems.

The real problems of Indian dispute settlement may be summed up as follows :

(a) an overt reliance on the OD system as a method of dispensing justice ;
(b) a "gap" between the RLDS notions on which the OD system is based and the operational morality which guides the use of the OD system ;
(c) the persistence of an unrestrained "free for all" system which reduces the viability of the OD system ;
(d) a commitment of injecting resources into the OD system without examining whether the OD system is suited to India ;

(e) a low-key commitment to reform of dispute settlement methods because certain people, groups and institutions are quite happy with the OD and NOD systems that exist ;

(f) a low-key commitment to deal with the problem of "access" and especially ignoring the problems of "motivational access" ;

(g) the development of an uneasy relationship between OD and NOD systems in that there is a tendency to extend the control of OD systems over NOD systems ;

(h) an inability to look at "law" and dispute settlement from a wider point of view.

These are not the only problems. Our perception of problems depends to a great deal on our expectations. To that we now turn.

(ii)

Any plan for the reform of any system must depend on what we expect from the system. To begin with, we should consider whether dispute settlement institutions should be judged from the point of the democratic principles of "accountability" and "participation". We would like to support the view that the notions of "accountability" and 'participation' should be used to guide the creation, reform and critical evaluation of dispute settlement mechanisms. The reason for this is that all OD dispute settlement mechanisms tend to make very important decisions. These decisions affect the parties and others. In appellate court hierarchies, such as those which exist in India, courts at the higher end of the hierarchy make decisions which affect the whole legal system and those subject to it. Decision making should proceed on the basis that those affected by it should have a chance to control or influence the process of decision making. In this way, people can participate in the process of decision making which will be accountable to them. It is possible to various kinds of dispute settlement systems which permit a greater element of lay participation.

As a concommitant to notions of accountability and participation, it is also important to examine the notion of "choice". People should have some kind of choice about the manner in which they should resolve their disputes. Needless to say, there is always a danger that some people may—and do—impose their choices of dispute settlement mechanisms on others whom they dispute with. Clearly the notion of "choice" does not extend to "enforced choice". If we explore the notion of "choice" further, we would need to revaluate both the basis of RLDS systems as well as the relationship between OD systems and NOD systems. People may not want to resolve their disputes through externally designated "norms". They may prefer to follow "negotiatory" patterns rather than pursue their "designated entitlement". In fact, it is well known that much of the working of even OD systems has been assisted by the persistence of some non-RLDS mechanism. Equally, people may feel that their life is overrun with external standards which they have little hand in making. This leads us to look at the relationship between OD systems and NOD systems. OD systems should not dominate NOD systems in such a way as to limit the various choices that people may have about their choice of dispute settlement mechanisms. People must be able to create NOD systems which are suited to their genius. There is, no doubt, the problem of ensuring that both OD and NOD systems do not operate to the disadvantage of some people. Various correctional techniques need not just be imposed by and through OD systems. They can also arise in NOD systems *suo motu*.

"Access" based strategies are not enough. We need to ask what we are providing this "access" to and why? It is not enough to provide resources to support the legal order. It is also a question of making up our minds on the kind of legal order we would like.

Conclusion

In a sense there are no conclusions that a managerial "establishment" can draw from much that has been said earlier. No panacea or even immediate processual or institutional remedy has been suggested to deal with the many problems that the constitutional and legal order in India faces. There is only an implicit warning that the range of reforms envisaged by the "establishment" has really exhausted itself. It has gained partial success in the awareness that many of the projected changes could not have been made. There is also an implicit assumption in respect of some of the changes that it was not really desirable that these be achieved.

Apart from the mechanics of power—and the social *status quo* which gives rise to this power—the major impediment to even a "management" oriented reform has been an implicit belief in Indian "establishment" circles that India's polity will, despite its domination by the social *status quo*, muddle through the problems which India faces. Although protestations abound and there has been a lot of rhetoric to the contrary, the "establishment" looks at the problems that India faces as being management problems. They are problems that simply have to be dealt with because they are there. The mode through which they are dealt with is not to try and resolve the problem. Much rather, the objectives in dealing with the problem are to take the sting out of the problem so that its extreme features are minimized and social tension is reduced. These objectives have met with some success. The failures have not really surfaced. Social tension has been expressed in various ways and been dealt with in various ways. Sometimes the social tension has simply been re-channelled; sometimes it has been bought off by promises; sometimes it has cooled down by the achievement of immediate results and sometimes it has been ignored and suppressed.

The problem that the "establishment" in India faces is not to devise new and more efficient non-feudal methods by which social tension can be harnessed to achieve a greater efficiency in respect of planned change. The real problem is more fundamental. It consists of the establishment making up its mind whether they want to treat the governance of India as a purely management question or whether they want to lay the foundations of an efficacious participatory democracy before the latter catches up with the "establishment"? At present, the "establishment" seems very heavily committed to looking at India and India's problems from a highly personalized management, even if feudal, point of view.

FOOTNOTES

1. *Arthasastra* (Samasastry edition, 1967) Book III.
2. R.C. Majumdar in R.C. Majumdar *et al.* (ed.), *The History and Culture of the Indian People : The Age of Imperial Unity* (1968) 334.

3. For a study of the operation of these provisions see Rajeev Dhavan, *President's Rule in the States* (1978) generally.
4. (1969) Cmnd. 4040, Volume II, 159.
5. The arguments canvassed here are more fully explored in R. Dhavan, *Judicial Decision Making* (1979, Mimeo, Delhi University).

* This paper consists of and edited version of the introductory papers written by Rajeev Dhavan to a project edited by Rajeev Dhavan, Visiting Professor, University of Delhi, and Professor D.K. Singh, Dean, Faculty of Law, University of Delhi. The project is entitled : *Reform of the Indian Constitution : The Establishment Looks at Itself* (Faculty of Law, Delhi University, 1979, in two volumes). I am delighted to offer a revised version of these papers to a volume in honour of Sir Alladi Krishnaswami Aiyer whose undoubted contribution to the making of India's Constitution cannot be underestimated.

APPENDIX

THE "ESTABLISHMENT" LOOKS AT ITSELF : THE VIEWS OF THE "ESTABLISHMENT" ON CONSTITUTIONAL AND LEGAL REFORM

This is intended to be no more than a list of "official" and "semi-official" documents which express the establishment's views on reform. Needless to say, the selection is not intended to be exhaustive. The pattern of classification which is followed here is the same as the pattern that has been followed in the main paper. The basic classifications, as before, are as follows :

A. Perceptions on Constitutional Development in India .
B. Political Mobilization-Participation, Accountability and Responsibility.
C. The Regional Distribution of Power.
D. Rights and Duties in the Indian Legal System.
E. Dispute Settlement in India.

A. Perceptions on Constitutional Development in India

This section is really concerned with how constitutional reform was perceived before 1950. The main documents which take the form of symbolic representations of what the leaders of the "freedom" movement wanted included in their basic political testaments for the period. Reference should also be made to the Debate on the Draft Constitution in November, 1948. This debate is significant because it was the only occasion when the "establishment" discussed the proposed Constitution for India as a whole. The last and final debate in 1949 which resulted in the adoption of the Constitution was not really an effective debate. It was a mixture of eulogy—well intended or otherwise—and reactions to what had already become a *fait accompli.*

The significant documents for this section are :

(i) *Home Rule Scheme*, 1889.
(ii) *Constitution of India Bill*, 1925.

(iii) *Commonwealth af India Bill*, 1925.
(iv) Debate in the Constituent Assembly re : *Motion on the Draft Constitution* : VII *C.A.D.*—44-47, 209-394 ; 4-6 and 8-9 November, 1948

B. Political Mobilization, Accountability and Responsibility

This really concerns itself with the major moves made to acheive a new kind of political mobilization other than the mobilization envisaged under the Constitution of India, 1950.

By and large, there was no real plan to move away from the liberal democratic structure which had been adopted in the Constitution of 1950. In 1958, the *Balwantrai Mehta Report on Panchayati Raj* had concerned itself with local mobilization but this was concerned with the administrative delivery system rather than political mobilization. This is equally true of the *Ashok Mehta Report on Panchayat Raj* in 1978. Those reports have been included in the next section on "The Regional Distribution of Power".

Explicit proposals on the manner in which the declared pattern on political mobilization ought to change emerged only as a result of the Emergency. The most important of these proposals was an anonymous document which wanted to decrease the flexibility of the liberal democratic structure in the Constitution of 1950 and centralize the system of power, decision making and patronage. This move failed because the existing social and political *status quo* put up the rather clever fight of taking the controversy outside the elite "establishment" to a wider "establishment". This served as an effective bluff. A series of other moves followed which were recorded in the documents which have been referred to in this section.

The significant documents for this section are :

(i) Anonymous : *A Fresh Look at the Constitution*, 1976.
(ii) Interim and Final Reports of the Swaran Singh Committee, 1976.
(iii) The Constitution (Forty Second) Amendment Act, 1976.
(iv) The Constitution (Forty Third) Amendment Act, 1977.
(v) The Constitution (Forty Fourth) Amendment Act, 1978.

C. The Regional Distribution of Power

Soon after 1950, when the Constitution of India was promulgated, it became clear to at least a few of the members of the "establishment" that no planned changes were really possible unless there was a delivery system which took the planned changes to the villages and towns. This led to the *Balwant Rai Mehta Report* (1958) and the *Ashok Mehta Report* (1978). These—and the policies and institutional arrangements which they gave rise to—have to some extent been academic exercises because the social *status quo* in these villages and other smaller units was able to dominate and control the administrative machinery which had been inducted to introduce the planned change.

In the middle sixties the Administrative Reforms Commission (A.R.C.) (1966-8) considered a large number of aspects of the delivery system through which planned change was being introduced. Many of the Reports put forward by the Commission and its Study Teams considered the need to reassess the regional distribution of power.

Finally, there have also been political moves to review the distribution of power between the Centre and States. The first move in this regard was the *Rajmannar Report* (1971)—predictably from a non-Congress ministry in Tamil Nadu. The other move in this respect came from the Communist Party (Marxist) (CPM) which obtained power in West Bengal after the "Emergency" ended in 1977. The CPM in West Bengal did not have any share of the power in the Union government which was in the hands of the Janta Party.

The significant documents for this section are :

(i) *Report of the Team for the Study of the Community Projects and National Extension Service*, 1958 (Balwant Rai Mehta Report).

(ii) *Report of the A.R.C.'s Study Team on District Administration*, 1966-8.

(iii) *Report of Committee on Panchayati Raj Institutions*, 1978 (Ashok Mehta Report).

(iv) *Report of the A.R.C.'s Study Team on Centre-State Relations*, 1966-8.

(v) *Report of the A.R.C. on Centre-State Relations*, 1966-8.

(vi) *Report of the A.R.C.'s Study Team on Machinery of Planning*, 1966-8.

(vii) *Report of the A.R.C. on the Machinery of Planning*, 1966-8.

(viii) *Report of the A.R.C.'s Study Team on Financial Administration,* 1966-8.

D. Rights and Duties in the Indian Legal System

The basic strategy that has been used has been the designation of certain "preferred" rights in the Constitution. These are contained in the Fundamental Rights part of the Constitution (Part III). Part III has been amended various times by various constitutional amendment acts. There have been several reformist attempts to change the ordinary laws of the land. This has included social reform (i.e., the Hindu Code of 1955-6), re-distributive reform (land legislation in various states) and planning reform (legislation giving the government various kinds of planning control). Needless to say, all these kinds of legislation have suffered some kind of damage at the hands of the social *status quo*. There is no single document which states the views of the "establishment" on these matters even though various reports of the Law Commission of India can be consulted in addition to reports of parliamentary and other committees and commissions.

The documents listed in this section are in the main concerned with the "preferred" rights rather than the large number of other rights which have been incorporated as part of the Indian legal system other than the Constitution.

The significant constitutional document for this section is :

(i) Part III : Fundamental Rights, Constitution of India as amended.

E. Dispute Settlement in India

There have been several attempts to look at the mechanisms of dispute settlement in India. The basic trust of the "establishment" in this area has been to make the system more efficient (i.e., not to pile up arrears of cases in courts) and more accessible. The latter quest is a more recent concern. The solution provided has been to provide increased financial and personnel resources for this area while making a few procedural changes. These goals have been expressed in various reports of the Law Commission of India and in the Report of the Shah Committee which was specially appointed to consider ways and means by which the backlog of arrears of cases could be reduced in the High Courts of the various states. The question of legal aid has been discussed in the Krishna Iyer and Bhagwati Reports.

In addition to considering "resource" questions, the Committee on Nyaya Panchayats also considered the perpetuation of some "quasi-officialised" "grass-root" dispute settlement methods.

The significant reports in this area are :

(i) The Fourteenth Report of the Law Commission of India : *Reform of the Judicial Administration*, 1958.

(ii) The Fifty Eighth Report of the Law Commission of India : *Structure and Function of the Higher Judiciary in India*, 1978.

(iii) *High Court Arrears Committee*, 1972 (Shah Committee).

(iv) *Report of the Committee Processual Justice to the People*, 1973 (Krishna Iyer Report).

(v) *Report of the Committee on Juridicare : Equal Justice : Social Justice*, 1978 (Bhagwati Report).

(vi) *Report of Study Team on Nyaya Panchayats*, 1962.

U.S.S.R.

NINE

V. YE CHIRKIN

LAW AND SOCIAL PROGRESS IN DEVELOPING COUNTRIES

SOCIAL life and behaviour of people in the countries which threw off the yoke of colonial dependence (they are also called developing countries) are regulated by various social norms: customs and traditions, norms of morality, religious dogmas (Islam, Buddhism, etc.), norms of various organizations of which those or other people are members (corporate norms), and lastly, legal norms.

In the Eastern countries legal and non-legal norms are often closely interconnected. In some cases we see their syncretic nature (Hindu law), personalism of their functioning (a special range of legal and non-legal norms regulates relations in the given tribe or caste). Nevertheless, the law proper, while being still connected with morality or religion has already singled itself out of other social norms. It is a regulator only of such types of human behaviour as are considered socially important in the given State (though the evaluation of the socially important differs from country to country), which is characterized by an objective possibility of influencing such relations with the help of State coercion, for example, by legislative enactments in respect of Muslim and customary law. The ruling class (classes) of the developing countries with the help of law, using its ideological influence (for instance, the idea of a proper behaviour) and its role as the creator of models as well as the threat of State coercion, channels (attempts to channel) development along a definite course.

Consequently, the question of social purpose of law, its creative role in forming a new progressive order or defence of conservation of old and obsolete one is inseparably connected with the question ; which classes expressing their will in law are at the helm of power in that country which liberated itself from colonial yoke ?

Social Nature of Law in Developing Countries

This question is connected with certain difficulties because in developing countries sometimes there is no clear-cut polarization of class forces and the structure of law is very complex. In these countries, for instance, many Acts of colonial period are still in force (for example, the French Civil Code of 1804 in French-speaking African countries, some laws of the Ottoman Empire in Iraq and the Criminal Code of 1862 in India), mediaeval Muslim law (covering a part of the Indian population), customary law the sourccs of which are rooted in primeval-communal relations and, lastly, newly adopted comprehensive legislation.

New legislation is also not uniform. Some Acts were passed immediately after winning independence but are still in force after the direction of development of the country has radically changed (as for instance, as a result of revolutions in Congo, Madagaskar, etc., stopped capitalist development and took the road of socialist orientation). There are other countries which have broken up capitalist development and now are socialist-oriented states. How can social character and social role of a complex set of legal norms in developing countries be evaluated in these conditions ?

It must be stated, first of all, that despite the functioning of legal norms stemming from different socio-economic formations and types of State (feudal one in Ethiopia, bourgeois one in Nicaragua, capitalist oriented in Madagaskar etc.) each country has one system of law, though it may be not uniform and sometimes possessing inner contradictions. Old and obsolete legal norms which are survivals of the past are preserved by new governments to the extent to which they do not contradict interests of the ruling class (classes). Being filled with a new content these norms are used for the aims which do not correspond to and sometimes contradict, their original purpose. Thus, the will of the ruling class (classes) transforms the whole structure of law, breaking up old forms of customary, Moslem, and colonial law, changing their functions and directing the development of law in accordance with a new system of ties and relations.

Hence, the social character of law in developing countries is determined by the class nature of the State. In those developing countries where strata of the bourgeoisie, or bloc of the bourgeoisie with the landowners, is at the helm of power, and the State is of a bourgeois type, law is also, on the whole, of a bourgeois nature and functions in the interests of capitalist development of the country. In the countries of capitalist orientation (these are mainly small and backward countries of tropical Africa and Oceania) where power belongs to a pro-bourgeoie social entity representing a farming class of the bourgeoisie (now it is called bureaucratic-bourgeoisie) tends the law towards a bourgeois type. In the States of socialist orientation (Algeria, Angola, Ethiopia, People's Democratic Republic of Yemen, Nicaragua etc.) law tends towards a socialist type.

It must be emphasized, however, that this general evaluation of law is possible only if we take the whole aggregate of legal Acts and take law as a whole. The essence of law cannot be evaluated correctly (because of its complex structure in developing countries) if individual acts or separate, isolated norms only are taken, for instance, housing or criminal legislation. A conclusion on typological nature of law can be drawn only on the basis of the whole aggregate of norms, the law on the whole, concentrating attention on the fact how law regulates issues affecting vital interests of various classes of society (workers, peasants, the bourgeoisie and landowners).

The Old and New in the Law of Developing Countries

The old which is preserved in the law of developing countries is heterogeneous. It seems that a distinction must be made between the two basic strata of the old. First, the old is represented by legal institutions inherited from even pre-colonial, semi-colonial or old feudal society (for instance, judicial authority of tribal chiefs, or absence of the institution of private ownership of land in common African law), institutions of marriage and divorce in Muslim law, laws of Ottoman Empire. Second, a special stratum of the old law is formed by the acts passed during the colonial period and are still in force. Besides that, in a number of countries of socialist orientation, there function acts passed after the independence, but during the development along capitalist lines.

The attitude of new governments towards various acts of the old law is not uniform. The traditional institutions connected with tribalism and feudal structures are being abolished. This policy is most resolutely pursued in the countries of socialist orientation, but in the countries of capitalist orientation this also takes place for paving the way for capitalist development (for instance, abolition of administrative authority of chiefs). It was exactly for this purpose that legislation was passed on abolition of communal land and ownership was abolished and plots of land were allotted as private property of peasants in Senegal in 1964 and 1976.

At the same time some traditional institutions continue to exsit. Even in some socialist-oriented countries during the implementation of land reforms Islamic norms were used, and some norms of customary law were used during the formation of local state organs (for instance, in creating Ujamaah in Tanzania and Fukunuluna in Madagaskar).

As already noted, Acts passed during the colonial period are used more widely. In India many laws passed by colonialists were revised but even now many old Acts are still in force. These Acts passed by imperialist colonialists correspond by their typological nature to capitalist development of liberated countries. That is why the question of complete abolition of colonial legislation does not arise in the given group of countries, and only those Acts and norms are abolished which contradict the sovereignty of the new State.

Many old Acts of the colonial period including codes are in force in countries of socialist orientation as well. In Tanzania and Zimbabwe some British court precedents are used. In fact, an almost complete renovation of legislation has been carried out only in Algeria.

In order to overcome old legal institutions various methods are used. They include : (1) adoption of new Constitutions (they are in force in all countries) and renovation of the old legisiation on this basis ; new legislation enables organs of the new State to function freely without being limited by legal Acts of former metropoly ; (2) filling old Acts with new content, their new interpretation, which in fact equals to their abolition "from within" ; (3) actions by popular masses "from below", the masses practically break up old norms (for instance, liberation of the Algerian government from limitations imposed upon it by 1962 Evian agreements which did not allow nationalization. As a result of actions by popular masses managing committees were set up at enterprises and farms left by colonialists. Thus popular masses actually carried out nationalization and laid the foundation of a self-governing sector of economy). The partial nationalisation de facto before the adoption of a law has been brought about by working masses directly in Angola, in Guinea-Bissar, in Nicaragua etc.

Contemporary development of law in liberated countries is, to an ever increasing extent, determined by new legal Acts and institutions. This, to a greater extent, pertains to countries of socialist orientation where new legal institutions are set up as a result of revolutionary activities of the new government, of creative activities of popular masses, and, ultimately, as a result of the impact of ideas of socialist law which are used in concrete conditions of respective countries of socialist orientation. Below we shall analyse four main spheres of social life—economic, social, political and intellectual, where some new institutions have been set up.

Influence of some ideas of socialist law can be found also in some capitalist-oriented countries (for instance, legal institutions connected mainly with protection of State property, adoption of development plans in the form of laws and the taking into consideration national, territorial and linguistic movements in creating a federation or granting autonomy).

It must be noted, however, that even in the countries of socialist orientation old legal norms are squeezed out by new legislation, they in turn also penetrate it, and they are sanctioned by it (for instance, constitutional norms of some Arab countries concerning Islam as the source of legislation and state religion, new laws permitting in some cases polygamous marriages, etc.).

Role of Law in Economic, Political and Cultural Development

Emergence of new States on the ruins of colonial system is always a result of the victory of revolution regardless of the nature of the national liberation struggle, whether it is peaceful or armed. As a result of the victory of the revolution State power is transferred from the hands of colonialists of the metropoly into the hands of that or other classes of former colony, and "the passing of State power from one class to another", V.I. Lenin pointed out, "is the first, the principal, the basic sign of a revolution, both in the strictly scientific and in the practical political meaning of this term."[1]

After the victory of a national liberation revolution (countries of capitalist orientation) or in the conditions of a democratic revolution's growing into a socialist one (States of socialist orientation) State power becomes more active in order to consolidate or create a new order, and therefore legal regulation becomes more active too. The aim of political regulation in the countries of capitalist orientation is consolidation of capitalist system with the use of both original institutions (for instance, Pakistan, Guyana, Papua-New Guinea) and models of capitalist countries (the so-called political modernization).

To transform society along capitalist lines institutions made by bourgeois law are used. In the sphere of economy it is the institution of private property, freedom of treaties, joint stock companies as a form of mobilization of capital, capitalist monopoly (monopolies exist in India, Egypt and some other developing countries) institution of a private company (etc.), which is used for an accumulation of capital, etc. In the sphere of social relations it is the institution of the power of the owner of an enterprise, alliance of the bourgeoisie with other exploiting strata, etc. In the sphere of politics it is the institutions of bourgeois parliamentarism, "division of power administration", bourgeois concept of State employees, bureaucratic centralization and administrative trusteeship by appointed officials over the activities of local representative organs, etc. In the sphere of intellectual life of society it is the creation of such legal conditions which promote consolidation of bourgeois ideology in using specific conceptions (Negritude in Senegal, Mobutism in Zaire, Arab or African "socialism" which actually conceals capitalist road of development, etc.).

However, in the countries developing along capitalist lines the active role of law is limited by the fact that the new society maturing there is an exploiting society, similar in its nature to former socio-economic formations.

In the countries of socialist orientation it is another matter. Here law plays not only a more active role, it also plays a creative role. This is due to the fact that in this case prerequisites of such a society are being created (socialist) which principally differ from all preceding formations.

As the 26th CPSU Congress noted, despite the existing distinctions the main directions of development of countries of socialist orientation, which takes place in complex conditions, are similar. "These include gradual elimination of the position of imperialist monopoly, of the local big bourgeoisie and the feudal elements, and restriction of foreign capital. They include efforts by the people's State to secure commanding heights in the economy and to go on to planned development of the productive forces, and encouragement of the cooperative movement in the countryside. They include enhancing of the role of the working masses in society, and gradually reinforcing the state apparatus with national personnel faithful to the people. They include anti-imperialist foreign policy. Revolutionary parties expressing the interests of the broad mass of the working people are growing stronger there."[2]

To ensure non-capitalist transformation of society, first of all, new legal institutions are used as well as old legal norms are filled with new content. In order to create a non-capitalist economic system legal institutions are used which ensure priority of the development of State sector, co-operation of small producers, gradual limitation and ousting of foreign monopolies, State control over their activities, the use of national capital in the interests of the development of the country limiting simultaneously the sphere of its activities, perspective planning, etc. Aims of creation and consolidation of a political system of socialist orientation are served by institutions strengthening the leading role of a revolutionary-democratic party (though sometimes this role is interpreted as the "supremacy of the party", constitutional power of the party), unity of State power, implementation of democratic centralism, the role of the Soviets as a political basis of the State, promotion of activities of mass public organizations, socio-economic rights of citizens, etc. New social relations become increasingly strong as a result of implementation of constitutional norms consolidating the alliance of the workers and peasants, creation of a bloc (united front) of all petriotic forces, participation of the working people in the management of enterprises, development of education and culture, new way of life, etc. Intellectual life in countries of social orientation is formed under the influence of such legal institutions which promote consolidation of revolutionary-democratic and emergence of embryos of the Marxist-Leninist ideology.

In other words, law of the countries of socialist orientation actively promotes the emergence of social relations of a new type. However, levels of the development of law are different. In this connection a distinction is made between national-democratic law and national-democratic people's law of socialist orientation the latter being a direct stage of transition to law of socialist orientation.

But this way is difficult and long, due to the backwardness of developing countries inherited from colonial times, the interference of imperialism and inner reaction, striving to stop socialist orientation by intervention or military coups d'Etat (coup d'Etat in Ghana in 1966, American intervention in 1983 in Grenada, etc.). If socialist orientation is broken up or gradually lost (as in Egypt or in Somalia in 1970), the socialist "embryos", elements in socialist oriented law are being liquidated, the nature of law becomes bourgeois or capitalist/oriented one.

Conclusion

Law is an active tool of State power in transforming social relations. Application of this tool is determined by the social nature of State power. Therefore, in developing countries law is used either to form and consolidate capitalist order or to ensure socialist orientation of the country. In the first case its positive role is connected, first of all, with abolition of backward, precapitalist forms because bourgeois society represents a higher degree of development compared, for instance, with feudal society. However, here the creative role of law is limited. The genuine social progress of newly-liberated countries is connected with socialism. That is why a truly creative role of law, and better use of its possibilities, exists in the countries of socialist orientation.

FOOTNOTES

1. V.I. Lenin, *Complete Works*, Vol. 24, p. 44.
2. Report of the CPSU Central Committee to the 26th Congress of the Communist Party of the Soviet Union and the Current Tasks of the Party in Home and Foreign Policy delivered by Comrade L.I. Brezhnev, General Secretary of the CPSU Central Committee, February 23, 1981. *Moscow News*, Supplement to Issue No. 9, 1981 p. 3.

YUGOSLAVIA

TEN

BOZO ZEPIC

RIGHT TO SELF-MANAGEMENT IN THE CONSTITUTION OF YUGOSLAVIA

Introduction

Many theoreticians in the world, and in Yugoslavia, who are considered to be experts on Yugoslav Constitution, define this basic legal document as a genuine document of self-management. According to most of its characteristics, it really is a genuine one : a man has the inviolable self-managing position in the society ; people have freedom and equal rights (no matter what is their social background, nationality or religion) ; people and nationalities are equal, they are united and fraternized freely in the federative socialist community ; the governmental (social) structure is based on the authority of the working class and all working people. Many constitutional norms regulate the untouchable rights of workers to self-management that give rise to many other legal and self-managing right of working class.

Establishing, in its basic principles, numerous facts which represent the inviolable base for the position and the role of a man in Yugoslav society, among other things, the Constitution emphasizes "the right to self-management on the basis of which each working man has the equal right to decide about his work, the conditions and results of his work, his own and common interests in the direction of social development, he can create the authorities and manage other social affairs." In fact this attitude expresses the essence of self-management. The point is to establish a society in which each worker and each man will participate indirectly in managing and making decisions concerning his work and his existence. That is why the Constitution defines the rights to self-management as the inviolable right of working people which means that these rights belong to them by The Constitution and nobody can deprive them of these rights ; if ever it is done, then it is an unconstitutional act. Self-management is not only a right but also an obligation, which means that the worker is obliged not only to participate actively in the work of self-managing bodies but also to make decisions responsibly and consciously together with other workers. The decisions are the result of the best proposals, their joint consideration, selection and adoption, while the essential social and individual interests are considered.

Constitutional Changes and the Development of Self-management

Although it is considered that Yugoslave self-management is deeply rooted in the essential events and heritage of the socialist revolution when the people's liberation committees, which were the first bodies of the people's authority and the embryo of the future socialist State . . . were formed, in fact the genuine self-management started later. The period from the victory of the socialist revolution in 1945 to 1949 is considered to be the period of reconstruction of the country. That period is characterized by the administrative central economy management.

Owing to dynamic development, and the quick and deep changes Yugoslavia has changed the Constitution several times for relatively short periods of time. Each change meant the enlargement and the deepening of self-management, or the ending of one stage of development and beginning of a new one.

The first stage lasted from 1945 to 1953. During this period self-management was not on the level of a constitutional right. In this period the first steps were towards introducing and legal-standardizing of the right to self-management. Before passing the law, in 1949, "Instructions for forming the workers' Council" were issued. The first workers' council was formed in the cement factory at Solin near Split. Experimental workers' councils were also formed in other working organizations. Introducing the experimental workers' council the workers got the insight into the defined problems of enterprise managing. They started indirectly to influence the decision-making and to get the first experience which confirms the correctness of this orientation, that is to say, to rely on own working class. This one-year experience was a base for passing the law in 1959 on Transmitting the Managing of Enterprises to Working Collectives. Tito, in his report referring to the law, said in the National Assembly : "There may be someone who thinks that this Law is passed too early that workers could not overcome the complicated procedure of managing the factories and the other enterprises. Whoever thinks so, is wrong to have such an opinion for it would mean that we do not trust our workers, that we cannot see that their participating in decision making will develop their creative force. This law will open the larger perspectives for their future, for the future of community."

By this law self-management was introduced not to all economy branches, nor to the public sector but only to factories, mines, transport, traffic, trade, agricultural and forest economy enterprises. The role of State and State plan is still given importance. The workers' council as the managing body of an enterprise is introduced but directors are appointed by the competent state authorities. The workers' council or Managing board recommends dismissal of the director of an enterprise. The role of the managing board is very important as it can make important managerial decisions. The director is the member of the board ex-officio, and is the representative of the State in this enterprise. The workers' council allows the essential plans and annual balance-sheet of the enterprise, elects and dismisses the managing board, makes the distribution of part of funds available to the enterprise, issues the regulations of the enterprise which are confirmed by the competent body and does other things.

With the passing of the Constitutional law in 1953, the second stage in the development started. For the first time self-management became a constitutional right of the working people. The number of branches and organisations in which self-management is to be introduced was enlarged and some vital branches such as railways, postal services could be organized on self-management basis. The enterprise independency from the State increased, especially, when income is in question or earnings realized by operating profit. Nevertheless the total accumulation of social means are owned by the State. Considerable experience was gained and for a short time good results were achieved. It was a base for further changes towards the development of self-management.

With the passing of the Constitution of 1963, the third stage started. It was primarily characterized by the broadening of working collectives' rights to independent managing and organizing. The self-management decision making was enlarged, in this stage of development, to managing the means of social reproduction. The investment funds of socio-political communities ceased to be regarded as funds of accumulation owned by the State and State apparatus. Accumulation was more and more available to working organizations.

Socially-owned property on the means for production, which excludes the returning of any system of exploitation of one side by the other, and the worker's self-management in his working organization and municipality as the basic socio-political community, became the important factors of the inviolable base of the new position and the role of man. They enabled him to develop his personality by various activities in social life, primarily in the self-managing bodies and the other associations which he could freely create in order to satisfy his own rights and interests.

At this stage the role of the director was changed and was brought into conformity with the changes that took place. He continued as the representative of the State in the enterprise, but was not appointed by State authorities any longer ; he was appointed by the workers' council. He was elected on proposal of a mixed commission consisting of the workers of the working organisation and representatives of the State and its bodies. The reappointment of the director every four years, was introduced.

The 1963 Constitution brought about the enlargement of self-management on the whole, the decentralisation of decision making and the democratization of social relations in every respect. Towards the end of this phase, in 1971, Constitution amendments were adopted, which were the introduction to the preparation for the New Constitution. By passing the amendments self-management was deepened especially in the sense of strengthening of direct forum of worker's decision-making. The new forms of organizing the associated labour (enterprise) were established.

By passing the 1974 Constitution, the new phase began, the fourth phase in the development of self-management, the one which is still going on.

Both the sympathizers and opponents admit the fact that the present Constitution of Yugoslavia is one of the most democratic Constitutions in the world, for it brought to social life the realisation which present the further democratisation and decentralisation in all areas of social life.

The Constitution inaugurated the essential changes relating to the organising of associated labour of material production, by which further development was enabled as well as the realisation of inalienable self-managing workers' rights. Besides the inalienable self-managing workers' rights to decide with whom and under which conditions they will associate their labour, the Constitution emphasises the basic organisation of associated labour, where the workers directly realize their rights to self-management.

The 1974 Constitution enlarged considerably and in a new way decided the question, of realizing the workers' right to do the self-managing workers' control. It is performed by three ways: First, directly, which means by all who are employed in the working organisation; Second by their delegates in the workers' council; and Third by special authority of self-managing workers' control, which is elected directly by voting in all organi ations of associated labour.

The particular characteristic of the Constitution is the new redistribution of competences between Federation and the Republics. The role and the importance of Republics as the social political communities, where working people are organized and nationalities realize their sovereign rights, are increased. In other words, the sovereignty of the Republics is accentuated and by it, their responsibility for togetherness by conforming to State law, which is common to the whole country. Because of this the nations and nationality of Yugoslavia determined to live in fraternised and federative community. The matters of federal concern are the integral Yugoslav market, the uniform financial and economic system, the integral territory and national defence etc. By these changes new conditions for successful solving of problems among nations on self-managing bases are created.

In Yugoslav conditions the workers' self-management is regarded as essential, and as the best way for coordinating and further developing relations between nations on the basis of complete equality.

Finally, this Constitution defines the place and the role of socio-political organisations which are now the intergral part of the total self-managing socio-political system. It means that they are not affected from outside by the authority of the political party, but from inside through their members and delegations. By the power of their arguments they bring about political decisions at all stages of self-managing organisation of the society.

CONSTITUTIONAL ORGANIZING OF SELF-MANAGEMENT

The working people realize their constitutional rights to self-management in the organisations of associated labour and work communities, then in self-management community of interests, local neighbourhood community as well as in assemblies of social political communities.

The organisation of associated labour is the common notion for three basic forms of pooling of labour and means : the basic work, and composite organisation of associated labour.

The basic organisation of associated labour (*BOAL*) is defined by the Constitution as "the basic form of associated labour where the workers realize their social, economic and other self-managing rights directly and equally and decide about the other matters of their socio-economic position." Each act that violates the rights in any way is anti-constitutional. The possibility for workers to realize self-management and self-managing rights in the scope of such an organisation is anticipated as one of the constitutional element for establishing and registering of the basic organisation. But in order to realize real self-management, the workers should be completely informed in time, and the Constitution provides the workers' rights to be regularly and completely informed about the entire dealings and material-financial situation of the organisation, generation and distribution of income, the use of means as well as about the other matters which are important for decision-making and the control of the organisation.

Work organisation is "an independent self-managing organisation of workers linked by common interests in work and organized in basic organisations operating within it or directly linked by the unified process of labour." It is a higher form of organizing which arises by pooling two or more basic organisations. Its independence is pointed out, for the basic organisation cannot exist as the law subject if it is out of the work organisation.

Composite organisation of associated labour (*in further* text : composite organisation) is further and higher form of pooling in which the work organisations are associated. But in contrast to basic organisations of associated labour, the work organisation do not need to be pooled into the composite organisation, which means that they can exist out of them as the law subject or they can be pooled into two or more composite organisations if there is any interest.

Self-management community of interests are such forms of pooling which arise for the purpose of the exchange of labour and means between the users and givers of certain services such as medical care and services, disability and old-age pension insurance, or life and goods insurance. They represent such associations which arise as the result of gradual dying out of and taking over the appropriate State functions by the workers.

Local neighbourhood community is organized according to territory in order to realize the common interests and to satisfy the common needs in the area of residence settlement, public services and the other aspects of life and work.

Socio-political communities are municipalities, autonomous provinces, republics and Federation. Self-management of working people is spread from the base of the society to the decision-making in all these socio-political communities by delegations and delegates in the assemblies of these communities.

Forms of direct personal expression of views and decisions in the organisations of associated labour are : workers' assembly, and others. Neither did the Constitution work out details, nor did it objectively develop the way of decision-making. It was done by Associated Labour Act and other Law regulations. Self-managing organisations regulate some problems by their self-managing documents of enactment (statutes, regulations) independently.

By personal expression of views in BOAL the workers decide on their inalienable rights by : referenda, at workers' assembly, making a special statement in written form or in other forms or by law, statute or self-managing agreement.

Referendum is the form of direct personal and secret decision-making of all employed workers in the organisation of associated labour. Associated Labour Act sets a large number of questions about which the workers decide by referendum.

The workers decide by referendum :

1. to make decision of organizing the BOAL,
2. to make decision on separation of basic organisation out

of work organisation,

3. to make a decision of adoption of self-managing agreement about the associating into the basic, work or composite organisation and business community,
4. to make a decision on status changes in organizing of basic organisation,
5. to pass self-managing documents of enactment : statute of BOAL, work community and composite organisation as well as the regulation on distribution of means on personal income and joint expenditure,
6. to make decision referring to waiving rights on returning of associated means.

By self-managing agreement and statute, the workers themselves can set the other questions about which they may decide by referendum, but of course, they cannot decide on the matters for which workers' council is authorized by Associated Labour Act and the Constitution. As we can see by referendum a large number of questions are covered. The citizens in local-neighbourhood community and socio-political communities can decide by referendum.

In contrast with referendum *Workers' assembly* is the form of direct personal decision-making, by voting in public (by aclamation) not secretly. Primarily, the workers discuss and prepare the matter which is going to be decided by referendum. The reason for that is that workers always decide personally when their invulnerable rights are in question and before decision is made the time for dispute must be reserved. Besides, at workers' assembly the workers make suggestions, give and coordinate their opinion about realizing their self-managing rights, they agree about their suggestions to instruct delegates and delegations who will represent their genuine suggestions and interests in delegate-assemblies. At workers' assembly they can make decision about the things that law, self-management agreement or statute provide for.

Finally, the Constitution of Yugoslavia gives a possibility, and Associated Labour Act binds the workers, in some situation, to make decisions personally in a third manner making *a special statement.* This way is used in cases of adoption of self-management agreement of pooling workers' labour, when it is necessary that each worker directly and personally has to agree for something, although it was discussed and adopted by the majority of votes on referendum. If an individual (worker) does not sign such an act, then it means that the provisions do not oblige the worker.

We can see that the Constitution insists on direct and personal decision-making by the workers, if possible. In cases when it is impossible, and because of the efficiency of self-management decision-making, the different forms of decision-making through delegates and delegations are provided for. In that case they make decisions on behalf of workers they represent and by their instructions.

Workers' council is the most important, and in practice the most representative form of decision-making. Since thirtyfive years, when the workers' self-management was introduced, it has been the managing body which manages work and business. This body exists in each work organisation, basic work and composite. The exception is only a working organisation with fewer than 30 workers. In such cases all workers shall perform the function of the workers' council and shall make decision by expressing their views on questions, which under law fall within the province of the workers' council.

The composition of the workers' council must fit the social structure of the employed, and workers from all areas of work process must be represented by their delegates and delegations in workers' council. The delegates in workers' council act by the workers' instructions through workers' assembly or delegation, and the delegates in work organisation, workers' council on the instruction of basic organisation workers' council. The delegates are responsible for their work to the workers by whom they were elected.

It is important to note that the members of the workers' council cannot be elected for a period longer than two years, and nobody can be elected more than twice in the same workers' council, and the director or the other managing person who is specially authorized or has the particular responsibility, cannot be the member of the workers' council. They can take part in the work, but have no right to decision-making.

The function of the workers' council as the managing organ is seen from the constitutional competencies. The workers' council sets the proposed statute as the most important self-management act of the organisation, makes decision on the other documents, makes the plan and programme of the development, sets the business policy, elects, appoints and dimisses the executive board and operational body (directors) of the working organisation and considers the workers to be completely informed in time. Workers' council can decide on other matters, which are set by the workers through the statute, self-managing agreement or any other self-management act of the organisation.

In addition to workers' council there are two other important self-managing bodies : the workers' self-management control and delegation. The election, the way of work and the responsibility of these two bodies refer to working collective as a whole, which act as the workers' assembly. That is why selfmanagement workers' control and delegation coordinate with the workers' council. These bodies are elected by direct secret voting, in the same way as the workers' council.

SELF-MANAGEMENT WORKERS' CONTROL

According to the Constitution and the Associated Labour Act, self-management workers' control must exist in each organisation. In the Constitution it is precisely said : " . . . in order to realize and to protect their self-management rights, the workers in the BOAL and other self-management organisation have the right and the obligation to realize their self-management workers' control" among the others, " . . . through the particular body of self-management workers' control."

On behalf of the workers and in order to realize their rights, this body controls : putting into effect the statute and other documents of enactment, carrying out of workers' decision, as well as workers' council and executive and operational boards. As it is the body of internal protection of self-management and self-managing rights, besides the other permanent bodies, its right is to evaluate the accordance of the documents and the decisions with self-managing rights, obligations and interests of the workers, which means that it can intervene, if this body notices any discordance or deviation. It is especially important to say that this body controls the accomplishing of work and self-managing obligations of workers as well as the other bodies and services of the working organisation. The realizing of self-management and workers' self-management rights does not mean one-sided insisting on realizing the rights and neglecting the duties, which would impede the efficiency of business organisation, but includes the simultaneous and responsible accomplishing of all duties. The workers' control supervises the use of social means which are available to the organisation : the control of distribution according to the work, distribution of income and the means for personal income. It is very important because in practice, there are two unacceptable tendencies. Either techno-bureaucratic structure usurps, or deprives the workers their rights, or in certain circumstances, among the workers of themselves, the tendency of irrational handling and illegal distribution of means predominates. It must be pointed out that workers' control takes care of complete, prompt and correct informing of workers about all matters which are important for self-managing decision-making.

Finally, the constitutional right of self-managing workers' control is to take care of realization and protection of workers rights, while they are employed, as well as the realization of other self-managing rights, duties and interests of workers. The body of self-management control has rights and is obliged to inform the appropriate authorities in the organisation about any defect which is noticed as well as about their opinion about it. It may ask for intervention, help or collaboration out of the organization of social or state body which is duly authorized. The efficiency of its work, considerably depends on the circumstances under which it performs in each organisation, and is especially effected by socio-political organisation, particularly by Trade Union (labour-union).

Delegation is the self-management body for authentic transmitting and representing workers' interests in assemblies of self-managing communities of interests and socio-political communities. It is, in fact, the basic rod for workers' self-management realization out of factory areas. It is the continuation of a hand in self-management to the matters, and means that are separated for the realisation of general social interests in self-managing communities of interests and socio-political communities. The Yugoslav Constitution defines the assemblies of socio-political communities, from the municipality to the Federation, primarily as the bodies of social self-management and then as the highest authorities of the defined socio-political community. Namely, the duality is specially here expressed, the duality between State and self-management, and the assembly expresses a dialectic unity of these two essential social factors. As the expression of authentic workers' interests through delegation system, this assembly is as self-management body, the highest authentic body acts, as the State body.

Delegations are formed in basic self-management organisations and communities in order to realize directly workers' rights and to participate in function-performing of assemblies of socio-political communities. The members of delegation are also elected secretly but the complete delegation must have representatives of workers from all areas of production process. The directors and the other authorized persons with special responsiblity and authority cannot be the members of delegations as in workers' council.

As the principle of responsibility and exchange in managership and self-managing bodies is consistently used, the same is the case in delegation. Delegates are responsible to self-managing base that elected them. It means that "delegation as well as delegate in the assembly could be replaced." Here the same procedure as in the case of election is used. The mandate of delegation lasts four years. Nobody can consecutively be elected twice as the member of the delegation in the same self-managing organisation or community.

Delegation assignment is to follow and register workers' opinion, suggestions and interests concerning the matters which are discussed and decided on assemblies of self-managing communities of interests and socio-political communities. The opinion of the delegation is conveyed through delegates who present them authentically at the assembly. The delegate is not "a free shot", he does not come out with his own opinion or suggestion, but he always does on behalf of delegation. In this way delegation is the link between workers and people on one side and the delegate and assemblies on the other, and the whole delegate and assembly system is losing the characteristics of representative system. By the Constitution there is no "indirect self-management" but the direct personal decision-making through delegates. A Delegate always comes out with the delegation's opinion concerning the matters which are discussed, they always represent the delegation, organisation or community they were elected by. The delegate is responsible for his work to them and must inform them about the work of assembly as well as about his own. It must be pointed out that the Constitution allows the delegate to decide and vote independently, which means that delegates are not strictly limited by the imperative mandated principle. The personal decision-making is very important when suggestions and interests of numerous delegations of self-managing and socio-political communities are coordinated among themselves as well as with common and general social interests.

Among self-managing bodies, there is a *collegiate executive body* which occupies an important place. This body exist as the executive body of workers' council in the organisation of associated labour (previously-enterprise). The members are elected by the workers' council, part of them are the members of the workers' council and another part are others employed in the organisation. According to the previous Constitution this body was called operational-managing board and was anthorized to manage and make decisions. Its duty, according to the new Constitution is to take care of the execution of workers' council decisions and to instruct the managing board (director). A director used to be the member of the management board, but now he cannot be the member of the executive body. He may and it is his duty (obligation) to be present at the session where he can suggest and warn if there are unsuitable and illegal decisions but he himself cannot make decisions. The executive body also proposes the draft of a statute and other self-management documents of enactment as well as the proposal of the plan of dealings in the organisation.

The assemblies of socio-political communities, from municipality to Federation, have their executive bodies, the executive councils. They are responsible for the situation in the socio-political community, for the execution of regulations, for carrying out of the defined policy as well as for the directing and coordinating of managing state body work.

According to some theoreticians a function of a director belongs to the organisation of self-managing bodies. Each organisation has a director (bussiness-managing organ). By his essential functions, he is workers' self-management body. He is also a representative of the State and its interests as well as the bodies of socio-political community.

The Constitution established two kinds of management body: one-man managing body (director), where one person manages, and the collegiate management body where a few persons manage. The workers themselves through the statute decide if there will be one-man or collegiate management body.

Business-managing organ is a specific self-managing organ for it is appointed by workers' council. It is responsible to the workers' council, executes its decisions, represents work organisation, examines the plans before they are adopted, suggests business policy and the measures for its carrying out, organises and coordinates the process of work in the organisation. At the same time, the business-managing organ can be considered as the State organ and the organ of broader social community in the organisation, for a director or the chairman of the business-managing board, is elected by the competition commission where the representatives of socio-political communities obviously participate as the members of the commission, and he is responsible for the legality of work of the work-organisation and his obligation is to warn workers' council if there are some unsuitable or illegal decisions (he has right of veto on such decisions).

The Assembly of Working People, workers' council, collegiate executive and business-managing organ, can have permanent or ad hoc commissions and the other bodies for preparations, proposals and pronouncing of certain measures. Workers' council, for example, has a permanent commission for employment, disciplinary commission and if necessary it can form others too.

SOCIALIST SELF-MANAGEMENT AS THE SOURCE OF NEW RIGHTS AND FREEDOM

One of the essential characteristics of socialism, as a system, is to provide higher degree of rights and freedom. In contrast to bourgeois society and its formal rights, it provides real freedom, fights for equality for all people. Instead of formal equality by law (which capitalism really provided and stepped forward from feudalism) it provides for real equality in the whole society, as to nations or nationalities or as to individuals.

Disregarding the protests of bourgeois antisocialist propaganda stating that human rights are endangered, and disregarding the disgressing of socialism as it happened in some countries, it is indisputable that socialism has the priorities. Not only it provides classic civil rights and freedom (freedom of choice of work, opinion, association, scientific and art creation, nationality and religion) but also provides a new substance and deepens it in all matters of its real realization.

Socialist self-management goes further enlarging and deepening socialist democracy by introducing new freedom and rights. The Yugoslav Constitution guarantees that "each worker in the organisation of associated labour, in basic organisation where he works and in all forms of pooling labour and resources jointly and on equal terms, manages work and business of the organisation of associated labour, and dealings and resources in whole related to social reproduction, settles the realizations, during the work, among themselves, decides on overall income earned through joint work in various forms of pooling labour and resources and earns his personal income (Article 14)."

From the rights to work with socially owned resource : and to manage the labour and dealings of the organisation, which are considered to be the essential and inalienable rights of worker emerge a lot of other rights which are typical for self-management system. For example, as the worker has a right to settle the relations in the associated labour, he has a right to self-management and social agreement as instruments which push out the State as the agent. The workers themselves pass directly the statute, the regulations on income distribution for personal income, collective consumption and housing construction etc. They pass the other acts through the workers' council, by which they settle the other relations that are not regulated sufficiently by law. So the workers establish independently various self-management rights, depending on the material standing of work organisation. The whole system of new self-management standards (norms) and rights are arising as the expression of workers' autonomous will. In its totality they are named self-management rights which are being enlarged. In that way the State rights are gradually (but permanently) transforming to new self-management rights, which show the legal tendency to enlarge and deepen the workers' freedom and rights in organising a man in the society.

PROTECTION OF SELF-MANAGEMENT AND SELF-MANAGING RIGHTS

Disregarding the constitutional and legal solutions, the fact that working class came to power, that there are numerous self-managing bodies, in practice, it happens that workers' self-management and self-managing rights are usurped. Although they are protected by workers themselves, through socio-political organisations, workers' council and self-management workers' control, the Constitution provides their social protection. By the Constitution, the self-managing rights and socially owned property are under special social protection. It is realized through assemblies of socio-political communities and the organs which are responsible to them, the court and the court of associated labour, as a specific form of court, then constitutional court, public prosecutor and self-managing attorney. The self-management attorney is the body which controls the socially owned properties and self-managing rights of workers on behalf of the society.

Final Remarks

Self-management in Yugoslavia, which has been existing for thirty-five years, proved the correctness of our determination, the vitality of system and the ability of working class to take over the managing in the society. Owing to numerous difficulties and contradictions in development, however, all conditions, where self-management could show its priority and equality have not been acquired yet. For that reason, it is the system of the future. Not only the Constitution proved the achieved degree of development in previous phases, but it opened the horizons and perspectives of development. The achieved results, in practice are the confirmation of theoretical assumption from which we started. The leading theoreticians are of the opinion that self-management is the form of social structure where the process of gradual exemption of labour and man from all forms of alienation, has started and can successfully go on. Self-management can be developed, only on the bases of socially owned resources of production but its development is the condition for further development and affirmation of social property relations. The specific kind of dictatorship of proletariat and a form of gradual dying of State goes on parallelly with the State. Law is regulated and is being developed within the framework of law, and law standards but at the same time in the specific form of dying of classic State law and its gradual transformation into new self-management law which is the expression of self-manager's genuine will. Self-management is, finally the alternative way to socialism. In Yugoslav circumstances it is the way without any other alter-n atives. In short, self-management is Yugoslav's way to socialism.

INDEX